Race, Romance, and Rebellion

Race, Romance, and Rebellion

LITERATURES OF THE AMERICAS IN THE NINETEENTH CENTURY

Colleen C. O'Brien

University of Virginia Press

Charlottesville and London

University of Virginia Press
© 2013 by the Rector and Visitors of the University of Virginia
All rights reserved
Printed in the United States of America on acid-free paper
First published 2013

9 8 7 6 5 4 3 2 1

Library of Congress Cataloging-in-Publication Data

O'Brien, Colleen C., 1969–
    Race, romance, and rebellion : literatures of the Americas
in the nineteenth century / Colleen C. O'Brien.
        pages cm. — (New World Studies)
    Includes bibliographical references and index.
    ISBN 978-0-8139-3488-4 (cloth : acid-free paper)
    ISBN 978-0-8139-3489-1 (pbk. : acid-free paper)
    ISBN 978-0-8139-3490-7 (e-book)
    1. America—Literatures—History and criticism. 2. Race
relations in literature. 3. Insurgency in literature. 4. America—
Ethnic relations—History—19th century. I. Title.
PN846.O27 2013
809'.897—dc23
                                                    2013004487

A book in the American Literatures Initiative (ALI), a collaborative
publishing project of NYU Press, Fordham University Press, Rutgers
University Press, Temple University Press, and the University of Virginia
Press. The Initiative is supported by The Andrew W. Mellon Foundation.
For more information, please visit www.americanliteratures.org.

Contents

Acknowledgments

MY CAREER AS A SCHOLAR has taken me to so many places that I cannot measure the debts incurred along the way. My mentors at the University of Michigan—Simon Gikandi, Arlene Keizer, Carroll Smith-Rosenberg, and Patsy Yaeger—helped me build a foundation in postcolonial and feminist American studies. Ron Walters and Rafia Zafar have continued to support me intellectually in the years since I finished my Ph.D. I also attended Dartmouth University's Futures of American Studies Institute in 2009, where Anthony Bogues and Elizabeth Dillon offered feedback and encouragement that shaped this manuscript, especially in terms of its transnational argument. I likewise thank Don Pease, not only for running the institute, but for exhorting me to finish the manuscript.

The friends I met in graduate school and since have made my early career, a long string of postdocs and visiting positions, worthwhile. I thank them for their enduring friendship and kindness. They have also read this manuscript in many incarnations and with great care. Without Sondra Smith Gates, Karin Spirn, and Jocelyn Fenton Stitt, I may not have made it out of Ann Arbor. Rian Bowie and Rynetta Davis not only offered me places to stay while I worked on archival research, they practically insisted that I get my work published. My "oldest" friend, Kelly O'Connor, has been not only a limitless source of hospitality, wisdom, and laughter, but also a great example of succeeding and flourishing in one's career regardless of its challenges.

The expertise and insight of outside readers, some whose names I do not know, have helped to refine and expand this book in innumerable ways. The readers for the University of Virginia Press have been, simply put, amazing. *African American Review* published earlier versions of chapters 5 and 6, and their outside readers gave outstanding advice for revision. I thank *AAR* and *ESQ: A Journal of the American Renaissance* for allowing me to republish work that appeared previously in those journals. *ESQ* published a version of part of chapter 1, and their readers and editors, especially Jana Argersinger, were equally insightful and generous with their time.

I began an early version of this book while a fellow at the St. Mary's College Center for Women's Intercultural Leadership (CWIL) and completed it as a Fulbright Research Chair in North American Studies at the University of Western Ontario. I thank CWIL, Fulbright Canada, and Western for supporting me at beginning and end. In the interim, I was an assistant professor at the University of South Carolina, Upstate. My colleagues there—especially Peter Caster, Esther Godfrey, Celena Kusch, and Rich Murphy—provided ongoing feedback and read most of the manuscript several times. More importantly, without the friendship, laughter, and sense of perspective that they and their families provided, time spent writing this book would not have been as joyful. Several students also inspired me and urged me on: Lateka Beasley, Jerrell Dunham, Domonique Finley, Trayonna Floyd, Christina Henderson, Carmelita Lopez, Victor Ochoa, and Bayla Ostrach have eagerly awaited this book and engaged in its subject matter in the many classrooms we shared.

My parents, David and Valerie O'Brien, spent their careers teaching, coaching, and mentoring adolescents. I thank them for their support and for believing (or suspending disbelief) that my efforts as an academic are as strenuous as their work with middle-school students. As I wrote this book, my mother and my sister, Jennifer, provided me with summers at Moon Lake, a family tradition we inherited from our late uncle, Fred, and will pass on to Alex, Natalie, Tyler, Henry, Sadie, Elijah, and Tess. My father supported the fervor with which I wrote because his own father, my grandfather, was as passionate about literature as I am. My only regret is that my grandmother, Evelyn, the grandfather from whom I inherited my passion—Edward O'Brien—and my maternal grandparents, Alice and Walter Szancilo, whose support and enthusiasm were unflagging, did not live to see this book published. It is to my phenomenal parents and grandparents that I dedicate my work.

Preface

THIS BOOK IS ABOUT romance and rebellion, amalgamation and expansion, a set of interrelated terms that reshape the way we might think about race, gender, sex, and the revolutionary concept of rights that emerged in the New World in the long eighteenth century. The idea of equality, which evolved in the Americas as colonies became states, was always troubled by exclusions that came to be defined as racial and gender differences. In the revolutionary era and throughout the era of reform, however, the act of righteous rebellion substantiated claims to equality. Thus representations or incidents of rebellion correlated with historically changing and contested definitions of race, gender, and human rights.

Simultaneously, what might be called romantic ideals of political equality infiltrated the literary genre of romance. What Hayden White identifies as the romantic emplotment of the novel both responds to the political changes going on and is reflected in the rhetoric of the public sphere. Politically, romanticism's ideals of universal emancipation led to acts of rebellion; in historical romance, the quest for freedom often materialized as a rebellion against racial and gender subordination. Therefore, both romanticism and romance are inextricable from the act and idea of rebellion.

The texts at hand epitomize the inseparability of the tropes of romance and rebellion from attempts to imagine universal freedom. The endurance and resilience of these stories during the era of reform (1835–1870) is my primary focus. Many imagined this era as the revolutionary moment revisited, the moment when the unfulfilled promises of 1776 would expand throughout the populace, or even the hemisphere. As I will illustrate, concomitant images of that other revolution—1791—permeate the imaginative and political discourses of the era as well.

While rebels like John Brown saw insurrection as an expression of filial love for black men, very rarely do proslavery or antireform writers envision political collaboration between white women and black men in particular as a platonic relation. Novels like Gertrudis Gómez de Avellaneda's *Sab* (1841), Harriet Martineau's *The Hour and the Man* (1840), E.D.E.N. Southworth's *Retribution* (1849), Elizabeth Livermore's *Zoë; or, The Quadroon's Triumph* (1855), Lydia Maria Child's *Romance of the Republic* (1867), and, of course, *Uncle Tom's Cabin* all flash back, in differing measures, to the spectacle of the Haitian Revolution, and they all explore cross-racial love of some kind. The juxtaposition of cross-racial relationships (romance) and violent uprisings (rebellion) takes root in the iconography of the Haitian Revolution and continues to appear in novels and nonfiction documents that address issues of radical equality and freedom for white women and African or Native Americans right up until the Civil War.[1]

In many of the New World's historical romances, racial and gender differences dissolved in the transcendent power of love affairs that were often cross-racial. Relationships between races, of course, could bring about the "amalgamation" of those races.[2] These forbidden romances imagined a world where a dialogue between lovers could level racial and gender boundaries and usher in new forms of equality. Amalgamation also broke down other kinds of boundaries and borders, both intellectual and geographic. Therefore, the dialogue between lovers could also be an allegory for the dialogue between U.S. and Haitian ideas of revolution.

While the expansion of enlightened political ideals allegedly led to new definitions of rights, the expansion of rights themselves was also a function of geographic expansion. Not only the opportunities that the New World afforded Europeans, but also the challenges to their sovereignty waged by the indigenes and unfree African laborers they enslaved, figure into the narrative of territorial expansion. These contending forces— romance and rebellion, expansion and amalgamation—had the potential to strike a radical break from Old World hierarchies and traditions. Supposedly natural boundaries between the races broke down through the process of biological amalgamation, different cultures and intellectual movements were amalgamated by geographic expansion, and all of these factors rebelled against the restrictions of the past.

This changes the way we view the literatures of the Americas because it reflects the mobility and fluidity of all the borders and limits that were thought to restrict the definitions of race, gender, and nation. Eventually, as many scholars of American studies have illustrated, the United States would become an exceptionalist, imperial nation. But before this solidi-fied, a handful of reformers would imagine more cosmopolitan, utopian, and millennialist alternatives. Racial discrimination and the hegemonic discourse of inferiority that shaped American laws contributed to the rise of an Anglo-supremacist worldview at home and abroad, but the discourse of inferiority did not go unchallenged by the reformers who participated in the creation and redefinition of citizenship rights from 1776 to 1865. The "exceptional" theories of the U.S. Revolution would become the uncontested truths of democracy and freedom by the twen-tieth century, but the Haitian Revolution stood in the shadows of that emerging mythology just as other Caribbean colonies contested those truths throughout the nineteenth century.

Because it connects the expansion of romanticism's political ide-als with the hemispheric processes of revolution and amalgamation that shaped the Atlantic world, this book also challenges the way we think about the romance genre, romanticism, heterosexual romances, and amalgamation in the literatures of the United States. For exam-ple, several other studies have attempted to explain the obsession with cross-racial romance or the biological "amalgamation" of the races that appears so frequently in nineteenth-century United States literature,[3] but none have really linked that phenomenon with the myths of revolu-tionary origin in United States and Haiti and the definitions of freedom each created. Much recent nineteenth-century American literary criti-cism has addressed the dichotomy between what might be called "amal-gamated" or pluralistic concepts of nation and the exigencies of con-structing a purified and homogenous image of a national subject.[4] What Lauren Berlant and Dana Nelson would call anxieties about or fantasies of Anglo-American superiority echo through the writings of those who seem to despise the "amalgamated" and aspire to the "purified" version of nation. But there is an alternative to that model.

This alternative—an unconventional strain of romance—had formi-dable rivals in its day. Douglas Anderson illustrates how Rufus Choate advocated the writing of "a body of didactic, national romances modeled on Walter Scott's Waverly novels" to "turn back our thoughts . . . from controversies about negro cloth" to proud memories of "the day when our fathers" heroically fought "the War of Independence" (35–36). By subduing concerns over slavery with grand narratives of inherited free-dom, Choate undoubtedly aspired to create a sense of national identity that assumed whiteness and a sense of virtuous masculinity derived from military valor.[5]

Whereas the expansion of the nation's borders in the nineteenth century did engender Choate's rational call for "didactic national romances," stories of romance and rebellion could not be contained by the boundaries of official history, nation, gender, or race. In terms of this book, the concept of romance and rebellion opens up the other mind-set of expansion—an eye toward expansion that was not for the purpose of conquering or controlling new territories, but for making peaceful transnational connections in a cosmopolitan spirit. The cosmopolitical desire for union paralleled the imaginative restructuring of race and gender relations in the Americas. Romance and rebellion imagined the potential for bonds of affection to unite men and women, black and white, through an expansion and interconnection of souls that also had millennial and radical Christian republican implications.

This cast of romantic rebel-authors, including Charles Emerson, Margaret Fuller, Harriet Jacobs, Gertrudis Gómez de Avellaneda, Elizabeth Livermore, and Julia Collins, recognized the indeterminacy of romance. They used that open-endedness to disrupt or rebel against the narratives of race and nation that attempted, as Dana Nelson describes, to create "imagined affiliation" between "men who have power over groups of people—the power to objectify, to identify, to manage" (*National Manhood* 3). Romance was not always a fertile genre in which the certainty and authority of an Anglo-masculine imperialist destiny could take root. I am interested not only in the indeterminacy of the genre, however, but also in what I interpret as a very concrete and decisive vision of a possible world. Whether as Avellaneda's romantic hero, Sab; Livermore's millennial "real Christian Republic"; or Collins's New (Black) South, the political future of the Americas envisioned by the main authors discussed in this book is decidedly counterfactual and radically soulful.

When romance meets rebellion, exclusionary meanings of race and nation can become unstable.[6] Characters who previously would have removed themselves to a different geography, like Rebecca in Sir Walter Scott's *Ivanhoe* or Lydia Maria Child's Hobomok in the eponymous novel, or performed rituals of self-sacrifice in the alleged interest of Anglo-American racial purity—like Cora in *Last of the Mohicans*—are transformed into the heroes and heroines of a romantic quest for political freedom.[7] In fact, the extent to which the literary cultures of African Americans and women constituted what Nancy Fraser calls subaltern publics invites us to explore stories of romance and rebellion as antithetical to a Waverly-type romance.

These romances envision a quest for the unattainable but convert the dialectic of hero and enemy into a dialogue between lover and beloved. These romances (referring both to the genre and the relationships they feature) are rebellious, thwarting the "social scripts" and heterosexual marriage plots that Rachel Blau DuPlessis and other feminist literary critics (including Sandra Gilbert and Susan Gubar) have found so insipid and self-defeating for female protagonists. Their plots take on scenes of racial rebellion, and they always weigh a transnational definition of freedom against its Anglo-American counterpart.

Looking back from this century, David Scott's *Conscripts of Modernity* challenges the postcolonial construction of historical romance, arguing that the legacy of the Enlightenment in the Caribbean might better be read as a tragedy. This certainly might be true for the twentieth century, but I think it is also important to see romanticism and the romance as something that Caribbean writers and activists contributed to in the nineteenth century. *Race, Romance, and Rebellion* looks at the Caribbean Enlightenment through the eyes of U.S. romanticists in a historical moment *before* "gender, race, sexuality, and empire . . . shaped Romanticism's sensibilities" into a didactic, Eurocentric pedagogy of the white center and the exotic colonial periphery (Scott 59). In part because many of its authors imagined themselves as colonial subjects, the clashing novelistic genres of romance and historical romance unveil the competing senses of history and identity that circulated in the antebellum United States and throughout the Atlantic world.[8]

Although previous critiques of the genre tend to see romance as an obstacle to political engagement, concepts of sexuality and embodiment or even of intimacy have been in critical favor. Peter Coviello's *Intimacy in America* considers how what he calls "anti-state" authors, including Walt Whitman, Harriet Beecher Stowe, Edgar Allen Poe, and Herman Melville, drew upon a sense of "present-tense mutuality, of a far reaching connectedness, to vouch for their coherence as a nation" (4). Citing Christopher Looby's *Voicing America*, Coviello distinguishes the antebellum concept of an "affect nation" from European traditions of nation; thus "for a range of antebellum authors dissatisfied with the claims of the state, American nation-ness existed, and had meaning, as a kind of relation—for some, an intimacy" (5). This largely homosocial relationality, which was complicit, as Coviello indicates, in the production of whiteness, may have been very important to some antebellum writers. As he points out, the relationality that produced whiteness was not universally or unproblematically absorbed by all Anglo-Americans and replicated uniformly in the literary public sphere. Relying largely on historians well known within whiteness studies such as David Roediger, Noel Ignatiev, and Matthew Frye Jacobson, Coviello explains why, in the two decades before the Civil War, political economy and national identity converged to correlate whiteness with entitlement to property, promulgate the myth of the vanishing Indian, and relegate blackness to a permanent state of dependency, of what Patricia J. Williams calls being the object of property.

In contrast to a somewhat predictable, if intriguingly more relational and affective narrative of nation that comes from Stowe, Whitman, Poe, and Melville, this study questions the idea of narratives of nation, or at least retraces, in racially transgressive imaginative romances, the counterfactual past that would have written that narrative differently. In spite of being "anti-state," the authors Coviello discusses seem to have been driven, almost presciently, toward the idea of nation that eventually manifests, in 1898, as the vehicle of the white man's burden or the champion of Manifest Destiny as far as the Philippines. Perhaps in a naturalistic or realistic sense, intimacy functioned as a political tool for white racial cohesion and the production of an Anglo-masculine national identity. But romance and rebellion, often as a bold rewriting of the genre of historical romance, figures sex, intimacy, politics, and history rather differently. This is, in large part, because rebellion provides a key ingredient to the romances under consideration.

Race, Romance, and Rebellion tells the story of a cultural obsession with romance and rebellion that was at once oppressive and potentially liberating. It is neither a homogenizing story nor one that revisits the romance genre via the usual suspects, but rather an exploration of disruptive, rebellious, and radically contingent ideas about race, gender, and freedom. As relationships between "mainland" and Caribbean colonies expanded, so did the ideas that circulated among them. The intellectual amalgamation of these geographies gave new meanings to romanticism's ideals; as these ideals expanded, so did the power of race and gender to inspire righteous rebellion.

Race, Romance, and Rebellion

Introduction

To Foment Freedom

I long to hear that you have declared an independency—and by the way in the new Code of Laws which I suppose it will be necessary for you to make I desire you would Remember the Ladies. . . . If perticuliar care and attention is not payed to the Laidies we are determined to foment a Rebelion.

—Abigail Adams to John Adams, March 31, 1776

We have been told that our Struggle has loosened the bands of Government everywhere. That Children and Apprentices were disobedient—that schools and Colledges were grown turbulent—that Indians slighted their Guardians and Negroes grew insolent to their Masters. But your Letter was the first Intimation that another Tribe more numerous and powerful than all the rest were grown discontented.

—John Adams to Abigail Adams, April 14, 1776

EVEN IN ONE of the best-known romances of the American Revolution—Abigail and John Adams's marriage—we find the threat of rebellion. As Abigail reminds her husband, the potential to "foment a Rebelion" is a universal human right, not just an exceptional project that he and his cohorts undertook to break ties with King George. Therefore, as Adams and the other leaders of those North American colonies struggled to exercise a new concept of freedom, they experienced a concomitant anxiety about the limits they would place on that freedom. Although John's jocular response to Abigail's entreaty to "Remember the Ladies" connects her demands to the rumor that Indians were "slight[ing] their Guardians and Negroes [growing] insolent to their Masters," it does not necessarily envision a coalition among those three "tribes" that could loosen the "bands of Government everywhere." Nonetheless, he names these three "tribes" as separate entities from the newly independent colonies, whose "Masculine systems" he acknowledges are "little more than Theory." By no means do I intend to disparage Adams as a sexist or racist by emphasizing his point. Rather, I simply mean to illustrate his acumen in pointing out the exclusions (which he does not naturalize, but attributes to theory) that characterize the birth of a new nation.

This might be one of the foundational moments of the creation, not only of a new nation, but of what Giorgio Agamben calls a "state of exception"—a paradigm of government wherein the "sovereign, who can decide on the state of exception"—or the exclusion of certain subjects from the "Code of Laws"—logically defines himself by the exception (35). In other words, John Adams locates his own sovereignty not only in Philadelphia proper or in the new political body he has devised, but in his nontribal identity as an Anglo-American man. He is not an Indian, a Negro, or a woman (nor is he a child, a dependent apprentice, or a naïve student); therefore, he locates himself within the borders of belonging that will define the new nation. Yet as that nation eventually expanded to incorporate more territory and develop direct relationships with the Caribbean in the triangular trade, the anxiety about the boundaries of revolutionary freedom increased. Even for Adams, a rebellion of indigenes, blacks, or women was not really unthinkable—but the ability of Anglo-American men to maintain their sovereignty within such a context was.[1]

The precedent for such rebellions was very familiar to Adams, who had defended the actions of the British soldiers in the Boston Massacre six years earlier. Pointing out that Adams characterized the black native Crispus Attucks and the "mob" he led as "a motley rabble of saucy boys, negroes, and molattoes, Irish teagues and out landish jack tars . . . screaming and rending like an Indian yell," Tavia Nyong'o asks, "What is the relationship between a potential nationality and the circum-Atlantic class of slaves, sailors, and commoners" that Attucks represented? (50, 41). Insisting that "we must suspend our dominant conceptions of multiracialism as a hidden source of redemption in the American past," Nyong'o reads Attucks as a quintessential exception to the image of citizenship in a potential nation (51). It might be premature, however, to read incipient nationalism in colonies that, for the next thirty years or so, tried to remain a loose confederacy of distinctly different and autonomous states, particularly when the relationship of those states to Caribbean trading partners was often paramount to their relationship to one another. Even Boston was extremely divided over the meaning of the 1770 uprising, so I would not hasten to assert that concrete racial meanings solidified in that moment or even that century.

Fears of revolutionary excess reached a new peak in the American political imagination, however, when news of a massive slave rebellion in Saint-Domingue reached the shores of the United States in 1791. This second defining revolutionary moment in the Americas had a resounding impact, in part because it proved that the desire for freedom and righteous rebellion could not be limited to white men. Stateside reports of events in Haiti, furthermore, emphasized the slaughter of white men and the ensuing vulnerability of their wives and daughters to the black revolutionaries. The specter of Haiti haunted the new United States' political and literary imagination because it evidenced the vulnerability of a system that denied the natural rights of the majority of its constituency in the interest of protecting the privileges of propertied white men. The fictions of the Haitian Revolution that always stood in the shadows of the exclusive U.S. Revolution often fixated on the African insurgents' capacity for "savage" and bloody violence and their attendant lust for white women, which made rape a primary expression of black revolutionary freedom. The sanguine language of bloodshed and the sexual language of "blood mixing" were the essential gothic tropes that characterized the effect of the Haitian Revolution on race and gender relations.

With increasing frequency in the nineteenth century, however, fiction and nonfiction writers alike throughout the Americas began to imagine potential relationships that crossed racial and gender lines differently. As a powder keg that could explode the boundaries of patriarchal or colonial nationhood, these cross-racial affiliations could be imagined in two almost diametrically opposite ways. As I mentioned, gothic memories of the Haitian Revolution could conjure scenes of rape and violence as the casualties of a violent slave insurrection. If interpreted in a romantic context, however, these affiliations could also appear as amorous heterosexual relationships—romances of sorts—or filial ties that transcended the discourses of blood so pervasive in the gothic version. Their explosiveness was then a function of romantic ideals of freedom, the struggle for liberation against seemingly insurmountable obstacles. Often, these stories were written in the genre of historical romance.

But when it comes to the intertwined themes of romance and rebellion, there is a rather fine line between print culture's illustration of the political imagination and the literary world of historical romance. The genre of romance takes on a distinct shape in American reform literature, particularly because of its focus on rights for the disenfranchised, its compulsive (if sometimes subtle) references to the Haitian Revolution, and its attempt to imagine the future identity of an ever-expanding republic. Therefore, I use the term "romance" to signify all of the possibilities that the idea of cross-racial affiliations produced—in love stories, in romanticist stories of righteous rebellion, and in a metahistory that crosses the lines of fiction and nonfiction.

The terms "romance" and "rebellion" are inextricable from one another, and they organize a narrative of the quest for equal rights that exceeds the boundaries of the United States, or John Adams's original state of exception. Many woman abolitionists took inspiration from the Haitian Revolution, as did the leading figures in African American print culture. The Caribbean revolt thus inspired various types of rebellion in the United States, particularly in the main texts I discuss in this work. Like the term "romance," the term "rebellion" takes multiple aspects in this book. First, it refers to the revolutionary fight for freedom and personhood that characterized the American and Haitian Revolutions and other slave insurrections; second, it describes moments when the "Tribe more numerous and powerful" rejects patriarchal authority and the "protection" of white men. In the third sense, however, rebellion is the backlash of white-supremacist violence that tries to contain the expanding rights demanded by white women and all Americans.

It is also important to consider the relationship between stories of romance and rebellion and the geographic expansion that took place in the United States at the time the stories were produced. The ruptured cartography of the Atlantic world caused by the Haitian Revolution in 1791 contributed to the transnational dimension of the idea of romance and rebellion and its possible effect on national boundaries. Images of romance and rebellion persisted in debates over the possible annexation of former colonial spaces like Santo Domingo and Cuba by the United States in the 1850s and contributed to the predicted cultural outcomes of the war with Mexico. The proximity of Haiti to the United States' territory, and of the idea of cross-racial romance to the fear of violent rebellion, provides a new map of social and political anxieties about race and sex. Yet rebellion and romance also produce an alternative narrative of American history. This alternative narrative is an alternative genre of romance, one that blurs all sorts of boundaries as it imbricates race and sex with expansion and rebellion.

Reform literature grapples with images of cross-racial romance and violent rebellion because reform literature, like the Haitian Revolution, challenges the racialized manifestations of citizenship that colonizers or the founders of a slaveholding nation developed in order to maintain an exclusive purchase on power. The Caribbean, for these reformers, signified rebellion against a singular masculinist and Anglo-American definition of nationhood. Geographically outside the United States but close enough for ideas to spread rapidly, the Caribbean was a liminal space where other cultures could take root, where not-so-masculine theories of government could develop, and where non-Anglo and nonmale people could foment a rebellion.

However, the "masculine systems" that Adams used to characterize the government of his thirteen American colonies were geared as much toward maintaining property rights as protecting life and liberty. The fomentation of rebellion through the Americas, of course, also challenged property rights. Slave insurrections not only contested the laws that rendered slaves property; they also threatened the very lives of those who tried to hold the insurgents as property. In addition, the practice of violent rebellion disrupted the passing of wealth from generation to generation. Consider one of the most powerful propagandistic tropes that appears in stories of the Haitian Revolution: white infants impaled on spears or dashed headfirst against trees.

This recurring nightmare suggested that the heirs of freedom in the revolutionary New World would not be the biological sons of the Founding Fathers. As American Prosperos, then, Anglo-American men often foresaw a future wherein the insurgents had "people[d] the island with Calibans" (*Tempest* I.ii.352–53).[2] Perhaps these images are so powerful in the political unconscious because they avert the mind's eye from the reality of what Jared Sexton identifies as "the state-sponsored social organization of violence and sexuality" that still troubles the promises of freedom and radical equality that constitute the revolutionary myth of the United States (9). Similar images also characterized earlier American captivity narratives and accounts of Indian wars. Eventually, they upheld the logic of lynching that became epidemic during Reconstruction and the supposedly "Progressive" Era in the United States. They effectively concealed white male sexual predators and the regimes of violence that they justified.

Stories of collusion also haunt antislavery examples in a way that is more sexually charged than in captivity narratives. Whereas Mary Rowlandson and Hannah Dursten insisted that they escaped sexual contact with their indigenous captors, white women were not perceived so "virtuously" when they came in contact with black men. Leonora Sansay's 1808 epistolary novel *Secret History* witnesses not just the "horrors of St. Domingue" but also the scandalous intimacy between Josephine Bonaparte and future (mulatto) president Jean-Pierre Boyer. As Jeremy Popkin notes, memoirs by white Creoles mention "white women who were assumed to have granted sexual favors to Toussaint Louverture after he had become the de facto ruler of the colony" (24). Among the many differences between the "Negro" and "Indian" tribes of men and the threats they posed to a white America was a myth of black sexual prowess and virility that might be irresistible. After all, Thomas Jefferson acknowledged that Indians "lacked ardor" whereas black men were preternaturally attracted to white women. In similar Anglo-American narratives of nation, native women are drawn to white men—Pocahontas warns John Smith against Powhatan's planned attack—and native men are clearly resistible. Even James Fenimore Cooper's octoroon Cora plunges to her death rather than accept the knife-wielding hand of Magua, but white women are not so trustworthy in the midst of black power.

The possibility of a willing, consensual alliance between a white woman and a black revolutionary like Louverture is the most pejorative of these images. The constant coincidence of representations of interracial sexual liaisons with representations of violent insurrection, both when slaves fight for their freedom and, less progressively, when white men riot to "protect" white women, also reflect a tremendous preoccupation with the prospects of amalgamation, both biological and cultural. For instance, according to John Fletcher's racist 1852 treatise *Studies on Slavery, In Easy Lessons*, the public spectacle of white woman activists walking down the streets arm in arm with black male abolitionists led to the burning of Freedom Hall in Philadelphia in 1839. Leading antislavery activists like Lydia Maria Child were also considered "amalgamationists." As Elise Lemire points out, "the anti-slavery women of Massachusetts . . . between 1838 and 1843 petitioned their state legislature to overturn the law banning interracial marriage as part of their effort to 'obtain for . . . [blacks] equal civil and political rights and privileges with whites'" (115).

The concepts of expansion and amalgamation, then, became indispensible tropes of the language of romance and rebellion. As each of the chapters in this book illustrates, the expanding borders of the United States during the era of reform provided a source of simultaneous hope and anxiety about what would happen to the nation when geographic expansion led to cultural amalgamation and freedom, if not radical political equality, for all. Just as romantic relations among black, white, and indigenous lovers symbolized a political coalition that would bring citizenship rights to all Americans, the new generation of Americans that would emerge from this union would create a culturally amalgamated body politic. The echoes of romance and rebellion rippled out, like concentric circles, through powerful cultural and political metaphors of racial and geographic amalgamation. The idea of amalgamation—one of the most salient and historically specific terms found in mid-nineteenth-century writing—resonates from the personal to public and political meanings in three concentric circles, or spheres, of influence: first, as literary representations of cross-racial love affairs; second, as the hope for the amalgamation of abolition and suffrage interests through the expansion of citizenship rights; and third, as the geographic amalgamation of the United States as its territories expand from the original thirteen colonies to Louisiana and Mexico and possibly even to the Caribbean.

The cultural and political significance of images of romance and rebellion in the novels and narratives of Gertrudis Gómez de Avellaneda y Arteaga, Elizabeth Livermore, or Harriet Jacobs is even more pronounced when compared to the corresponding yet opposite references to the same imaginary spectrum in antireform print culture. The stark difference between the playwright Charles O'Bryan's *Lugarto the Mulatto* (1852) and Avellaneda's *Sab*, or between Maturin Murray Ballou's magazine novella *The Sea Witch; or, The African Quadroon* (1855) and Livermore's *Zoë*, illustrates the contested nature and powerful symbolism of stories of cross-racial romance and racial rebellion in the mid-nineteenth-century circum-Atlantic world. The heroes and antiheroes of these rebellious romances appear in diverse places, ranging from well-known U.S. Senate speeches by William Henry Seward or Charles Sumner to archival pieces like the 1835 proslavery pamphlet by Massachusetts Attorney General James T. Austin, or Paul Broca's early race-science texts. The champions and opponents of romance and rebellion not only reflect the political milieu that produced them, but they also illustrate how the idea of romance and rebellion actually shaped political rhetoric, particularly as it pertains to race, gender, and rights.[3]

Although I do read the themes of romance and rebellion in the work of O'Bryan and Ballou or in political pamphlets, medical texts, and various other forms of racist literature, it is not my intention here to rehearse what Robert Levine calls "the certitude of traditional arcs of American literary nationalism" that narrate the development of an Anglo-masculine idea of nation-ness (*Dislocating* 11). Whereas antireform writers tried to undermine new concepts of equality, I want to explore the pathways of romance and rebellion that, from about 1835 to 1870, provided alternative possibilities for the development of a national consciousness, perhaps even a transnational one. This emerging political consciousness was full of chaos and disruptions that could potentially yield positive transformations and new social commitments to equality rather than a teleological impulse toward Anglo-masculinity. These stories unveil theories of race that were protean and contingent rather than essentialist or biological, and they suggest that many abolitionists and women's rights advocates may have imagined their political role, not as marginalized groups seeking inclusion in an emergent idea of nation, but rather as insurgents—colonial subjects of a sort—seeking to disrupt and reshape the contours and boundaries of the "nation" entirely.

Although American literary critics and historians have been heavily invested in nationalism and nation-ness, yielding many compelling and politically relevant readings of mid-nineteenth-century literature, the role of romance in the literary public sphere has received less attention. Neither millennial visions of an egalitarian future nor heroic figures who blur the boundaries of race and nation have been linked to the creative potential of romance as a genre.[4] Part of what is so fascinating about romance—and in this case I mean romance as what Northrop Frye describes as a "quest" whose form is "dialectical: everything is focused on a conflict between the hero and his enemy, and all the reader's values are bound up with the hero" (187)—is that it offered a way to imagine radical democratic possibility. The reader identifies with the hero and begins to champion his or her quest, which in the 1850s is often a demand for inalienable property. The romantic quest becomes even more intriguing when we consider the woman suffragist suit for property ownership or the black abolitionist assertion of property in the self. The kind of self-possession that Harriet Jacobs claims when she chooses her lover translates into her quest for a home of her own. This home is not just in a house that she owns, but figuratively in a place where she belongs—a place that is clearly not the white space of Anglo-American nationhood.

Although the following chapters focus on sources that enable us to read narratives of race, gender, and nation in new ways, the first chapter navigates the terrain of antireform print culture. These sources depict the dangers of romance and rebellion; they include speeches, pamphlets, and medical texts that invoke the memory of the Haitian Revolution to argue against the expansion of rights to women or the abolition of slavery.[5] Harriet Jacobs's narrative, however, delves into the theme of expansion in remarkably different ways. Her writing not only reflects a demand for the expansion of rights, but also a desire for mobility that places her story outside the geographic borders of the ever-expanding white space of the United States. The second chapter considers the transnational and anticolonial dimensions of *Incidents in the Life of a Slave Girl* (1861); it also discusses Jacobs's rebellion against patriarchal nationhood, which grows from her experience in a failed cross-racial affair. Jacobs, however, goes beyond rebellion to imagine a different constituency in which she might belong—a Christian republic that recognizes the radical equality of human souls as well as the sanctity of human bodies. In this way, her vision has much in common with the Radical Abolition Party.

The third chapter reads Cuban romantic poet and novelist Avellaneda's epistolary autobiography and 1841 novel *Sab* as representative of a hemispheric American fixation, not only on the possibility of cross-racial love affairs, but also on the potential for black insurgents to "avenge" the "copper-colored race," Native Americans. Avellaneda's discussion, however, also turns to romantic ideals of expanding and radically equal souls that might engender the forms of freedom she seeks. It also incorporates the Cuban landscape in a way that equates its integrity and autonomy with the bodily integrity and sexual autonomy of its rebellious characters. The fourth chapter recovers Elizabeth D. Livermore's transatlantic antislavery novel *Zoë* and her literary magazine, the *Independent Highway* (1856), both of which advocate a romantic, amalgamated, millennial, and expansionist vision of racial equality and women's rights. The power of the soul and the corporeal nature of an activist Christianity that can take on the forces of Anglo-masculine nationhood provide new tools for Livermore's rebellion much as they do for Jacobs and Avellaneda.

Julia C. Collins's political essays and her Reconstruction romance, the newly rediscovered serial novel *The Curse of Caste* (1865), are the primary texts for the fifth chapter, which introduces two cross-racial Creole heroines who redefine the inheritance of slavery and its implications for entitlement to American citizenship. Rather than imagining the "tragic mulatta's" liaison with a privileged white man as disastrous, Collins creates a symbolic "national family" that is creolized, its Anglo-Saxonness diluted, and therefore more connected to the cultures of the Caribbean.

In the sixth chapter, Frances Watkins Harper's letters and fiction, including her 1869 novel *Minnie's Sacrifice*, mark the end of the era of reform's romantic representations of interracial love and righteous rebellion, leaving only the exploitative nature of interracial sex and the irreparable loss of civility caused by rebellion. Harper pivoted away from her former alliances with white northern suffragists during Reconstruction, choosing instead to focus on her work with the freed people and the prospects of a free black nation within the treacherous borders of a postbellum United States. Yet all is not lost—Harper's vision of this free black nation, like the free black nation of Haiti that the United States officially recognized in 1862, is a place where labor and belonging can level the boundaries of race and gender that govern the white space of U.S. nationhood. In the conclusion, I briefly consider Lydia Maria Child's long career; her writings coincide with various moments when romance and rebellion took on different meanings, and her final analysis of the problem in *Romance of the Republic* is symptomatic of the unresolved issues of race, gender, and rights that persisted long after the Civil War.

Just as the idea of romantic relationships between black and white mediated the issues of rights presented in the abolition and suffrage movements within the geography of the United States proper, it also signaled the complexities and contradictions within a United States that wanted to think of itself as an exceptional, revolutionary, and anticolonial nation but also quickly assumed a role very similar to colonial domination over indigenes and people of African descent throughout the New World. The era when abolitionists and suffragists contested the very definition of citizenship and individual rights domestically was also an era of expansionism, annexation, and filibustering; thus the antebellum cultural fascination with interracial relationships that suffused fiction, political rhetoric, and even medical and biblical treatises had as much to do with geographical amalgamation as racial mixing.

In the work of many of these writers and reformers, I find an intriguing set of ideas that run contrary to most of our understandings of American literature. These authors exemplify a brief moment in American literary history that explodes with romance and rebellion—a creative intervention in the definition of citizenship that sought to disrupt and obliterate the perceived boundaries between male and female, black and white, or nation and colony.[6] Romantic reformers who transgressed these boundaries did so not only as millennial perfectionists and race radicals; they also did so as geographic and cultural amalgamationists who would bring the spirit of rebellion to every struggle for human rights that emerged in the expanding United States.

1 "What Mischief Would Follow?"

Racial Boundaries, Antireformers, and White Space

The strong attractions of mind, person, manners, fortune, should be able to break through the barriers we now consider impregnable . . . the descendants of the European should covet alliance with the descendants of the African. There is no harm in the supposition, be the improbability of the thing what it may—the only question is, if the fact should happen so to turn out, what mischief would follow?

—Charles Emerson

IN A LETTER DATED October 17, 1849, Wendell Phillips thanked Ralph Waldo Emerson for the use of a set of volumes that he described as a "valuable contribution to the scanty stores of Haytian history."[1] Phillips's apparent claim that "Haytian history" existed only in "scanty stores" is interesting, not only because African American newspapers had been publishing stories about Haiti throughout the first half of the nineteenth century, but also because Phillips himself would consequently discover and contribute to a broad Haitian archive, lecturing on the heroics of Toussaint Louverture by the beginning of the Civil War.[2] For many reformers, rewriting the Haitian Revolution provided a corrective to the providential narrative of freedom that characterized United States history. Situating the Anglo-American concept of righteous rebellion in a hemispheric context, Charles Chauncy Emerson's 1836 antislavery lecture, quoted above, places Haiti as the "other" foundational site of American Revolution. In the eyes of American romanticists like the Emersons, Haiti sometimes signified what Nick Nesbitt describes as "the capacity for self-determination that is a universal, immanent potential" (22), a nation whose founding fathers did not condone what David Brion Davis identifies as the sin of slavery—what Charles Emerson referred to as "sewing up the body politic . . . in a sack with a living viper" (quoted in Bosco and Myerson, *Emerson Brothers* 163). The two poles of representation that characterized Haiti in the nineteenth-century United States, however, were as distant as Nesbitt's space of immanent potential and Charles Emerson's viper-infested sack.

But Charles Emerson's lecture also offered a site of radical possibility in postslavery society, one where "barriers we now consider impregnable" give way to alliances between "the descendants of the European" and "descendants of the African" (15). He expressed this vision of peaceful racial coexistence by suggesting that intermarriage between black and white might some day signify equality, a concept that many of the women in his circle and beyond would explore in their own writing. Although the longing for union was an ideal for some reformers and transcendentalists in the 1840s and 1850s, however, it was anathema to most slaveholders and even the more liberal sectors of American society. In the context of more conventional narratives of American identity, ones that affirmed the white republican gentleman's benevolent care for and just representation of the women and slaves in his "family," the potential for either of these "tribes" to demand their own rights spelled nothing more than an attack on the very tenets of Anglo-American culture and civilization.

Harking back to the foundational myth of white women who performed sexual favors for Toussaint Louverture, the confluence of women's rights and abolitionist activism caused great anxiety for many mid-nineteenth-century Americans, who often imagined the abolitionist as a black man and the suffragist as a white woman. Mason Stokes explains, for example, how proslavery and antisuffrage lecturers and propagandists promulgated a version of the Eden story in which the snake was a black man and Eve an unruly activist woman who transgressed racial and gender boundaries through her illicit relationship with the snake. Just as the abolition of slavery presented a potential disunion within the nation, the abolition of masculine and feminine spheres would certainly disrupt the patriarchal family. The possibility of legally recognized unions between black and white seemed high; it was difficult for even the slave power to deny that such encounters had long taken place between white men and black women despite the barriers of patriarchy and racial slavery. De facto cross-racial marriage and the presence of so many people with mixed African and European lineage among the black population in the Americas was a social reality that emphasized the "naturalness" of cross-racial unions despite the law's repeated attempts to define them as "unnatural" by forbidding or not legally recognizing interracial marriage.[3]

However, the transmission of property and the necessity for Anglo-Americans to envision the ever-expanding landscape as white space also motivated laws against intermarriage. The infamous Manifest Destiny tract attributed to the literary nationalists called the Young Americans, "A Great Nation of Futurity," declares that "American patriotism is not of the soil . . . it is essentially personal enfranchisement" (qtd. in Wald 111). In other words, although "American patriots" have no indigenous claim to the territory they take up, their presence is justified by the ideals of a political experiment that converts the wild and untamed landscape into a civilized and productive sovereign territory. The inherent contradiction of disenfranchising enslaved laborers, however, had well-known consequences. Rousseau's suggestion that the right of first occupancy applied only to settlers who cultivated and made "improvements" to that land should have caused some anxiety to slaveholders who never actually dirtied their hands with that soil. Although not all Americans agreed with the "Great Nation of Futurity" philosophy, the idea that the men and women who had performed virtually all of the agricultural labor in Haiti could lay claim to that landscape, rising up against their masters and demanding allotments of the land they had cultivated, certainly lingered in the political imagination. Both rebellion and cross-racial romance could yield an "amalgamated" landscape, the province of black and white rather than the patriotic space of white "personal enfranchisement."

Even abolitionists who welcomed the tropes of romance and rebellion had trouble relinquishing the assumption that the American landscape should remain white space. Charles Emerson's antislavery lecture invoked the topics of amalgamation and rebellion as central concerns in the slavery debate. Oddly enough, however, he assumed that a similar situation, brought about peacefully in the United States, would not involve any redistribution of land or property. Slaveholders would not be impoverished by emancipation because "their land will not be emancipated. There will be no abolition of the cotton tree, or the sugar cane, or rice or tobacco." He thus maintains the fantasy of the American landscape as "white space" that becomes so central, four years later, to the Young Americans.

The project of defining the New World as white space required racial boundaries that were far more solid than national borders. As the United States, in particular, defined its Anglo-American mission and stretched the limits of white space to Louisiana and beyond, excluding the first occupiers or enslaved laborers from citizenship helped whiten the space. That the transmission of property and entitlement were passed from father to son made it imperative that white women be kept away from black or indigenous men. Emerging in the late 1830s, "medical" and "anthropological" texts that legitimated white male authority and explained the necessity for restrictive marriage laws focused intensely on the hypersexual black male body as a source of contamination, much as gothic tales of the Haitian Revolution devised what Angela Y. Davis has called the myth of the black rapist.

Attempting to use reason and scientific knowledge as the basis for defending the marriage contract as constructed through racial patriarchy, antireformers resorted to descriptions of the sexual act to draw distinct biological lines between racial groups and deny the reality of sexual relationships between black and white. Dr. Paul Broca, a distinguished member of the London Anthropological Society who was known as the founder of French anthropology, explained the dangers of allowing proximity between white women and black men very clinically: "One of the characters of the Ethiopian race consists in the length of the penis compared with that of the Caucasian race. . . . There results from this physical disposition, that the union of the Caucasian man with an Ethiopian woman is easy and without any inconvenience for the latter. The case is different in the union of the Ethiopian with a Caucasian woman, who suffers in the act, the neck of the uterus is pressed against the sacrum, so that the act of reproduction is not merely painful, but *frequently nonproductive*" (28). As a justification for "breeding" practices that would increase the quality of one's chattels, this shocking excerpt advocates white male sex with black women but depicts sex between black men and white women as painful, perhaps dangerous, and so unnatural as to be "non-productive" (28). While sex between an "Ethiopian" and a "Caucasian" woman was obviously not unthinkable, its implications concerned nations that reaped the benefits of slavery. Broca's cosmopolitan résumé, furthermore, reminds us of the transnational dimensions of the politics and practice of constructing racial boundaries, even in a supposedly enlightened and rational Atlantic world where the boundaries of knowledge were porous.

This genealogy illustrates how, as Jared Sexton puts it, "the politics of interracial sexuality are fundamental to racial formation" (15). The convergence of race and sexuality, however, is more than a prurient preoccupation or a "persistent focal point of psychosocial anxiety" (15). Defining race through biology—particularly by obsessing over the differences articulated in interracial reproduction—"is foundational for racial difference—the field for its production, contestation, and containment" (15).[4] Whether through coercing sexual submission or forcing labor, the reality of racial slavery was that one could be coerced *because* he or she was black and therefore had no sovereignty of self. Lacking self, one could not own any other kind of property; thus the racist construction of blackness also protected an American landscape envisioned as white space from infiltration or encroachment. In this case, the ideal of cross-racial sexual relationships as a type of romance collapses; they can take place only through coercion and violence.

The psychosocial connection between interracial "romance" or heterosexual relations and acts of rebellion, in the writings of antireformers, much as in writings by experts from colonial powers, also unveils the critical role of property and entitlement to the creation of racial boundaries. Because insurgents who took over territory were also believed to take white women, this kind of romance and rebellion renders human bodies and geographic bodies metaphorically interchangeable. Just as encounters with black men could supposedly do great damage to the bodies of white women, black property ownership was perceived as threatening and destructive to the sovereign political body built upon what Anglo-Americans imagined as white space.

Politicians, scientists, and medical doctors alike went to great lengths to prohibit sexual relations between black men and white women. For example, Dr. Alexander Walker's treatise *Intermarriage: or, The mode in which and the causes why beauty, health, and intellect result from certain unions and deformaty* [sic], *disease, and insanity from others . . .* , first published in London in 1838, was reprinted and, according to advertisements and endorsements printed in the front matter of one of these editions, enthusiastically received in the United States. The book's title page touts it as "essentially scientific" and "transcendently important" in its illustration of the "laws of nature." While England was the political vanguard in abolishing the slave trade and emancipating its colonies, its print culture clearly worked in the opposite direction. Walker's basic premise is that intellectual and moral characteristics are inherited from the father and physical strength and vital organs from the mother's "blood." This argument conveniently supports "breeding" between white men and black women, certainly a boon to slave masters and overseers who were "fathering" a burgeoning mulatto population and expanding their property, both real and chattel, in the Americas. Conversely, since intellectual vigor is passed down from the [white] father, Walker sets the stage to demonstrate the inherent danger of crossing a black man with a white woman—the birth of an imbecile, physically degenerate child. A few years later, American Dr. Josiah Nott registered his concern about passing on "intellectual vigor" from the white race to the black because "every one at the south is familiar with the fact that the mulattoes have more intelligence than the negroes, make bad slaves, and are always leaders in insurrections" (28). In this case, it seems that Vincent Ogé rather than Louverture serves as the iconic Haitian example.

A chain of events beginning with cross-racial sex and culminating in the presence of rebellious, amalgamated bodies that would lay claim not only to freedom but also to the landscape through acts of insurrection is typical in mid-nineteenth-century writing about race and sex. Anxieties about racial "mixing" shaped political rhetoric in the United States, both in terms of race and gender rights on a national level and in terms of new territories, such as Louisiana, that might absorb new racial groups into the constituency. A public obsession with the idea of "blood" as an essence that differentiated between male and female bodies as well as between Anglo and African or Native bodies made political rhetoric very carnal and sexual rather than abstract and intellectual. Both proslavery and antislavery factions used the term "amalgamation" to describe the blending of black and white blood that took place when these cross-racial sexual relationships produced offspring. Early American legal documents and political writing, including Thomas Jefferson's *Notes on the State of Virginia*, reflect a similar obsession with amalgamation. As A. Leon Higginbotham illustrates, the concept of "racial purity" had a foundational role in defining "what it meant to be white and superior" in the United States and to lay claim to territory or property within its expanding boundaries (41). The historical reality of amalgamation, therefore, had a seminal effect on the very definition, and the exclusionary parameters, of American citizenship. According to Higginbotham, "the 1662, 1705, and 1723 Virginia statues have always been analyzed for their use of race to define who was a free person, who was a slave, and who was a servant. This sort of analysis is certainly crucial to understanding how the form of slavery that the colonists developed in the New World was unique, in that it relied exclusively on race. But the statutes also have another meaning that is equally important. With the legislators' rather compulsive preoccupation with interracial sex, the statutes grounded the precept of inferiority firmly in biology. If black blood was the mark of inferiority, sex became the instrument by which it was transmitted" (41). Thus the spectacle of interracial sex marked the erasure of whiteness and its attendant privilege: it defined whiteness as "no black-ness" and tied black inferiority to black sexuality.

Expressions of cross-racial desire seem least frequent among black male authors and orators, suggesting that the fixation on the sexually ambitious black male body was, in large part, a white fantasy. Despite David Walker's assertion in the *Appeal . . . To the Coloured Citizens of the World* (1829) that "I would not give a *pinch of snuff* to be married to any white person I ever saw in all the days of my life," black demands for justice and calls to action often translated, in the white imagination, into demands for access to white women (Gilyard and Wardi 1047). Again, it is ironic that antireformers knew that the majority of mulatto children were born to black mothers and white fathers, yet they still demonized black men as the sexual aggressors. Representations of and anxieties about the Haitian Revolution fixated on the potential dangers of mulatto or free black populations. Vincent Ogé, the free black man massacred by the colonists in 1791 for demanding French citizenship, was the son of a wealthy mulatto woman in Port au Prince. That his murderers liter-ally split his body apart after torturing him publicly suggests a deep psy-chological hatred toward blackness and the desire to eradicate it from the body politic just as they violently tore apart and bashed Ogé's cross-racial body. This is a revolutionary moment that the Russian theorist Mikhael Bakhtin would have understood—a moment where "the scene" of political upheaval "is consistently portrayed as a tearing to pieces," a carnivalistic dismembering of the body (*Problems* 161).

Similar antipathy toward black incorporation into the body poli-tic existed in the United States and often confused the very presence of cross-racial bodies within the republic with a bestial desire, on the part of blacks, to infiltrate and corrupt the white female body and the Anglo-American body politic. Somehow, spectral images of cross-racial sex erased white men's violations of the black women's bodies and focused on panic-ridden predictions of the black male rapist overtaking (and con-taminating) the white woman's body and the body politic of the United States. This impulse toward Anglo-Saxon or white nationality, though pronounced, did not go unchallenged, as I will discuss below. If aggres-sion was a racial trait, there was a wealth of evidence that it was endemic to Anglo-Saxons, particularly in the conquest of the United States and its expanding borders. Many activists were well aware—and critical of the fact—that the British Empire, the font of Anglo-American "greatness," established its "dominion" through violence rather than innate cultural or intellectual superiority. Theodore Parker, for example, announced in

1854 that the early settlers of Plymouth Bay "had in them the ethno-logic idiosyncrasy of the Anglo-Saxon—his restless disposition to invade and conquer other lands; his haughty contempt of humbler tribes which leads him to subvert, enslave, kill, and exterminate; his fondness for material things" (quoted in Frederickson 100).[5]

It is interesting that antireformers, who often invoked the powers of Anglo-Saxondom, projected these hypersexual, violent stereotypes upon the black male body. One example of the antireform hysteria over abolition and its supposedly "amalgamationist" undertones comes in an 1835 treatise by Massachusetts Attorney General James Trecothick Austin, written in response to William Ellery Channing's denunciation of slavery. As part of a volume of short works on slavery that Senator Charles Sumner had bound and eventually donated to Harvard University, Austin's *Remarks* provides a quintessential example of U.S. paranoia about racial coexistence in a postslavery society, or "amalgamation."

Austin argues that even if black men emerge from slavery "intelligent, moral, and industrious, with all the capacity and inclinations of the white man. . . . [t]hey would be negroes still" (45). Basing his predictions, perhaps, on the precedent set by Toussaint Louverture and deeply invested in an assumedly immutable biological difference between black and white, Austin continues and echoes Jefferson: "The more their intelligence, the greater would be the mutual hostility of the two races; and the final possession of power would be the result of a war of extermination, in which one or the other race would perish" (45). Compare Jefferson's sentiments in *Notes on the State of Virginia*: "Deep rooted prejudices entertained by whites; ten thousand recollections, by the blacks, of the injuries they have sustained; new provocations; the real distinctions which nature has made; and many other circumstances, will divide us into parties, and produce convulsions which will probably never end but in the extermination of the one or the other race.—To these objections, which are political, may be added others, which are physical and moral" (145). This flashback to the Founding Fathers is another consistent move in debates over insurrection, whether articulated by the likes of Austin or as a justification for uprisings voiced by abolitionists.

Yet the most consistent move was to connect rebellion to cross-racial sexual relations. In the next paragraph, Austin questions the concept of amalgamation, seemingly envisioning the result of this war as the extermination of white men and the ensuing sexual availability of white women to black men. His rant reflects the anxieties of both insurrection and cross-racial romance that emerged from the antireform sector of the public sphere in the United States and that would persist in white-supremacist ideology for one hundred years, at the least. In response to the specter of mulatto citizenship that he has just proposed (and that he blames on reformers rather than on Anglo-American men like Jefferson), he says:

> But I fearlessly aver that if this [amalgamation] be the tendency and the result of our moral reformation, rather than our white Saxon race should degenerate into a tribe of tawney-colored Quadroons, rather than that our fair and beauteous females should give birth to the thick-lipped, woolly-headed children of African fathers, rather than the nice and delicate character of the American woman, which in its freshness and its pride is at once the cause and the consequence of civilization, should be debased and degraded by such indiscriminate and beastly connexion, rather than the negro should be seated in the halls of Congress and his sooty complexion glare upon us from the bench of justice, rather than he should mingle with us in the familiar intercourse of domestic life and taint the atmosphere of our homes and firesides, —I WILL BRAVE MY SHARE OF ALL THE RESPONSIBILITY OF KEEPING HIM IN SLAVERY. (45)

The collision between public and private, between an imagined threat to the national and domestic sanctity of American life, is striking. Austin does not distinguish between cross-racial sexual relations that debase and degrade the "nice and delicate character of the American woman" and the disruption of public power that results in the "negro . . . seated in the halls of Congress and his sooty complexion glar[ing] upon us from the bench of domestic life"; in fact, the "Negro" judge or congressman seems to go home, at the end of the day or at the end of Austin's rant, to enjoy the "familiar intercourse of domestic life" and the "atmosphere of our homes and firesides" (45). His irrational—even hysterical—response does not specify whether insurrection or amalgamation have brought about this spectral future for the republic—the two seem as inseparable as the public and domestic spheres of influence in which he perceives a white male crisis.

The anxious language of proslavery Anglo-American men is just one of the conventional narratives of American identity that figured race and gender—in this case, white masculinity—as central characteristics of citizenship and entitlement to land. Their use of revolutionary rhetoric justifies Anglo-American supremacy, while other activists would turn to other revolutions to challenge that supremacy. The prevalence of references to the Haitian Revolution in African American political arguments both asserted a radical concept of equal rights and envisioned Haiti as the appropriate home for freedom-loving Americans of African descent. Understandably, many African American men looked to emigration—either to Haiti or to Africa—rather than continue the struggle to be integrated into "white space." The language of rebellion is singularly important in black emigrationist rhetoric, which introduces a different type of expansion and rejects the idea of amalgamation as a form of inclusion. Martin Delany's 1859 novel *Blake; or, The Huts of America* even seems to reject the idea of inclusion in a national body politic in favor of insurrection. Although he was an activist who demanded recognition in national politics and asserted his belonging in the United States (he stood by Frederick Douglass and opposed William Lloyd Garrison's burning of the Constitution in 1848), Delany's tale of transnational slave rebellion as well as his expanding interest in emigration in the 1850s suggest that he kept other paths toward freedom open. Should we assume, then, that his contemporaries imagined inclusion in the body politic established by the Founding Fathers as the only means toward freedom?

Many African Americans overtly rejected the idea of inclusion or the ideals of amalgamation that some white abolitionists, like Lydia Maria Child, believed could resolve problems of racial difference. If nationality itself was a white creation designed to imagine filial connections between white citizens of the United States, the likelihood that the national family could recognize its black members seemed slim. Citing the *Douglass Monthly*, Mark Noll says:

> In 1863 a free black from Washington, D.C., John Menard, wrote to Douglass's newspaper to argue that republican principles were so interwoven with white American racism that blacks should simply give them up: "The grand plea" of the "great American people" is republicanism and the perpetuity of white nationality. . . . Republicanism is the family god of the American people; it is their all—their meat and bread and religion. . . . The inherent principle of the white majority of this nation is to refuse FOREVER republican equality to the black minority. . . . the prosperity and happiness of our race and their posterity lay [*sic*] in a separation from the white race. (405)

Menard, in this case, is arguing that the development of a pluralistic or amalgamated national family is unlikely to take place. His awareness of the white majority's power to exclude African Americans from the body politic casts doubt on the ubiquitous symbols of an amalgamated nation or family that surround him. But what kinds of alternatives did Menard envision? To what extent did Delany, or Harriet Jacobs, consider other options and alternatives? The presence of options suggests that many antebellum Americans were highly critical of a "white nationality" built upon essential ideas of racial difference. They also lacked the attendant faith in the national government to resolve the issues of slavery and gender subordination. The next chapter illustrates how, waging such a critique, many activists perceived their role more like insurgent colonial subjects than potential citizens. Rebelling against the fixed and oppressive forms of racial meaning was one way that these activists imagined themselves as insurgents, and the metaphor of heterosexual romance was one vehicle through which they voiced that challenge. Much of the archive presented in this book demonstrates how some antebellum Americans thought well beyond the limits of Anglo-masculine nationhood.

Although "nation" has been a salient term in literary criticism for some time, it may not be an all-purpose vehicle to understand the literary and political imaginings of subaltern groups because it stems from a national ideal that was exclusive, exceptional, and elitist.[6] As Priscilla Wald illustrates, groups in conflict with the U.S. government, such as the Cherokee, recapitulated a state of "imperium in imperio" that had much in common with the prerevolutionary colonies' relationship to England (28). Thus when women's rights activists invoked a term like "slavery" to describe their condition, they most often echoed the revolutionary rhetoric of slavery under colonial domination rather than a sense of identification with the experience of transatlantic slavery. Similarly, African American activists positioned themselves as a colonized people by identifying with Haitian revolutionaries. The political imaginary of many residents of the United States, rather than aspiring toward inclusion in a homogenous U.S. national identity, produced a model of political activity that looked very different.

To get to the space of freedom and equality, furthermore, required engagement in embodied acts of rebellion. As the rebellious figures of American letters pushed the borders of belonging that defined the revolutionary moment of 1776, they reconsidered the revolution of 1791 as a lesson for white men. While it was often characterized by fear, bloodshed, and rape, the lesson of Haiti also had radically egalitarian potential. John Stauffer's *Black Hearts of Men* (2002) discusses the Radical Abolition Party founders—John Brown, James McCune Smith, Gerrit Smith, and Frederick Douglass—in light of their belief that white men needed to acquire "black hearts" so they might recognize the rights of black men and develop a radically egalitarian society. W. E. B. Du Bois's biography of Brown attributes his strategies of insurgent warfare to an almost metaphysical connection to Haiti, stating that Brown "had posted himself in relation to the wars of Toussaint L'Ouverture" (126). Racial longing and Brown's faith in cross-racial love, in this instance, are spiritual rather than sexual. Discourses of the soul in that period also keyed to the "black heart" and its ideal of platonic love. Utopian, communitarian, and even "free love" groups endorsed the romantic concept of equal souls in a manner that signified political equality, which they sometimes extended to white women and people of color. What John Spurlock calls a "New View" affected the way people understood "religion, literature, and social thought throughout the United States," and "anchor[ed] the dignity of man in his inner being" (43–44). The kind of love that guided John Brown to Harpers Ferry, then, drew from a romantic concept of the soul with radically equalitarian political implications. Rebellion, once again, was linked to a romantic ideal, undergirded by the fact that John Brown took inspiration from none other than Louverture.

Of course, a politicized concept of love could also be used to deny rights to people of color. Joan Dayan illustrates the perverse linkage of the concepts of love and romance to the "business of race"; the twisted type of dependent and submissive love that "a slave, a black pet, or a white wife" might have for his or her master (or husband) "is not possible between two equals" (189, 193). Whereas "racialist arguments . . . depended on the negro's lack of *proper* 'love' or refined feeling" and even Thomas Jefferson argued that "love seems with them to be more an eager desire, than a tender delicate mixture of sentiment and sensation" (quoted in Dayan 191, 194), many reformers used love as a metaphor for political equality. It is important not to forget that both the form of love that would spur cross-racial heterosexual relationships (biological amalgamation) and the idealization of Toussaint are facets of romantic racialism: each imagines the potential for racial union through white recognition of and attraction to distinct qualities in blacks that had been "unthinkable" in the moment of the Haitian Revolution. According to notable historians like George Fredrickson, racial meaning in the mid-nineteenth-century United States emerged within a constellation of biologically deterministic race science, the expedience of chattel slavery, and occasional abolitionist attempts at romantic racialism. The terms of race science were couched in the same stereotypes and horror stories that white Creole refugees told about rebellious Haitian blacks, emphasizing savage violence and lasciviousness. Yet Lydia Maria Child and Charles

Emerson refuted these stereotypes. Beginning in the 1830s, both Child and Emerson, following suit with the writings of many black authors, retold the story of the Haitian Revolution quite differently.

Quoted in the epigraph, Charles Emerson's speech also considers the significance of cross-racial love and violent rebellion in a Haitian context. It illuminates the way that amalgamation, or the "melioration" of races, rather than the rise and fall of distinct and discernible civilizations, is a transnational cultural project, not just a biological one. Haiti, then, becomes a test case in the making of racial meaning for Charles Emerson and his contemporaries.[7] Charles Emerson cites the *Liberator*, Benjamin Lundy's *Genius of Universal Emancipation* (founded 1821), and his English cohort Harriet Martineau's *Illustrations of Political Economy* (1834). What Emerson and other transcendentalists understood about Haiti also came from sources like *An Appeal in Favor of That Class of Americans Called Africans* (1833), wherein Lydia Maria Child makes it a point that "when the general rising of the blacks took place in 1791," Toussaint declined to participate in unnecessary bloodshed and actually saved lives (*Appeal* 175). Martineau also penned a historical romance, *The Hour and the Man* (1841)—starring the magnanimous and unimpeachable Toussaint—that also shaped, and distorted, New England's views of Haitian history during the most vigorous era of U.S. abolitionism. Charles Emerson's "Lecture" also speculates and theorizes on racial meaning in general.[8] Ralph Waldo Emerson refers only a few times to "the arrival in the world of such men as Toussaint, and the Haytian heroes, or of the leaders of their race in Barbadoes and Jamaica," yet his idea of Toussaint (*Antislavery* 31), the man who Lydia Maria Child insists refused to join the rebellion until he had "procured an opportunity for the escape" of his master" (*Appeal* 175), shares similarities with many of the writings of other transcendentalists.[9]

For Charles Emerson, cross-racial encounter offers the potential for an amalgamation that is a form of cultural syncretism, a postslavery United States where men treat one another with the same exemplary love and respect that Toussaint showed his former master.[10] The true origin of equality, in this example, is of course the Haitian, rather than the American, Revolution—but the idea of amalgamation is less biological than Broca, Walker, or Nott see it.[11] As an early example of how reformers intervened in the proslavery claims about race and biology that were tied to amalgamation and insurrection, Charles Emerson's lecture draws a distinction between the romanticized, loving image of blacks and the more spectral figure of black rebellion.

After citing the commonly held fear that blacks will "rise in a mass to massacre the whites" in the United States, he names Haiti as a "first witness" in the case against slavery, an object of study that can reveal the keys to racial harmony in a post-emancipation United States (13, 17). Conscious of the effect of historical narratives on political power, he writes, "owing to ignorance or misrepresentation the history of [Haiti] has often been quoted as showing the atrocities," whereas Charles Emerson sees only men who fought for their freedom and reported duly to work when they had secured it. He interrogates the irrational contradictions of "race science" by asking how slaveholders can claim that people of African descent are inherently ferocious and simultaneously insist that their captives are "tame and affectionate servants" (14).[12] As Michel-Rolph Trouillot illustrates, French colonists on the eve of the Haitian Revolution "devise[d] formulas to repress the unthinkable and bring it back within the realm of accepted discourse" by writing about "the Negroes" as "tranquil and obedient" (72). In the wake, not only of the Haitian Revolution, but of Denmark Vesey's alleged 1822 plot in Charleston and Nat Turner's 1831 insurrection in Virginia, U.S. slaveholders could no longer cling exclusively to the "tame and affectionate" formula. Yet Charles Emerson inhabits the space of contradiction to question the assumption that "freedom for the Negroes is a chimera" and propose a new narrative of slavery and freedom in the Americas (72).

As he advocates immediate emancipation, his initial invocation of stories of extreme antiwhite violence in the Haitian past shifts into a possible future for the United States. This future is one wherein "the strong attractions of mind, person, manners, fortune, should be able to break through the barriers we now consider impregnable," and "the descendants of the European should covet alliance with the descendants of the African" (15). He also juxtaposes the claim that blacks are naturally lascivious with the claim that blacks are "physical[ly] repugnan[t]" to whites, undermining both arguments with a reference to the vast mulatto population of the United States, which turns the argument about lasciviousness back on white males and reveals the desirability, rather than the repugnant quality, of black women (15). While his "first witness," the Haitian Revolution, culminated in a notorious description of an "independence act" that would use "the skin of a white man for parchment, his skull for a desk, his blood for ink, and a bayonet for a pen," Charles Emerson ignores this imagery of ruptured race relations, rewriting the Haitian Revolution and anticipating the end of slavery in the United States with a conjugal conclusion.[13]

To move between specters of violent racial conflict that are well-known "facts" of the Haitian struggle for freedom and an ideal of romantic love that resolves the problem of racial difference seems equally chimerical. Yet the juxtaposition of gothic images of the Haitian Revolution and stories of cross-racial love reappear, almost obsessively, in early-nineteenth-century print culture. The two poles of representation—tearing apart a white body to gain independence versus bringing together black and white bodies in an amorous embrace—persisted in New England newspaper reports of Haiti in the 1830s and 1840s. In 1830, reprints of the announcement that "one of the daughters of Madam Christophe, Ex Queen of Haiti . . . is engaged to be married to a very handsome Prussian Colonel of high reputation. Mademoiselle Christophe is described as a charming and accomplished young lady; her complexion is the purest ebony"[14] contrasted with reports that "intelligence has been received from St. Domingo . . . of the blacks taking possession of the Island and murdering every white person except the English and American consuls."[15]

Charles Emerson knew that more than a decade of bloodshed surrounded Toussaint's campaigns, and newspaper reports in the 1830s and 1840s depicted ongoing racial violence in Haiti. Yet the geography of freedom in his lecture is transnational, a freedom he claims already exists in Colombia, Mexico, Brazil, and other parts of the Americas. Nonetheless, he acknowledges that the violence that race inspires is the fault of whites and contaminates the promises of 1776. The history that the United States must reckon with, as Charles Emerson explains when he moves on to the example of the Haitian Revolution, is the legacy "of the Sin," not only in the slave trade, but in "the prejudice against the free colored citizens" (20). "The Sin" is particular to the United States because, since the Revolution of 1776, "instead of forming a Union to establish justice, promote the general welfare, and secure the blessings of liberty to ourselves and our posterity, we have set our feet in the stocks and loaded Liberty with a chain heavier than that from which she was just set free" (20). Charles Emerson cites examples of the benefits of emancipation throughout the Southern Hemisphere and severely criticizes the American Colonization Society's plan to deport free blacks, "compelling him to leave the country which is as native to him as to us" (19). The insistence that African Americans not only belong, but also deserve the same rights as Anglo Saxons continues in a protest against the shameful persecution of Prudence Crandall (for educating black children in Connecticut); the perpetrators of these injustices, Anglo-Americans, clearly suffer from a dearth of ethics. As Charles Emerson says, "The persecution . . . stands conspicuous amongst the mortifying evidences of narrow-mindedness . . . that characterise us as a people" (19).

Charles Emerson's query about the biological amalgamation of the races concludes with a condemnation of the violent amalgamation that characterizes racial slavery. When he asks "what mischief would follow" if "the barriers we now consider impregnable" should break and "the descendants of the European should covet alliance with the descendants of the African" (15), he frames slavery and racism as a huge historical mistake. If those barriers broke, he asks, "would it not be a matter of rejoicing with the men of that distant age?" (15). While he seems to advocate a model of cross-racial love, he does not treat the topic of amalgamation during slavery in the United States with the same optimism. Rather, Charles Emerson says, "the intercourse that now subsists between master and slave, whites and blacks, is a thousandfold worse than legal marriage": "The whole country south of the Mason's and Dixon's line is a Nursery of the mixed breed, and that the amalgamation of the two races is going on much more rapidly and with much more fatal influence on the character of the people than would be possible in the case of emancipation" (15).

Charles Emerson attacks the problem of amalgamation, but from the opposite angle that antireformers tackle it. While the romantically racialized traits of "benevolence," joy, and even docility are troubling stereotypes, retelling the story of the Haitian Revolution, as Charles Emerson indicated, would change the way people thought about race. He believed this retelling was characteristic of a new age. Charles makes an antiracist and constructivist, rather than romantic racialist, argument in his lecture. Since stories and lived experiences condition morally intrinsic racial qualities, they are mutable and take shape in the moment of articulation. They are not biological realities whose containment requires vigilant and violent policing. Like Theodore Parker's, Charles Emerson's version of recent history illustrates that whiteness—the qualities of the Anglo-American—is marked by aggression and greed. Charles Emerson's hemispheric construction of freedom extended as far as Brazil, but his brother Ralph Waldo Emerson failed to take up the project of imagining this expanding, amalgamated, loving world of freedom. Instead, women writers developed the metaphor of amalgamation as the productive outcome of cross-racial amorous affairs and righteous rebellion.

In the next chapter, Harriet Jacobs not only aspires to instruct white men on the limits of U.S. nationhood, she employs many of the dark gothic images of Haiti to characterize the restrictive and oppressive white space that is the U.S. South. In her revision of revolutionary history, the lesson of Nat Turner carries on the work of the Haitian Revolution and challenges white masculinity just as she, in her own rebellious manner, engages stories of failed romance to trouble the limits of freedom.

2 Colored Carpenters and White Gentlemen

Harriet Jacobs's Pedagogy of Citizenship

> After the alarm caused by Nat Turner's insurrection had subsided, the slaveholders came to the conclusion that it would be well to give the slaves enough of religious instruction to keep them from murdering their masters.
>
> —Harriet Jacobs

HARRIET JACOBS'S NARRATIVE is a fascinating example of the coincidence of cross-racial relationships and incidents of rebellion. *Incidents in the Life of a Slave Girl* contests the manifestations of cross-racial sexual violence that contaminate all unions, personal and national. In fact, cross-racial sexual violence in the United States served to demarcate the boundaries of the nation as white space, the cause for Jacobs's protest. This white space emerged not only because Anglo-American men had exclusive claims to property (both real and chattel) in the nation, but also because the mandate that slavery followed the condition of the mother served two purposes: not only were the offspring of cross-racial sexual encounters denied any inheritance from their white fathers, but those children's status as chattels also increased the value of the white father's property. The definition of freedom that the American Revolution generated not only made the legal and geographic contours of the nation into white space; it also indirectly justified white men's "right" to sexual coercion and, in its insistence on the right of white men to expand their property, equated enslavement with immobility and the denial of self-sovereignty.

Therefore, the white space of property and privilege that white men could claim, the place Jacobs endeavors to escape, enabled violent forms of amalgamation. This white space was literally the real estate upon which white men were entitled to use their slaves—their chattel property—to reproduce their own wealth. These privileges of nationhood, which emerged from the American Revolution, shape Jacobs's representation of Dr. Flint, who repeatedly tries to restrict her movement and contain her so he can exercise his "right" to his property—her body. Yet another form of amalgamation, and of rebellion, comes through in Jacobs's writing. In her own role as a rebellious slave, Jacobs protests the laws of the Anglo-American nation and the conditions of the white space to which Dr. Flint confines her. She escapes the sexual violence of white space, finding room to maneuver by taking two lovers of her own choice. Although her story ends "with freedom, not in the usual way, with marriage," she repeatedly invokes stories of heterosexual romance to illustrate her own personal form of rebellion.

Whereas the expansion of rights that constituted the American Revolution relied on the development of a sovereign—and homogenous— emergent nation that functioned through conquest and masculine power, the expansion of rights to which Jacobs aspires coincides with a concept of black nationalism that Robert Levine has identified as simultaneously transnational. Although, before her escape and for the balance of her narrative, Jacobs is confined to smaller and smaller spaces, she repeatedly envisions other spaces of freedom, from Florida to the North. Levine's work on Douglass, Martin Delany, and Whittier teases out the complexities of black nationalism within the emigration debates that were particularly vigorous in the 1850s; in this context, the very idea of emigration had many layers. Emigrationist thought, more specifically, did not have to entail moving to Haiti or Africa; rather, it could be participation in a school of thought that challenged certain aspects of the United States—of what I would call its limits and boundaries as a white space of nationhood. Thus imagining spaces outside of her restricted location enables her to critique the United States. Keeping in mind that Jacobs began writing *Incidents* in the 1850s, the expansionist and emigrationist ideas of the black periodical press were available to her.

Therefore, references to faraway places disrupt the white space of amalgamation that constitutes the United States. The distinctiveness of Jacobs's more transnational family history provides a glimpse of racial cosmopolitanism that vastly improves upon a restrictive Anglo-American model of nation. On the first page of *Incidents*, Jacobs projects a migratory idea of freedom that is connected to a similarly provisional idea of citizenship. She introduces her grandmother through a family history of interracial love and manumission: "I had also a great treasure in my maternal grandmother, who was a remarkable woman in many respects. She was the daughter of a planter in South Carolina, who, at his death, left her mother and his three children free, with money to go to St. Augustine, where they had relatives" (*Incidents* 12).

Although she mentions that she is unclear about the specifics of the story, the detail that her grandmother was captured and reenslaved en route to Florida, which was then a Spanish colony, offers up one of the first gestures toward geographic mobility. At this and other moments, Jacobs imagines being outside the United States entirely as the best option for freedom. The inability of her unfortunate great-grandfather to protect his heirs also provides one of Jacobs's early critiques of an Anglo-masculine nation. It seems probable that "patriots" fighting for independence, not British soldiers, captured her grandmother. British forces had a greater role in emancipating slaves than in capturing them during the war. Ironically, the first promise of freedom in her family history was likely thwarted by freedom-loving Anglo-Saxons who were either patriots fighting for their own independence or slaveholding Tories fighting to maintain the "freedom" of slavery. The promise of freedom falls apart because her grandmother never makes it to St. Augustine, where she has relatives who might be black or white—this is not one of the "particulars" Jacobs recalls. Tragically, her grandmother is confined by the white space of emerging Anglo-American nationhood.

As we learn from Zepheniah and Anna Jai Kingsley's stories, which I will recount momentarily, Spanish Florida offered free blacks more property rights and privileges than the early U.S. republic. Jacobs's reference to St. Augustine implies an understanding of the different models of rights that operated under different colonial regimes; her contemporaries would have recognized these differences as well. At the same time, her maternal great-grandfather, a white man, initiates a pattern of failed Anglo-American manhood that she replicates throughout her narrative.

As many critics have observed, Jacobs's critique of white patriarchy and fathers who fail their black children parallels the failings of a national government that does not recognize the nation's black family members. The failings of an amalgamated national family, however, also parallel the failings of a foundationally flawed nation that strives to expand and amalgamate its geography. While Florida, as a Spanish colony, is a place of refuge, formerly French New Orleans is a dangerous place for Jacobs's family, particularly after the Louisiana Purchase. In other words, a Florida untainted by Anglo-masculine power is superior to a Louisiana that is. Like the amalgamation of bodies that interracial sex can engender, the amalgamation of political cultures engendered by Anglo-masculine expansion is a form of contamination that corrupts the pure ideals of freedom. After her favorite uncle, Benjamin, makes his first escape attempt, her grandmother learns the devastating news that he has been captured and will not be resold until the trader reaches New Orleans, which would make it unlikely that he would see his family again. In this case, the reference to New Orleans has to do with its geographical distance from the family home in North Carolina rather than its reputation for sexual exploitation and plaçage, an elaborate system of concubinage focused on "cultivating" beautiful quadroon or octoroon women for the exclusive purpose of pleasing wealthy white men.

Because the expansion of Anglo nationhood, or white space, facilitates encroachment on black women's bodies, Jacobs attenuates those effects. The additional dangers facing women in the white patriarchal regime of Anglo-masculine nationhood, nonetheless, are crucial to Jacobs's narrative. She takes the opportunity to draw attention to this New Orleans system of sexual exploitation subtly, interrupting the story of her uncle's struggle to point out that the trader "said he would give any price if the handsome lad was a girl. We thanked God that he was not." The practice of amalgamation through plaçage, in this case, takes on a more negative cast than the practice of selling a young man so far away from his mother that the two will likely never meet again. Jacobs's allusion to plaçage, in this case, interrupts her family narrative to call attention to the dangers of sexual relationships between white men and black women. Whether situated in New Orleans, Florida, or even North Carolina, black women cannot expect protection from white men, even if those men have the best intentions, as did her grandfather, and eventually, the father of her own children.

A similar set of complaints appears, somewhat ironically, in the writings of the white slaveholder Zephaniah Kingsley (whose story was partially recorded by Jacobs's future editor, Child, in 1836). After marrying an African woman who had been his slave, Kingsley struggled, even as a white patriarch, to "protect" his cross-racial family within the boundaries of the United States. The limitations of Anglo-masculinity as a symbol of national leadership surface as readily in his writings as in Jacobs's. Kingsley emigrated, with his mulatto sons, to a colony he established in Haiti. The idea that one can escape the laws of slavery in the United States and live under some "law less absurd than that of color" clearly appealed to Jacobs's white patriarch as well (Stowell, Genovese, and Mormino 120). Nonetheless, Kingsley did not acknowledge that a nation built on the privileges of racial slavery could not contain racial and gender differences without subordinating them and effectively rendering nonwhite and nonmale as noncitizens. Just as Florida and Louisiana's "inclusion" in the United States limited the potential for freedom that each colony could offer, inclusion in an Anglo-masculine nation would compromise Jacobs's "pure" principles of freedom. Similarly, sexual involvement with white men would compromise her "pure" and sacred body.

Because Jacobs endeavors—and fails—to make the site of cross-racial romance into a pedagogical space where she can convert and transform the men who have power over her, she fundamentally critiques the idea of nation as an abstract political entity and container of natural rights. Rather than merely being "included" in the definition of personhood that governs an Anglo-masculine nation, she tries to insert her own articulations of self in the narrative of race, sex, and rights. To an extent, her objectives become like Kingsley's: she aspires to create a space of freedom for herself and her family, "some land of liberty" wherein their rights are inalienable (Stowell, Genovese, and Mormino 120). Ultimately, this space of freedom consists of what the feminist legal theorist Drucilla Cornell calls an "imaginary domain," a narrative space in which one has the right to think of oneself as "whole" rather than submit to the encroaching forces of Anglo-masculinity or the suffocating seclusion of white space.

Being immobilized by slavery's laws within the white space of the United States encroaches on Jacobs's "pure" principles of freedom. Although she never suggests that her patterns of migration should continue beyond the United States, Jacobs's definition of sovereignty—both the self-sovereignty of the sexual body and the sovereign personal property upon which one builds her home—cannot adhere in the northern or southern United States. She nominally completes her journey from slavery to freedom, but the progress she makes in understanding and conceptualizing the unfinished business of the American Revolution is a quintessential example of the political theorizing that accompanies stories of romance and rebellion. I posit that her imagined condition as an insurgent colonial subject challenges the racialized and gendered assumptions of U.S. citizenship; it disrupts and reshapes the contours and boundaries of an Anglo-masculine political hierarchy that many of her contemporaries accepted as an organic manifestation of the natural order of things.

Jacobs's rebellious romance with Mr. Sands, then, is her revolutionary attempt to redefine the terms of biological amalgamation by divorcing it from sexual coercion and the reproduction of white male property rights. Her affair with Sands allegorizes the forms of cultural and geographic expansion that undergird her revolutionary concept of freedom as sexual self-sovereignty, cultural syncretism, and geographic mobility. Other stories—particularly heterosexual romances—that feature this new kind of amalgamation had similar features: insurgent impulses toward white masculinity, egalitarian, or at least consensual and legitimate, sexual relations between white men and black women, and emigration. The story of the parents of the activist Robert Purvis, for example, reconstitutes the fear of insurrection, the scene of amalgamation, the transfer of property, and the right to geographic mobility in ways that mirror Jacobs's aspirations as she entered into her relationship with Sands. The summary of Harriet Miller and William Purvis's life together, recounted in the *Women's Journal* in 1870, offered a slightly unusual obituary notice. It read: "Harriet Miller, colored, widow of Wm. Purvis, a wealthy South Carolina planter, died in Philadelphia, Friday, aged 85, and worth 200,000. When a slave, she discovered a plot to murder her master, and disclosed it to him, and he, in gratitude, married her, leaving all his property to her at his death." For suppressing rebellious black violence and replacing it with love, Miller inherited the fortune left by her formerly slave-owning husband and passed it on to her biracial children, literally amalgamating the "white space" that had been his property.

The Miller/Purvis romance was unique because Harriet had been William's slave in South Carolina, but her children were well-known reformers by the 1850s (perhaps stimulating Jacobs's imagination), after the family emigrated to Philadelphia. As hopeful as their example may have been to contemporary reformers, the somewhat similar example of Zephaniah and Anna Jai Kingsley complicates the idea of cross-racial romance as a source of revolutionary reform. Zephaniah—who also married, manumitted, and left property to his slave, Anna—did not, like Purvis, become the patriarch of an abolitionist family. Kingsley did advocate an expedient alliance between free blacks and whites, but this alliance was meant to safeguard the system of slavery and prevent rebellion rather than further the cause of abolition. Whereas the Philadelphia Purvis family symbolized the peaceful and loving abolition of slavery and the possibility for equality in the North, the Kingsley family migrated farther and farther south to secure their version of freedom.

Harriet Jacobs's narrative falls somewhere between these two extremes, strategically restaging and critiquing the allegory of the nation/family that shaped political discourse. While it proposes the idea of cross-racial romance as a means toward freedom, it does not end happily, as was the case with Harriet Miller Purvis's successful family and secure home and property. Jacobs's story has more in common with Anna Jai Kingsley's, largely because her white gentlemen, like Zephaniah Kingsley, ultimately fail to secure the rights and privileges of their cross-racial family members within the United States. Jacobs's narrative, like Kingsley's, critiques the limitations of racial slavery and race prejudice within an Anglo-American nation; ultimately, Jacobs extends her critique of nation to question and subvert the tenets, not only of the nation's "protecting laws," but of the fundamental assumptions about race and masculinity that undergird those laws and shape the very idea of nation.

While Kingsley located himself, physically, in colonial territories, Jacobs can only locate freedom in a colonial territory of the mind—one that stands on the margins of United States nationhood, ready to rebel. Her insurgent stance against an Anglo-American nation mirrors her sense of self in relation to the men who encroach on her physically, either attempting to violate her bodily integrity and self-sovereignty—as does the sexual predator Dr. Flint—or refusing to recognize her right to freedom, as is the case with Mr. Sands, the white man with whom she chooses to form a union that proves irreparably illegitimate.

Jacobs's narrative representations of the possibility for egalitarian unions between black women and white patriarchs, or for the creation of an amalgamated and enfranchised "national family," are ultimately as disastrous as Zephaniah Kingsley's. Although he eventually set up a colony in Haiti, largely so his own mixed-race family members could enjoy the freedom that the United States denied them, he was a staunch defender of slavery.[1] The caveat was that he claimed not to advocate racial slavery because he claimed to be free of color prejudice. Child's "Letters from New York.— No. 30" published in the *National Anti-Slavery Standard* in 1842, features an interview with Kingsley that declares "the coloured race [are] superior to us, physically and morally. They are more healthy, have more graceful forms, softer skins, and sweeter voices. They are more docile and affectionate, more faithful in their attachments, and less prone to mischief, than the white race" (Stowell, Genovese, and Mormino 109).

This story, with which Jacobs was likely to be familiar due to her close relationship to Child, epitomizes the fine line between romanticism and romantic racialism. While Kingsley found the "intermediate grades of color"—the mulattos, quadroons, and octoroons—superior to black or white, he claimed that his African-born wife was "black as jet, but very handsome" as well as affectionate, faithful, and trustworthy (109). His pamphlet *A Treatise on the Patriarchal, or Co-operative System of Society* was republished several times between 1828 and 1934. The *Treatise* asserts many of the points articulated in Child's "Letters," particularly that "under a just and prudent system of management, negroes are a safe, permanent, productive, and growing property" who "have a strong attachment to their homes, to their wives and children, and domestic life" and who will "perform a great deal of valuable labor" for a benevolent master who can then "feel happy in experiencing the attachment, confidence, and good will of a grateful and happy people" (Stowell, Genovese, and Mormino 50). It is important, nonetheless, for these judicious and benevolent masters not to fall prey to the same "pride in denying the participation of equality to free colored people" that "caused the destruction of that flourishing and important colony"—Saint Domingo (46). In other words, when they have children with the women they enslave, these masters should treat their offspring with equality, not necessarily due to filial love, but to form a "grand chain of security by which slaves are held in subordination" (44). Once again, the memory of Haiti both opens and forecloses the potential for freedom.

Kingsley's vision of the amalgamated family never had legal grounding in the United States, where "mulatto" children followed the condition of the mother rather than being "admitted to most of the rights of Spanish subjects," as he believed they were in Florida (Stowell, Genovese, and Mormino 12). In the 1811 document "Manumission of Anna," he grants freedom to his wife and their three children, ceding his rights to them, and declaring "from today forward, they can negotiate, sign contracts, and buy, sell, appear legally in court . . . and do any and all things which they can do as free people" (24). Democratic ideals and liberal concepts of contract informed his definition of freedom, which is not surprising for the son of an English merchant whose family moved to Charleston, South Carolina, when he was five years old.

Yet a singular concept of nation does not seem particularly important to this Kingsley's freedom; rather, he has a provisional, if not opportunistic, idea of citizenship. For a brief period, Kingsley professed loyalty to the United States, but he was also intermittently a Danish citizen, then a citizen of the Spanish territory of Florida. Yet in his "Last Will and Testament" (1843), he descried the "illiberal and inequitable laws of this territory" which could not "afford to [his children] that protection and justice, which is due in civilized society to every human being" (120).

He urged his mulatto children to "remove themselves and properties to some land of liberty and equal rights, where the conditions of society are governed by some law less absurd than that of color" (120). The failings of Florida's laws, however, were even more pronounced in the laws of the United States. Kingsley's phrase "land of liberty" probably referred to Haiti, where some of his children and former slaves already lived, certainly not to the states to his north.

While Jacobs never emigrated geographically to some "land of liberty," she certainly rebelled against Anglo-masculinity and slavery's designation of the United States as a white space that excluded women, black or white, and all African Americans from freedom. The steps in Jacobs's rebellion mirror the upcoming sections of this chapter. First, I revisit Jacobs's seminal romance, in which she defines her self as a desiring subject through her first love—a thwarted affair with a free black man. Her "colored carpenter" serves as an ideal of masculine benevolence in marked contrast to the white men who benefit from the southern system of slavery as well as the republican free labor ideology of the North. Having contrasted Jacobs's political ideals with the discourse of free labor ideology, I then juxtapose her vision of Christian republicanism and sacred self-sovereignty, for women in particular, with a rather different and more rebellious political viewpoint—that of the Radical Abolition Party. In conclusion, I discuss the imaginary domain—the narrative space of freedom—that Jacobs occupies as a refuge from the geography of slavery and Anglo-masculine nationhood that is the United States.

"With All the Ardor of a Young Girl's First Love"

Jacobs's incident of first love depicts a rebellious romance that does not involve a white man; rather, the affair is radical because the marriage she hopes to contract with a "colored carpenter" represents a new ideal for masculinity, one that surpasses even northern regional ideals of the free laborer. In an ideal world, her right to choose the man she will marry—and to maintain her sense of sexual virtue—aligns her desire for autonomy with that of white women who aspire to negotiate gender relations through egalitarian marriage. Yet Jacobs does not originally figure the ideal of egalitarian marriage as a sign of cross-racial union or metaphorically amalgamated national family; her first love and romance looks more like a model of black community self-sufficiency. Before she becomes entangled in the liaison with a white neighbor who fathers her two children, Jacobs explains that he was not her first choice. The careful logic that she uses to narrate her sexual choices suggests that her stories of romance are strategic. Historical evidence affirms that she had a relationship with her neighbor, Sawyer, but the careful selection of details about her love life and the strategic juxtaposition of the carpenter, her tyrannical master, and her white lover amounts to a parable of rights and self-sovereignty as well as a reminiscence of lived experience that critiques and rebels against the ideas of white manhood and its associated political sphere of nationhood.[2]

Early in her narrative, she conflates her desire for freedom from slavery with her desire to love and marry a free black man whom she never names. In contrast to the contrived love affair that she engages in with Mr. Sawyer/Sands to protect herself from Dr. Norcom/Flint, her first love retains complete anonymity yet does not need to have his identity protected with a pseudonym. The idyllic memory of "a young colored carpenter, a free born man" whom she "loved with all the ardor of a young girl's first love" goes unnamed, perhaps because he embodies qualities that might be found in any number of upstanding black men (37). Her master forbids her marriage and the consummation of this first love, growling, "if I catch him lurking about my premises, I will shoot him as soon as I would a dog" (38). Therefore, Jacobs must reenact those "tender feelings" with Mr. Sawyer, a wealthy white neighbor who is legally protected from Dr. Norcom's vengeance. Jacobs invites the reader to see, nonetheless, how she used a personal, innocent, sensual experience of love and desire for a free black man as a starting point to redefine her strategies and tactics for voicing political and social desires.

This affair is radical because the woman is the desiring subject; Jacobs asserts her racial and gender identity free from any inherent assumptions of inferiority by narrating her own reality, by imagining a space of freedom that begins with her sovereign sexual body and eventually extends, metaphorically, to the ideal of a home wherein her rights are protected. Mark Rifkin astutely reads Jacobs's articulations of "home" as political theory, and I concur; the narrative power that she invokes throughout her story, in fact, constructs a nineteenth-century version of Cornell's "imaginary domain" because her narrative maps out new borders of the body and of national belonging.[3] As Rifkin argues, "Jacobs explores the ways that the possession of, and protection within, one's own domestic space indexes a national commitment to one's welfare as an American, reciprocally demonstrating how white wealth as coalesced in homes depends on direct and indirect government support for the expropriation and exploitation of African Americans" (75). The centrality of sexual self-sovereignty and bodily integrity to the way Jacobs can imagine a sovereign space of freedom—a home within or outside the boundaries of the United States—refigures the heterosexual metaphor of the national family and its protecting white patriarch. In her case, the white patriarch never measures up to the ideal of the free black man.

The difference between her two lovers is very important because the power she has in negotiating romantic relationships correlates with the power she lacks as a woman who is enslaved. Before she "bec[omes] desperate, and ma[kes]a plunge into the abyss," which is how she characterizes the beginning of her relationship with Sawyer, Jacobs *chooses* a free black man as her beloved (53).[4] Hoping, initially, to avoid white men altogether, she says: "This love dream had been my support through many trials; and I could not bear to run the risk of having it dissipated" (38). Aware, nonetheless, of this dream's impossibility, she describes the mental anguish that Norcom inflicts on her: "again and again I revolved in my mind how all this would end" (66). His power over her exerts psychological domination for its own sake, and she knows that her beloved cannot rescue her because "there was no hope that the doctor would consent to sell [her] on any terms" (66). Perfectly epitomizing what Ralph Waldo Emerson describes as "the love of power, the voluptuousness of holding a human being in his absolute control," the incorrigible Norcom exhibits the most perverse form of masculinity (17). "He had an iron will," states Jacobs, "and was determined to keep me, and to conquer me" (66). Norcom's vision for an amalgamated future is the antithesis of radical romance: it crushes the visionary world of romance, it asserts radical inequality to the extent of destroying his conquest's sense of personhood, and it engages amalgamation in the worst sense, as forced sexual relations between a white man and black woman written in the language of territorial expansion—"to conquer" (66).

In stark contrast, the carpenter's self-reliance endows him with a particular sense of bodily integrity. Among male abolitionists, gender and embodiment provided salient metaphors for political representation and citizenship; Theodore Weld advocated "body based personal piety" in the early 1840s, and the radical abolitionist James McCune Smith described masculinity much as Jacobs describes her carpenter: as a "tall, stalwart, hard-fisted . . . embod[iment] [of] a Hope of the Race" (Stauffer, "American Responses" 115–16, 148). Contrasting Norcom with her lover, "[who] was an intelligent and religious man," Jacobs illustrates two extremes of masculine power: uncontrolled virility and greed in Norcom and focused, concentrated productivity in the self-sufficient carpenter who generously offers his wages for the emancipation of another (42). Through these contrasts, she assumes what Elizabeth Spelman calls the place of "moral agent and social critic," commenting on the shortcomings of men's role as protectors of women (82). According to Ralph Waldo Emerson's definitions of power and self-reliance, the carpenter embodies the most refined form of moral and civil manhood, whereas Norcom suffers from the "excess of virility" and obsession with "miscellaneous activity" that dissipates the vital forces that nature lends the individual (*Prose* 281–82).

The notably *respectable* carpenter's desire to marry Jacobs indicates his sexual self-control and proper intentions to contract a legitimate family rather than Norcom's irresponsible and selfish desire to propagate illegitimate, disinherited offspring. The carpenter is responsible and self-reliant; his desire to marry his beloved childhood companion and to raise a family whom he can protect from the nation's laws (by working to purchase their freedom from slavery) places freedom outside the official national context of Anglo-masculine patriarchy. Significantly, Jacobs upholds a free black man as embodiment of virtue and moral sense in sharp contrast to the white men in her narrative. The unnamed carpenter, self-reliant, free, and responsible in his sexual intentions, serves as a model of civic virtue and sexual morality in sharp contrast to Norcom and Sands. Whereas, in the white space of amalgamation, the act of reproduction results in disenfranchised enslaved offspring who bring financial gain to the father, Jacobs imagines a different sexual relation. In the space created by the colored carpenter, the father invests his own work and resources to protect and free his children. The contrast symbolizes radically different models of political economy.

The anecdote about the carpenter also suggests an alternative to the northern free labor ideal. Unlike the tradesmen and laborers of the North, who actively endeavored to exclude African Americans from the promise of freedom, this southern man will sacrifice his own labor to free Jacobs and their potential children. Whereas northern free laborers were seduced by what James Fenimore Cooper referred to as the "subterfuge" of free labor ideology in hopes of saving enough wages to buy personal property, Jacobs's relationship to the self-sufficient carpenter implicitly critiques republican ideology (Roediger 45). Northern republicans may have believed that property in the laboring body had value, or, as Paine claimed, "man was free in large part because he held 'property in his own labor'" but Jacobs's experience and knowledge that a slave "being property, could hold no property" makes freedom impossible within an Anglo-masculine nation (Roediger 48; *Incidents* 3). As Frederick Douglass also points out, the body of the wage laborer is not much freer than the body of the slave—one is just slightly less beholden to his master.

Jacobs's emphasis on the carpenter's trade and financial self-sufficiency (which also echo her father's identity as a worker) depict him as free from the corrupt influences of a market economy that go so far to create imagined affiliations and a sense of national identity among Anglo-Americans. This critique of the fundamental concept of nation appears among the authors who envision romance and rebellion. In contrast to capitalism, Ralph Waldo Emerson's later writings extol the kind of work that Jacobs's carpenter, or even her grandmother, performs—manual labor that connects the worker to his or her community as opposed to what he describes in "New England Reformers" as the "business in Trade . . . that constitutes false relations between men" (*Prose* 223). In fact, workers like Jacobs's carpenter are on an equal plane with poets and artists by virtue of their labor; "whether the work be fine or course: planting corn, or writing epics," it is a venerable use of masculine power (*Prose* 232). Valerie Smith points out that, while other slave narratives "enshrine cultural definitions of masculinity" by "mythologizing rugged individuality, physical strength, and geographic mobility," Jacobs's assertion of power demystifies those qualities (35). Not only does she empower herself through connections to her family and to supportive members of her community rather than the ruggedly masculine qualities one finds in Frederick Douglass's narrative, but she characterizes her ideal colored carpenter's masculine virtues in terms of his promise as a father and his ability to build a happy home and contribute to a stable, ethical community.

Representations of self-sovereignty extend to an insurgent model of black womanhood because Jacobs's grandmother, like her father and her lover, has the potential to create a self-sufficient home. In contrast to the sovereign black feminine space of her grandmother's cottage, bankrupt tenets of Anglo-masculine nationhood encroach and contaminate this space of freedom in Jacobs's chapter "Fear of Insurrection." Briefly mentioning Nat Turner's rebellion, Jacobs turns to an anecdote about the "muster" that poor whites in Edenton undertook to authorize their social control and power over African American families.

In addition to referencing the Nat Turner uprising, her description of the white "soldiers" resembles James McCune Smith's disparaging representation of the "petit blancs" who victimized Vincent Ogé and the black middle class during the Haitian Revolution. Jacobs suggests that the logic of white supremacy that undergirds capitalist exploitation dupes uneducated white laborers into a false sense of power based on violent domination, one that takes the place of a sense of power based on property ownership and economic viability. McCune Smith berates the petit blancs for their artificial self-importance, as when they formed an army "in which every officer became at least a general, and every soldier an officer" (10). Generally referring to them as "scum" (13) and echoing historian J. Brown's assessment of petit blancs as "subordinate," "idle," and "dissolute" (6), McCune Smith also notes the passage of laws that deprived free blacks in Haiti of many forms of public employment, privileging petit blancs and ushering them into the labor market at the expense of free black men. Jacobs depicts white workers similarly.

In contrast to her first love or to her "father, [who] was a carpenter, and considered so intelligent and skilful in his trade, that, when buildings out of the common line were to be erected, he was sent for from long distances, to be head workman" (11), the poor whites of Edenton display artificial self-importance. In response to the Turner insurrection, "every white man shouldered his musket. The citizens and the so-called country gentlemen wore military uniforms. The poor whites took their places in the ranks in every-day dress, some without shoes, some without hats" (97). "[S]o-called country gentlemen" manipulate the crass, illiterate, and inarticulate "bullies" (97).

This display of white manhood revolves between Jacobs's snide account of their behavior in her grandmother's home, which she "arranged . . . as neatly as possible . . . put[ting] white quilts on the beds, and decorated some of the rooms with flowers" because "nothing annoyed them so much as to see colored people living in comfort and respectability" and rather graphic accounts of the violent assaults on the black population of Edenton that take place out of doors (98). The parallel between the poor men's appetite for "sweetmeats," their assumption that respectable blacks "seem to feel mighty gran' 'cause you got all them 'ere fixens. White folks oughter have 'em all" (100), and the extreme violence that they enact on the black population directly critiques the capitalist system and the free labor ideology, or subterfuge, that promises white laborers the opportunity to gain property and respectability on their own behalf. As Jacobs points out: "It was a grand opportunity for the low whites, who had no negroes of their own to scourge. They exulted in such a chance to exercise a little brief authority, and show their subserviency to the slaveholders; not reflecting that the power which trampled on the colored people also kept themselves in poverty, ignorance, and moral degradation" (100).

The fear of insurrection that drives this scene is as much inspired by the memory of the Haitian Revolution and the prevalence of race riots in the North as it is by the recent Nat Turner uprising. In fact, as a scene of insurrection, the muster has more in common with the Haitian Revolution because the persecution that poor whites inflict on the black community corresponds with McCune Smith's account of the events in Haiti and the well-known martyrdom of Ogé. McCune Smith's criticisms of illiterate northern whites who riot against free blacks in the name of free labor resembles Jacobs's assessment of the muster and the white citizenry that enjoys it: "What a spectacle was that for a civilized country! A rabble, staggering under intoxication, assuming to be the administrators of justice!" (102). In contrast, when Jacobs returns to the South to work among the freed people in the 1860s, she describes impoverished African Americans quite differently. She says: "I was hopeful for the future. The consciousness of working for themselves, and of having a character to gain, will inspire them with energy and enterprise, and a higher civilization will gradually come" (*Papers* 2:588).

Whether this civilization will come through inclusion in an already-established Anglo-American identity or whether it requires a significant rewriting of the idea of nation, perhaps in a revision that exceeds nationalist boundaries and considers other revolutionary projects, seems to be the question. Rifkin reads the domestic space so crudely invaded during the muster—the private space of the home—as a discursive parallel to "an enduring relationship between black bodies and American land" forged through black participation in the American Revolution (78). The rhetoric of the African American club movement, as Rifkin points out, identifies American territory as "our native land . . . our sweat and blood poured out on it," a national metaphor that he says makes the case for black "political inclusion" (78, 80).

Yet the native land or sovereign home that Jacobs desires exists solely in her mind, in her freedom to envision and theorize about what a space of freedom from Anglo-masculine nationhood might look like. The domestic imaginary that encompasses Jacobs's parallel vision of rights is not necessarily limited to American territory, nor was it limited in the rhetoric of African American club members, who often considered emigration as a viable solution to the exclusionary practices of U.S. nationalism. Thus limiting Jacobs's political theorizing to the limits of nationalist discourse implies a sense of trust in the forms of justice created by the Founding Fathers and the viability of free labor ideology. As Rifkin points out, "she puts more stress on the demands of free labor than the depredations of enslavement" (90). Perhaps the northern capitalist economic structure is as inextricable from Anglo-nationalism as is southern slavery. To say that freedom is not an abstract right, but rather a material entity guaranteed by ownership of property, not just in the sexual and laboring body, but for women to think of themselves as fully free and equal, goes well beyond the tenets of republican free labor ideology.

"God Is Your Father, and Ye All Are Brethren"

Although *Incidents* is largely based on her experiences in Edenton, North Carolina, during the 1830s, Jacobs wrote her story as a free woman living in New York and Boston in the 1850s.[5] Her narrative thus reflects many of the ideals of an intellectual community whose emergence in the 1850s brought an unprecedented religious view of the political world and of citizenship: the Radical Abolition Party founded by the eventual Harpers Ferry martyr John Brown, Frederick Douglass, James McCune Smith, and Gerrit Smith. Jacobs's brother lectured with Douglass, and she also participated in abolitionist work in the 1850s. Disgusted by the Compromise of 1850 and bolstered in confidence, perhaps, by the voices of her contemporaries in publications like the *Frederick Douglass Paper* and the *Provincial Freeman*, Jacobs began to write (Foster, "Resisting *Incidents*" 64; Yellin, *Harriet Jacobs* 125).[6] She first tested her public voice in letters to the *New York Tribune* in 1853 and then entered African American print culture, publishing her narrative to assert her voice as a black woman. Continuing this discussion of Jacobs's narrative as political theory, it becomes evident that virtuous colored carpenters alone cannot secure homes and protect rights. Jacobs thus articulates a specific meaning of rights for women, one that moves beyond her critique of republican free labor ideology and engages with the tenets of the Radical Abolition Party in a way that furthers the discourse of Christian republicanism.

The activities of poor white men during the postinsurrectionary muster in Edenton reveal the ways that capitalism and Anglo-masculine racial nationalism control and manipulate the majority of the nation's subjects for the benefit of a select few. In contrast, Jacobs's responsibility to her family and her reliance upon other members of the African American and abolitionist community to secure her freedom demonstrate that one must recognize and respect the sanctity of every individual. One cannot assume the role of speaking for or protecting others, which would imply that those others lack sovereignty of self. Although "the community and each individual in the community are ultimately responsible for every other person," the sacredness of the individual precedes his or her community engagement (Brown, "To Catch" 126). The fact that Jacobs wrote a chapter for her narrative regarding John Brown's raid on Harpers Ferry could have an important connection to the revolutionary and rebellious concept of the sacred individual's relationship to his or her community, one about which we can only speculate since Child elected to omit that chapter from the published manuscript.

The self-sacrificing honor of the colored carpenter and his respect for Jacobs epitomizes her ideal of sacred self-sovereignty, the interconnectedness between an individual and an ethical community. I borrow this term from John Stauffer, who notes an affinity between Emerson and the radical abolitionists, particularly in their idea of sacredness of self (*Black Hearts* 35–39). He calls this belief "sacred self-sovereignty"—the idea that God dwells within and without—a redefinition of the divine and of the self that likewise placed moral authority within the individual rather than in the stagnant world of social norms or the corrupt arena of political legislation (16–17). This idea of subjectivity —the individual's relationship to the divine that forges a revolutionary model for human empathy and ethical behavior—also governs Jacobs's narrative persona. The critical difference is the role that sexuality and bodily integrity play in Jacobs's construction of subjectivity. For many black Americans, the promise of a Christian republic guaranteed "their natural right of liberty and equality against the racial order of American society" (Glaude 81). Radical abolitionists like Douglass and Brown imagined a millennial identity, free from the sin of the external world, through which black and white identities could converge (Stauffer, *Black Hearts* 39).

While Jacobs would support John Brown in the aftermath of his attempt to initiate a major slave rebellion, she also initiated a very important rebellion of her own—one that was waged on the terrain of her own body. Radical abolitionists also valued the individual body, soul, and mind rather than the rule of law as the source of ethical action, but I think Jacobs sees some major shortcomings in their definition of freedom. Although they did not exclude women from their vision of equality, they, like Emerson, believed that masculine will was the most important quality needed to deliver the nation from its turpitude.[7] In contrast, Jacobs warns her reader about relying on male benevolence or virtue for self-defense. She makes freedom and salvation contingent on her own actions, ideas, and beliefs rather than those of men who are supposed to protect her. Nonetheless, her narrative conveys a sense of optimism similar to that of Emerson and the radical abolitionists—the hope that "divine sentiments" might guide American culture, that they might ameliorate culture's degeneracy: "poverty, solitude, passions, war, slavery" (Emerson, *Antislavery* 84).

Jacobs's spiritual justification for a series of sexual choices, therefore, has much in common with the language of radical reform. Yet her representation of masculine will also unveil its shortcomings and offers to teach a lesson in cooperation, perhaps, to her contemporaries Emerson and Douglass. Although radical romance as a cross-racial relationship that models radical equality does not work in her narrative, the narrative itself initiates a radical romance between the spiritual tenets of radical abolition and Jacobs's own concept of embodiment and women's rights. As Jacobs describes her religious justifications for engaging in a cross-racial love affair that would have otherwise scandalized her "gentle" northern readers, she narrates a sexual history that would be considered sinful if her assertions of divine influence were not so convincing. Thus while Emerson says that "self-reliance, the height and perfection of man, is reliance on God," Jacobs invokes a similar sense of self—a corporeal Christianity that allows her to think of her own body as sacred (*Antislavery* 84).

Because Jacobs speaks of her own sexual body in terms that are distinct from Emerson or Douglass, one might align her religious worldview with Elizabeth Livermore's "corporeal Christianity" in addition to "sacred self-sovereignty."[8] It stands to reason that the radical abolitionist climate of the late 1850s supported Jacobs's work. I hope to sidestep the question of influence and consider how they all were deeply invested in a culture that sought to redefine citizenship through the nexus of race and gender, as a corporeal Christianity. Jean Fagan Yellin's biography of Jacobs indicates that she had the opportunity to hear Emerson lecture as early as 1846 (*Harriet Jacobs* 88). No paper trail connects the two as of yet, but the concept of intertextuality suggests that influence between authors does not require direct correspondence; rather, it relies on the play between a variety of texts that are social, political, and literary.

Jacobs negotiates the issue of her rights through romantic relationships and through religious arguments. After asserting herself as a desiring subject in the romance with her "first love," she instructs white gentlemen of their role in the radical romance between black and white, man and woman. In her account of her white lover, Mr. Sawyer, Jacobs ultimately abandons the language of romance and relies on her self to negotiate her rights. Just as Emerson reminds his audience that divine providence "will not save us but through our own co-operation," Jacobs can only save her self from the hostile environment created by slavery (*Antislavery* 88). While the Emersons speculated on the power of love to transform race relations, the rebellious black subject who elicits the transformation in Jacobs's representative white men is not Toussaint Louverture. It is herself.

Incidents in the Life of a Slave Girl, however, is not just a personal narrative; it asserts the need for African American women to represent their own corporeal, spiritual, and intellectual needs in an historical moment when the definitions of race, gender, and citizenship are undergoing radical revision. The experience of cross-racial romance does engender Jacobs's rebellion. Scripted in sentimental tropes of love, piety, and idealized marriage, literary culture sometimes imagined a revolutionary model of race and gender equality.

To reach the optimal reality of equality that was radical abolition's goal, Jacobs added a woman's perspective. She initiated a radical romance between women striving for equality and radical abolitionism's masculine ideal of the citizen. The issues of bodily integrity and family responsibility offered a critical component to Christian republicanism. Although these issues can be assigned to the private sphere, Jacobs chose to make public her experience and thereby politicize her racial and sexual identity. Gayle Tate points out that "by making their personal lives publicly visible for moral scrutiny, they dared to appropriate political power to change not only their own psychological and material conditions but those for all black people" (108). Alternately, as Jacobs invokes natural law and religious discourse to validate her own identity as a black woman, she "privatizes social justice for black people by redefining that ambition as a black woman's desire to obtain a home of her own for herself and her children, a home in which slavery has no domain" (110–11). This closure, as in novels by Julia Collins and Francis Watkins Harper that will follow it, "is not meant as a reflection of reality but as that of a visionary world" (121)—an imaginary domain.[9]

The black feminist anthropologist Irma McClaurin uses Gayatri Spivak's term "strategic essentialism" to describe Jacobs's critique of liberal democracy, which calls for social transformation beyond the project of abolition (137). The sexual economy of slavery, as she illustrates through strategically selected anecdotes, subjugates black *and* white women because it permits a masculine dominance that corrupts all families. Her use of personal narrative to demand political rights and protection exemplifies McClaurin's point: "There is a materiality (derived from political and economic relationships and fields of power) to identity that must be acknowledged. . . . [N]otions of the self are intricately woven into the body politic of American culture" (52). As stories that relayed personal experience for political ends, McClaurin says, "Slave narratives resisted the conventional poetics of autobiography and shaped a tradition of black autobiography in which . . . the individual self and the collective were indistinguishable" (70–71).

This Christian republicanism is also rebellious because it refutes the images of Anglo-masculine political culture as protecting and benevolent. Jacobs attempts—and fails—to refigure the image of the national family, with herself as mother, Sawyer as the father, and her children as the amalgamated future, and the concept of love governing personal as well as political freedom. The hope that reformed racial and gender power dynamics, symbolized through egalitarian marriage and cross-racial love, could reform the national family is thwarted. Her second romance, the relationship with Mr. Sawyer, has more political resonance in this context because it is a conscientious effort to negotiate her freedom from slavery. Representations of radical romance in the writing of Jacobs and other African American women, as upcoming chapters will discuss, also reflect and often invert the dominant images of white manhood. Mr. Sawyer, the "white gentleman" who fathers fifteen-year-old Jacobs's first child, personifies Jacobs's imaginary departure from the very real brutality of slavery and the usual hypocrisy of southern "gentility." Jacobs believes he is a kind and gentle man, genuinely concerned for her welfare and sincerely trying to help her. The term "gentleman," as Orlando Patterson points out, referencing Rollin G. Osterweis's "chivalric cult" of Southern Gentlemen, embodies the essential features of the slaveholder's identity including "an excessively developed sense of honor and pride, militarism, the seclusion and idealization of women, and regional nationalism" (qtd. in Patterson 95).

Jacobs presents Sawyer as courting her, "constantly seeking out opportunities" to see her, and even writing to her "frequently" (54). He works to impress her and win her affection. His romantic overtures, in the narrative's retrospective view, seem deceitful, for she adds that she was "a poor slave girl, only fifteen years old" (54). Rather than creating prescriptive and didactic representations of African American womanhood, Jacobs starts to construct an imagined projection of "true white gentlemanhood." Even as she struggles to justify her own actions and rescue them from the moral condemnation of the cult of true womanhood, addressing "ye happy women, whose purity has been sheltered," Jacobs weaves an entirely new image into her narrative of justice and injustice (54). She constitutes two images of white manhood: the bestial Dr. Norcom, contrasting with the "white gentleman" who recognizes the beauty and intellect of a slave girl and treats her with respect and kindness. On the fringes of the slave girl's life stands a white man who *might* treat her like a person and enact the performance of equality between black and white, male and female, that Jacobs herself is trying to promote as a model for relations between individual and community.

By setting a fictive stage where she controls her own body as well Sawyer's attitude toward social equality, Jacobs uses her text as a site where race relations are governed by the ideals of true love and filial obligation. The reader learns, later on, that Sawyer falls short of these ideals. While Jacobs's sensual experience of "all the ardor of a young girl's first love" translates into a heightened awareness of her racial subjugation, she tries to replicate that ardor and romantic freedom in a manner that will translate into an escape from social and legal subjugation. Since Sawyer takes the place of her first love, a colored carpenter who offers her freedom, his actions must measure up to those of the free black man—but they fall far short.

The only place where Sawyer actually fulfills the ideals of radical equality is in the imaginary domain of her mind, which she translates into her narrative when she asserts her own right to freedom and respect. Jacobs uses the trope of romantic love to fabricate her fantasy of power when, in fact, she is virtually powerless. She transposes her initial hope to have the right to marry her beloved colored carpenter onto Mr. Sawyer, the surrogate lover, who (like the free black man) promises to buy her freedom. Love, in either case, resonates with freedom. Ideally, conjugal love would foster the recognition between the two lovers of an equality of souls—of the equal humanity that Jacobs and her colored carpenter share. Instead, she settles for "something akin to freedom"; she wants Sawyer to prove his love on the most material level, using his power to buy her from Norcom and manumit her (55).

Provisionally, however, her "love dream" enables her to imagine a situation that stems from her own desire, even as it forces her to settle for a white man—"creeping" into her heart to replace her original love for a black man. Valerie Smith argues that Jacobs's "relationship with Sawyer provides her with a measure of power," although the triumph associated with her sexual power is not individualistic; it represents part of the power she derives from her family (33). *Incidents* narrates a leap from a young girl's sensual and romantic love for a free colored carpenter to an awareness that, in a nation that defines citizenship and its attendant rights in according to race and sex, there can be no personal freedom. Claudia Tate argues that "black female-centered expressions of political desire for a fully functional citizenship" are represented in literature as idyllic marriages: "The idealized civility of black women and men in the private realm as wives and husbands becomes a gendered paradigm for responsible citizens in the public realm" (96). The decency and nobility of the black men in Jacobs's narrative, however, goes virtually unquestioned. The real dramatic tension and creative energy is directed into a paradigm of responsible citizenship for white men. While a great deal of critical attention has been paid to the heroines of late-nineteenth-century African American novels, the prescriptive and rather type-cast roles that their white lovers play shatter conventions and elicit a "cult of true white gentlemanhood" that is perhaps one of the most radical features of the sexual as well as race relations imagined in Jacobs's narrative and the novels by Julia Collins and Frances Harper that will follow it.

So that women like her might uphold their family's honor, be faithful partners to the "colored carpenters" of the world, and choose the fathers of their children, all women's self-sovereignty must be legally recognized and protected. As Anita Goldman has observed, narrative assertions of authority provide a metaphor for expanding the "purely contractual claims and obligations constructed in the liberal theory of government" (242). Her claim to bodily integrity invokes the liberal discourse guaranteeing citizenship and "full protection under the law," but it also extends beyond "the liberal wish for freedom and the racial tie that attaches her to her family" (242). Rather, bodily integrity—the assertion of self-sovereignty—is a critical condition for the creation of a republic in which every man and woman, black and white, enjoys full equality under the law.[10]

Jacobs tries, in her relationship with Sawyer, to re-create the sense of self that she enjoyed when she initially hoped to marry her first love. She describes the love between herself and the carpenter as "honorable," adding "he would not love me if he did not believe me to be a virtuous woman" (39). When she reveals her first pregnancy to her master, Norcom assumes that the "colored carpenter" has taken Jacobs's virginity. An assault on the honor of her ideal black man is also an attack on her ideal of self, on the possible honor and virtue that she possessed when he loved her. The very assumption that the colored carpenter would irresponsibly father enslaved children leads Jacobs to strike back verbally

at Norcom with a passion and loyalty completely absent from her opinion of Sawyer. She no longer "feel[s] as proud as she had" when she first
schemed to deny Norcom's access to her virginal body, and she is "low-
ered in [her] own estimation" of her personal dignity, but she refuses to
"bear his abuse in silence" when he assumes that the carpenter would
stoop so low as to father an illegitimate child with a woman who is
enslaved (58). The fact that Sawyer has done this—joining a long line
of "Southern Gentlemen," some of them Jacobs's forefathers—does not
merit any comment, which makes it very clear that her standards and
expectations for masculine behavior were seriously compromised when
she consented to an affair with a white man.

Insulting the colored carpenter is another matter entirely: "But when
he spoke contemptuously of the lover who had always treated me honorably; when I remembered that but for him I might have been a virtuous,
free, and happy wife, I lost my patience" (58). Lamenting the fact that
"my strongest weapon with him was gone" because, having given up her
virginity, she has not maintained the boundaries of her body completely,
she nonetheless insists that she has triumphed over him because she
chose—and controlled—who could access her body (58). Jacobs rejects
the moral economy of slavery as she asserts sacred self-sovereignty over
her sexual body. She declares to Norcom: "I have sinned against God
and myself, but not against you" (58). This assertion of her own corporeal Christianity and bodily integrity is the starting point for her to theorize what freedom might be like.

According to Harryette Mullen, by "refus[ing] to be modestly silent,"
Jacobs "permitted a directness of expression . . . about matters . . . rendered unspeakable;" specifically, women need to control the boundaries of their corporeal selves in order to maintain intellectual and moral
integrity ("Runaway Tongue" 246, 251). It becomes eminently clear that
the sexual body, within a Christian republic, is sacred; its fate should be
determined between an individual and her God. More radically, Jacobs's
narrative posits the bodies of black women—inseparable from their
minds and souls—as the symbol of Christian communion and an amalgamated, truly representative democracy.

In controlling her own sexual body and denying Norcom her virginity, Jacobs defeats Norcom in a moral, though pyrrhic, victory. Jacobs
rejects the legal precept that she has no human status and thus no claim
to her own sexual body: it belongs to her and she is accountable to God
alone. Her assertion of her own divine nature and of the radical equality among all people regardless of society's assignation of racial and

gender inferiority also requires a higher ethical standard for how one treats others. Recognizing the radical equality of souls in a Christian republic brings with it a profound responsibility to others—to neighbors and Samaritans and even one's enemies—an ethos of mutuality in which degrading or uplifting the character of another directly reflects the descent or ascent of one's own character.

Weighing the virtues of the carpenter against the vagaries of Sawyer and the wrongdoings of Norcom, Jacobs sets up a series of equations that leave her in a compromised position. She argues that she cannot maintain the privileged, protected, and hypocritical standards of Christian sexual virtue that apply to the slave woman's white "sisters" (10). She laments the fate of another mulatta slave girl who, in contrast to her white sister's joy on her wedding day, "drank the cup of sin, and shame, and misery, whereof her persecuted race are compelled to drink" (29). Conflating sexual and religious imagery in this passage, Jacobs highlights the sacredness and ecstasy of the white sister's virgin nuptials with the ignominy of the mulatta sister's sexual degradation. The religious language of persecution begs comparison of slaves with Jesus Christ, particularly because the communion image of drinking of a cup of sin suggests forgiveness through the body of Christ. Christ, like the mulatta, was persecuted. Nonetheless, the mystical body of Christ, like the amalgamated body of the mulatta, offers a symbol of interconnectedness. The ideal of a Christian republic, much like the body of Christ through which radical abolitionists believed all people could commune and realize holiness, required a racially and sexually inclusive and accessible body politic.

In the political climate of the 1850s, the body of Christ as metaphor for the body politic proved ideologically consistent with salient political imperatives known as Bible politics and higher law. Chapter 4's Elizabeth Livermore, for example, endows her quadroon heroine, the "product" of amalgamation, with a Christ-like spiritual power that dissolves racial conflict. This conflict is not so easily resolved for Jacobs; resonance between the "blood of Christ" in communion and the supposed "cursed blood" of slaves again comes to the fore when Jacobs describes the aftermath of the Nat Turner insurrection. After vindictive whites demolish the black church, "benevolent" whites permit blacks to attend unseen in the galleries of white churches. Still denied full participation, Jacobs states ironically that, after the conclusion of services, they "partook of the bread and wine, in commemoration of the meek and lowly Jesus, who said, 'God is your father, and ye all are brethren'" (67).

These images of bread and wine call to mind the persecuted body of Christ and thereby sanctify the bodies of believers who are persecuted slaves. Under authority of God, Jacobs likewise claims the sanctity of her own Christian body and questions the meaning of filial connections to those who enslave her. Communion, in this case, has highly charged political significance and resonates with the memory of blood commingling as black women conceive children with white fathers. Communion happens in the aftermath of a crucifixion—the extreme bodily violation of Christ; thus, the suffering inflicted on black women's bodies through rape and forced reproduction might be followed by an era when white men's sinfulness can be purged and the nation can unify, communing through an expanded body politic.

Jacobs makes it clear that the sinfulness of slavery makes the actions of white men like her master inconsistent with the values of a Christian republic.[11] In one of their final confrontations, Norcom has joined the Episcopal Church and urges Jacobs to do so as well. In a consummately witty moment, she rejoins: "There are sinners enough in it already. If I could be allowed to live like a Christian, I should be glad" (75). It is not until she visits England, a free country, that Jacobs embraces organized religion and finds white friends who "inspired me with faith in the genuineness of the Christian professions. Grace entered my heart, and I knelt at the communion table, I trust, in true humility of soul" (185). In this profession of faith, she implicitly condemns racist Christians in the United States and affirms the oneness of her own body within the body of Christ. These acts of communion and inclusion in a spiritual body contrast radically with Jacobs's rhetorical construction of her own family's place within the United States body politic.

"My Narrow Mind Also Began to Expand"

When her initial "love dream" fails, Jacobs begins to develop another visionary world—her own "imaginary domain" wherein natural rights are inalienable. Knowing about natural rights and actually enjoying them are entirely different things, but she expresses her belief that "Nature" has the power to revive "the human soul" (83). Even in her sarcastic indictments of Christian churches, she identifies "souls that are thirsting" for "the water of life"—a collective spiritual striving, quenched by something that flows among people and nature, like water (73). Jacobs traces the evolution of her own intellect as freedom opens her mind. She uses the term "mind" almost fifty times in her narrative, beginning in the preface when she says: "When I first arrived in Philadelphia, Bishop

Paine advised me to publish a sketch of my life, but I told him I was altogether incompetent to such an undertaking. Though I have improved my
mind somewhat since that time, I still remain of the same opinion; but I
trust my motives will excuse what might otherwise seem presumptuous"
(1). As her sense of mental interiority develops free from the psychological and intellectual shackles of slavery, however, her sense of an "original" sexual or racial difference in intellect dissipates.

Her declarations of mental inferiority result from her state of mind,
because it was strained and darkened by the trials of slavery, and are also
caused by the deleterious effects of sexual harassment that any woman
could suffer—the impure "foul images" and polluting words inflicted on
her psyche by her master's verbal sexual abuse (54). Her initial evalua-
tions of her own intellect reflect the artificial "belief" in female mental
inferiority that she wants to eradicate. Freedom alleviates both the intellectual and psychological symptoms of slavery; as her "narrow mind
also began to expand . . . [she] gradually became more energetic and
more cheerful" (169). Notably, this expansion of mind also comes with
physical mobility—with the opportunity to travel north and seek a less
restrictive geography than the confines of Norcom's home or plantation.
In the home of black friends, she gains a moment of respite from "white
space" and the results are cathartic. The idea of the mind expanding,
furthermore, plays on the promises of the Enlightenment that helped to
bring revolution to the United States. Ironically, the enlightened claims
of the expanding Euro-American mind that traveled to the Americas
would not define her as a person. Nonetheless, Jacobs appropriates
those claims to assert her own personhood as she narrates the process of
"enlightenment" that inflicted inferiority on her race.

While theories of race that operated as early as the revolutionary era
posited that Africans were in a more savage or barbaric state, Jacobs
makes it clear that "enlightened" men put people into that state. She also
challenges conventional narratives of promiscuous and licentious slaves
by pointing to the depravity of white men in power. The sin and impu-
rity of the slaveholder's sexual behavior, not any innate characteristic,
contaminates the community of slaves. Enslaved men, Jacobs admits,
are sometimes so cowed by the lash that they turn their own wives and
daughters over to slaveholders. Jacobs forcefully inquires of her reader:
"Do you think this proves the black man to belong to an inferior order
of beings? What would you be, if you had been born and brought up a
slave, with generations of slaves for ancestors? I admit that the black
man is inferior. But what is it that makes him so?" (44). Inferiority is not

a product of intrinsic racial or gender qualities or even a state of arrested ethnic development; in fact, with the eradication of racism and patriarchal domination, those qualities will dissipate. Whereas Dr. Norcom embodies and epitomizes racist patriarchal culture, her colored carpenter embodies a model of virtue that can emerge outside racist economies of human value. Importantly, the carpenter is also a traveling man—he is free to seek out spaces that suit him because he is self-reliant and mobile. Free from the restrictive space of white property that encroaches on her very being, in the narrative space that Jacobs creates to voice her own autonomy and personhood, radical equality can be attained. Her temporary condition of inferiority diminishes with the development of personal autonomy and mental interiority, the creation of an imaginary, though psychologically freeing, space within which to narrate her own personhood.

The church symbolizes a space where the equality of souls should outweigh the economic, racial, and gender hierarchies of white space, and Jacobs articulates a specific kind of rage when slavery encroaches on that sacred space, much as she does when Norcom attempts to violate the "sacred temple" that is her body. Even after her affair with Sawyer, she deflects sin and shame away from her self very subtly, probably because a strident justification of her affair with Sawyer would have made her narrative obscene. When she enters the church with her grandmother to baptize her child, however, she recollects her mother and the memory that, in the same church, "she had presented me for baptism, without any reason to feel ashamed" (78). Jacobs laments that Norcom denied her the right to enter the church under the same circumstances, thereby deflecting shame on him. Even Jacobs's grandmother, who is heartbroken that she has chosen to have the affair with Sawyer, blames Norcom. In a heated argument over Jacobs's sexual behavior, her grandmother indicts Norcom, telling him that "he was the one to blame; he was the one who caused all the trouble" (82). She warns him, with biblical conviction, that "you ain't got many more years to live, and you'd better be saying your prayers. It will take 'em all, and more too, to wash the dirt off your soul" (82). After the exchange with her grandmother, Norcom gives Jacobs the choice to go to a cottage in the woods and become his concubine or to go to the plantation. She chooses the plantation. She never finds her material home, but her mind is freer there, in the place she chooses to travel to, rather than in the sexually proscriptive white space of Norcom's cabin in the woods.

Recalling Child's woodland cabins and spacious homes where quadroon maidens consent to illegal unions with white lovers, Jacobs's choice of the plantation emphasizes the importance of sexual sovereignty and its potential to combat the whiteness—the coercion and exclusion from freedom—that a confined cabin symbolizes. In the next chapter, images of mobility and the vast countryside of Cuba also signify freedom for a young mulatto slave, this time a man, who dares to love whomever he chooses.

3 Desire, Conquest, and Insurrection in Gertrudis Gómez de Avellaneda's *Sab*

> The earth that was once drenched in blood will be so again: the descendants of the oppressors will themselves be oppressed, and black men will be the terrible avengers of those of copper color.
>
> —Gertrudis Gómez de Avellaneda y Arteaga, *Sab*

THE EPONYMOUS HERO of Gertrudis Gómez de Avellaneda y Arteaga's 1841 novel *Sab* is a former slave with the potential to level social hierarchies in racially striated Cuba and, supposedly, "avenge" the conquest and genocide of Cuba's First Nations. His musings about equality, however, are inspired by his love for his former master's daughter. Couched in the language of the soul, Sab's definition of equality has much to do with his desire for Carlota, the master's daughter. Avellaneda's writing, which also includes autobiography and poetry, is heavily influenced by romantic ideals of the ever-expanding soul and has much in common with that of transcendentalist and radical romantic Margaret Fuller (1810–1850). As Carolyn Sorisio has argued, the idea of the radical equality of souls provides one of the most powerful transcendentalist refutations of racism (105). The personal similarities between Fuller and Avellaneda (who probably never met) are intriguing, but the primary interest of this chapter is not to compare the two. Rather, the goal is to map out the expanding revolutionary and romantic ideas about equality, embodiment, and the soul that writers throughout the Atlantic world share but that escalate, in Avellaneda's prose, into insurgent desires.[1] While Fuller's ideas about the transformative power of the soul touch upon the subject of racial equality, Avellaneda's depictions of the soul erupt into tempestuous relationships between man and woman, mulatto and indigene, Anglo-American and Cuban Creole, or colonizer and colonized. The spiritual force that connects her heroine and tragic protagonist, furthermore, is also integrally connected to the Cuban landscape. While the heroine, Carlota, communes with the landscape in a more limited sense than does the hero, Sab, Cuba's natural environs are completely inaccessible to Carlota's Anglo-American suitor, Enrique. The Cuban landscape itself seems to resist its demarcation as a white space; instead, it conveys memories of conquest and an insurgent spirit that are only available to the Creole heroine Carlota and her mulatto counterpart, Sab.

Our first exposure to the workings of the soul in *Sab* has to do with the transgressive cross-racial romantic attraction between the hero and heroine. In this respect, Avellaneda's romantic soul looks quite like that described by Fuller, who captures the spirit of cross-racial intimacy and gender equity in an 1844 scrapbook poem. She envisions an "era of social harmony" that will fall upon the world "When the perfect two embrace, / Male and female, black and white" (Murray 289). Figured through the image of a romantic embrace, Fuller transformed the romantic ideal of the ever-expanding individual soul to a conjugal metaphor for human equality; *Sab* does similar work, suggesting that the idea of amalgamation and the expansion of mind and soul shaped the politics of women's rights in the United States and in Cuba. Yet the more subtle workings of the soul—its connection to the Cuban landscape— make different claims about entitlement and sovereignty. Specifically, the major restriction upon women's intellectual and spiritual expansion, or freedom, is in large part the result of the natural world having been converted to property by patriarchal culture and the laws of contract. In other words, women's ability to gain an education or choose whom they will marry is circumscribed by property laws, especially those that govern the inheritance of lands claimed by colonial regimes. The simultaneous occupation of a colonial landscape and of a young woman's body, then, is Avellaneda's main complaint.

There is also a transnational dimension to this problem of sovereignty. Avellaneda, like her contemporaries, juxtaposes the idea of romantically intertwined and equal souls with the intertwined economic and political destinies of colonials and the First Nations; the romantic encounter between man and woman metaphorically represents the encounter, or relationship, between Spanish and Taino or Cuba and the United States. Just as biological amalgamation of races might take place when a cross-racial love affair resulted in offspring, foreign relations in a growing American empire created another kind of amalgamation. Since race was used to define the parameters of inclusion and exclusion in a political body that was also founded on a radical (though unfulfilled) concept of rights, the amalgamated body represented the challenges of incorporating new geographies and cultures into the body politic. Like racial amalgamation, the rhetoric of geographic amalgamation traveled through proslavery and antislavery rhetoric: in the former, it reflected slaveholders' desire for the profits and wealth through Caribbean expansion and a simultaneous, somewhat contradictory anxiety about incorporating cultural difference; in the latter, the expansion of rights takes on transnational dimensions as nations like Haiti become exemplary models of freedom and equality that the United States might emulate.

These encounters and metaphorical romances, either as relationships between individuals or a meeting between the political bodies of the United States and Mexico, Cuba, or Haiti, always have the potential to cause an uprising of some sort. Similarly, the cross-racial romance that Avellaneda foregrounds in her novel is inseparable from images of insurrection. As Eric Sundquist and Sibylle Fischer point out, segregating U.S. reactions to cross-racial relationships, both in terms of history and of literature, from the history of Haiti and Cuba or the effects of those histories on the political and literary imagination would leave us unable to account for the transnational anxieties that shaped U.S. ideologies of race.[2] Building on Ralph Bauer and Debra Rosenthal's transnational American literary work, I argue that the appearance of literary tropes of amalgamation and cross-racial romance provide a literary context for "hemispheric notions of cultural structure and the incorporation of persons into a constituency" (Rosenthal 1).[3] They also impinge upon and reshape republican ideals of citizenship and sovereign rights by engaging the public discourses of self and nation that changed dramatically in the United States during the era of reform.

Avellaneda's use of romantic tropes and the discourse of the soul has something akin to U.S. transcendentalists including Lydia Maria Child, yet so does her substitution of white female heroines for indigenous figures. Like Hobomok, Avellaneda's Taino characters disappear, leaving behind a white woman to carry on their legacy. Although her white heroine Carlota mourns the disappearance of the Taino and the death of her black hero, her own romantic prospects and interests are very much tied to the plantation that her Spanish father owns in Cuba. Wealth in land draws Carlota's American suitor, and her father's desire to protect her inheritance is an effort to maintain the landscape as white space by keeping his daughter's body white. As Shirley Samuels says of *Hobomok*, "Anxiety about racial mixing becomes imbricated in contracts about land, as well as legal constructs about the relation of the land to the nation" ("Women" 58).

Avellaneda's concerns about the amalgamation of land and culture and its impact on women's rights also share much with Fuller and Child. Again, this is not an argument about influence or social networks—it is more of a recognition that questions of race, rebellion, and women's rights expand beyond linguistic and national boundaries in the Atlantic world. Even if Avellaneda's work was not part of the reading list of Child or other transcendentalists, however, issues regarding Cuba were. In many ways, Cuba itself represents a series of contradictory ideas about "Americanness," citizenship, and self-sovereignty in the U.S. literary imagination. U.S. travelers frequented Cuba, seeking information about slavery or a cure for tuberculosis. American businesses became the major buyers of Cuban sugar and coffee, and, according to Rodrigo Lazo, "investors from the United States in 1828 founded Cárdenas, which due to its demographic makeup became known as the 'American City'" (8). The romance between the United States and its linguistic and cultural "other," Cuba, signified the potential for inclusion and exclusion within American identity itself. Even in Waldo Emerson's second series of essays, Cuba figures doubly, as a symbol of the torrid and ideal natural world as well as the site of slavery's worst crimes, which he emphasizes in "Man the Reformer." Both Charles Emerson and Sophia Peabody Hawthorne spent significant time in Cuba, Charles to recover from tuberculosis and Sophia for her myriad health concerns.

While social and personal connections are not clear, the cultural and economic connections between U.S. and Cuban culture in the earlier part of the century invite comparisons between Avellaneda's work and that of U.S. writers. Thinking of literary production in terms of what Frederic Jameson calls the political unconscious accounts for the similarities between Cuban and U.S. antislavery literatures, especially when we consider the impact of revolutionary romantic ideals on the reform writing of the period. *Sab* was one of the earliest antislavery novels in the Americas, following the first U.S. antislavery novel, Richard Hildreth's *The Slave; or, Memoirs of Archie Moore,* by only five years. Both the Cuban and the U.S. novel draw from Continental influences, particularly a set of romantic and revolutionary concepts. Avellaneda and Hildreth's protagonists—Sab and Moore —are spectacular romantic heroes. Alexander Saxton muses that "Hildreth must have believed he was enlisting Archie Moore among the ranks of Byronic heroes, dedicated, like Prometheus, to human liberation despite the gods" (234). Like Sab, the gods with whom Moore battles are the gods of slavery; he endorses righteous retribution, allying with the African insurgent Tom

to rise up against white men in a battle for freedom. Sab, too, understands his own freedom in a Lockean context; Saxton's assessment of
Hildreth, that he sought "to show that persons of 'powerful character'
and moral intellect could rise above unjust institutions," applies to Avellaneda as well (234).

Avellaneda's narrator plays with the idea that Sab might avenge both
his and the "bronze" (indigenous) race. *Sab* also considers the potential
for the mulatto hero and his mistress, Carlota, to attain the freedom to
love—to select a lover based on the dual recognition of divine souls rather
than to have one's lover chosen by patriarchal arrangement or biologically defined racial identities. Not only do Sab and Carlota have "superior souls" that draw them to one another, these souls also commune
with the natural world and with the deceased spirits of other rebels in a
manner that challenges the authority and entitlement of the white men
around them. Yet the man who stands in the way of both rebellions—
the project of racial retribution and the quest for freedom to love—is an
American. Carlota's suitor, Enrique Otway, the son of a social-climb-
ing and greedy Anglo merchant, has come of age in the United States.
Notably, the economic opportunist comes from the United States with a
desire to "annex" himself to a Cuban woman for financial gain.

Insurgent Affairs

On one level, *Sab* addresses questions of equality and entitlement
through romantic metaphors of a metaphysical connection to a sublime
natural world inhabited by the spirits of slain African and indigenous
rebels. In contrast to the contractual and commercial relations between
white men, a sublime energy connects insurgents to nature and to one
another —whether they are unruly white women, indigenes, or former
slaves. Unfortunately, these communications can take place only under
soulful, rather than physical, circumstances because Avellaneda reduces
Cuba's First Nations to a tribe of spirits. (Taino people still fight the
myth of genocide in the twenty-first century.) She limits the descendants
of Camagüey (her name for the ghost of the warrior Hatuey) to a single
old woman and her disturbingly needy and sickly grandson. Both grandmother and child believe Sab is their savior and a reincarnation of the
righteous rebels who preceded him. He seems to have a transcendent
connection to the land and nature, which he appropriates from its first
occupiers.

Antithetical to Sab's synergy with nature and the landscape, we find
the antagonist Enrique's desire to appropriate the Cuban landscape for

his own—to convert it into a white space of capitalist accumulation. While United States print culture divulged anxieties about incorporating Creole cultures into the United States, those Creole cultures had similar reservations about Anglo-American imperialism. Avellaneda's characterization of Enrique, then, conveys her contemporaries' anxieties about the United States annexing Cuba. As Lazo points out, Cuban exile writers in the United States sometimes struggled with the question of annexation, of substituting one form of empire for another, and at other times desired complete independence for their island home. Only seventy miles from the continental United States, Cuba was technically outside, but in close proximity to, national boundaries. It was also integrally connected to the U.S. public sphere. By midcentury, Lazo says, seventy-plus Cuban newspapers in the United States had developed upon "a long-standing, two-way flow of economic, political, and cultural exchange between the United States and the island" (7). Ambivalence among Cubans about whether Cuba should become part of the United States remained.

While Sab's own anxieties about racial difference preclude his ability to declare his love for Carlota, he is unquestionably the story's hero because he transcends stereotypes of inequality when he communes with the forces of nature to perform dazzlingly brave acts. In contrast, Enrique might be a villain or an antagonist if he was not so entirely boring and bland. The "love match" to which Don Carlos consents stimulates Carlota's romantic imagination, but her betrothed quite clearly engages with her because he and his father expect to become rich from Don Carlos's plantation. The anxiety about amalgamation, in this case, does not convey any dread about a possible coupling between Sab and Carlota; instead, it denotes a fear of U.S. encroachment on Cuba, an inversion of the kinds of amalgamation fears that circulated in the United States at the same time. In a more nationalistic and perhaps nascent anti-imperialist sense, Anna Brickhouse reads *Sab* as "a romance of interracial love that implicitly explores the looming possibility of US annexation" because the heroine eventually learns that her Anglo-American husband is far inferior to the authentically Cuban mulatto whose love she overlooked during his lifetime (173).

The potential for romance and rebellion in *Sab* also threatens to encroach on the white space of the landscape and the equally white body of the Creole woman. Sab has the potential to become the kind of "dangerous" mulatto who haunts the writings of James Trecothick Austin or Josiah Nott. Unlike Hildreth, who broaches amalgamation only by depicting white men's forced liaisons with the women they enslave,

Avellaneda integrally connects Sab's cross-racial romances to his potential to become an insurgent. Cuban Creoles certainly had not forgotten the Haitian Revolution, the Aponte uprising, the alleged Denmark Vesey plot in nearby Charleston, or the hemispheric insurrections during the 1830s in Jamaica and Guyana, much less the revolt aboard the *Amistad*, a ship originally headed to Cuba, in 1839. Sab's potential to supplant white masculinity, both romantically and politically, directly challenges the authority of patriarchy itself, a challenge that also registers Avellaneda's own desire to resist white male authority and power.[4]

Halfway through the novel, a holiday in the countryside introduces the prospect of rebellion. The landscape of the countryside, contrary to the plantation landscape, speaks of a history of contact and conquest. The narrator introduces us to Martina and, in doing so, introduces an indigenous angle to the plot. Martina claims to be a descendent of Camagüey, a chief of the province who welcomed the Spanish invaders with "generous hospitality" but was "treated despicably" by his "savage murderers" (73). Avellaneda's inclusion of this indigenous aspect in her antislavery novel gives her, a white Creole woman, two possible outlets for the expression of her personal frustration with Creole and Old World Spanish culture: not only can she critique the system of slavery that the Spanish introduced to the New World and that the Creoles perpetuate, but she also can critique the very idea of conquest. Ultimately, the white female heroine identifies with Sab and Martina rather than the Spanish. Yet the white female heroine becomes the only survivor of the New World culture clash.

If Carlota symbolizes one way that Sab might challenge the social structure—cross-racial romance—Martina represents another even more controversial and corporeal possibility—insurrection. Thus when the main characters ride in to Cubitas, Martina's "native" land, the memory of rebellion literally flickers in and out of view. When Carlota points out a mysterious light in the hills, Don Carlos asks Sab to recount a legend he has learned from the locals. We never know whether Carlos has a "rational" explanation for the natural phenomenon, but the fact that he asks Sab to tell an indigenous story suggests an attempt to relegate the story to folklore or myth. Sab explains that the light is a manifestation of the conquered native leader Camagüey's restless soul, which roams the hills of Cubitas and has returned to the earth to avenge the wrongs committed against his people and their descendants. As a disembodied spirit, Camagüey is not a terribly threatening insurgent, but by asking Sab to tell the story, Don Carlos might inadvertently spark Camagüey's spirit in Sab. Since Sab is not yet as divorced from his body as Camagüey, the story hints that Sab might use his body, his physical prowess, to lead a rebellion and radically change Cuba's racist social structure.

As he tells the story, Sab connects Martina to the legend, asserting her descent from Camagüey and mentioning that she is also a prophet. When Don Carlos asks Sab, rather hesitantly, about the nature of Martina's prophesies, Sab repeats one: "The earth that was once drenched in blood will be so again: the descendants of the oppressors will themselves be oppressed, and black men will be the terrible avengers of those of copper color" (73). Thus Sab introduces a possible way to subvert Creole culture—the slaves will rise up to avenge their Indian predecessors, shedding Creole blood and oppressing those who had enslaved them. Blood, rather than the prohibitive signifier of racial inferiority, becomes the liberating sign of emancipation from the racist discourse of "blood" itself. Don Carlos doesn't like the story of Camagüey any more than he would like to know of Sab's love for his daughter, particularly because, as the narrator points out, "the Cubans, [were] always in a state of alarm after the frightful and recent example of a neighboring island" (73). "The neighboring island" is, of course, Haiti. Cuba was not without its own conspiracies and insurrections, such as the Aponte rebellion of 1812. During the Aponte trial, prosecutors alleged that insurgents were inspired and motivated by drawings of Toussaint. The myth of Haiti, in this instance, calls to mind a spiritually, physically, and intellectually integrated leader—Toussaint—who might become Sab's role model. Thus the novel presents two radical and sanguine prospects for challenging patriarchal Creole culture: blood mixing and bloodshed.

Rather than being frightened by the echoes of Haitian insurgency as a proper Creole should, Carlota sympathizes with "those of copper color: "'I have never been able,' she said, 'to read the bloody history of the conquest of America. My God, how many horrors! It still seems incredible that men were able to reach such extremes of savagery. I am sure it must be exaggerated, for it is impossible; human nature cannot be that monstrous'" (73). It is no accident that Carlota's passion and emotion are stirred by something other than love for her fiancé. Recalling a moment of traumatic historical memory stirs her soul. The monstrous becomes an apparition to her, yet, unlike her father's memory of vengeance wrought against Creoles, the monstrous and horrible is not the figure of Toussaint. Carlota's monster is the Spanish conquistador.

Sab seems to interpret Carlota's openness to the humanity of the Indians and her condemnation of the Spanish as a sign that she might recognize his humanity and reciprocate his love. Moreover, Martina's prophesy works two ways: it suggests Carlota's detachment from Creole identity and simultaneously links Sab, the black man, to the indigenous people. Sab calls Martina "mother." All of Martina's children have died, and her last grandson withers on his deathbed. She considers Sab her adopted son and only heir. Without any reminder from the narrator, Martina's prophesy becomes hauntingly real. Could Sab, then, be the black man who will avenge "those of copper color"? (73). Is it possible that Sab can create the New World again by leading a violent insurrection? Would Carlota then recognize his soul as equal to her own? Of course, this insurrection never happens, nor is it even planned; instead, Avellaneda returns to her romance plot and locates Sab's desire for a different manifestation of freedom: the freedom to be a subject, to desire the other rather than be the other. Certainly, a marriage between Sab and Carlota would challenge racial hierarchies within Cuban society, but Carlota's extended family eventually disinherits her merely because of her betrothal to an English merchant—imagine the outcry if she married a mulatto and former slave.

Nonetheless, Carlota's condemnation of Spanish "savagery," which inverts the Old World logic of civilization and conquest, completely astonishes Sab and gives him hope that she might recognize the equal soul ensconced in his black body. Carlota's fiancé, Enrique, on the other hand, shows no sympathy for Camagüey or Carlota. We learn a great deal about Sab and Enrique from their reactions to Martina's prophesy and Carlota's empathy: "The mulatto regarded her with an indescribable expression; Enrique made fun of her tears" (73). The two extremes of sensibility and empathy of which Enrique and Sab are capable become central topics in the story, supplanting the brief reference to insurrection and refocusing the narrative on Carlota's love life.

This fixation on the soul, likewise, emphasizes one of Avellaneda's major romantic beliefs: that there are superior souls in the world. Carlota has one; Enrique does not. The novel hinges on this comparison and analysis of souls, locating freedom and equality within an economy of intellect, imagination, and passion rather than within the political and economic status of real bodies in everyday life. But it also hints that "beautiful souls" are capable of physical action. Flickers of possibility that interracial love might become real repeatedly occur in moments that refer to insurrection. Sab's "terrible passion" for Carlota suggests the possibility of amalgamation just as his relationship to Martina suggests, even more subtly, the possibility of insurrection. Avellaneda's historical context certainly curtailed her artistic license, and directly advocating miscegenation or insurgency to combat white patriarchy would have been absurd, but I find it intriguing that she broaches the unthinkable.

The novel's plot, and its suspense, hinges on a series of radical possibilities. There might be an insurrection, or there might be a wedding. Carlota might come to her senses, or her illegitimate cousin Teresa might recognize the liberating power of Sab's desires. A few chapters later, Teresa reintroduces the idea of insurrection. While the story of Camagüey is introduced because Carlota notices a "brilliant, pale light which flickers far away," the flickering of light sets the stage for another possible resolution to the story's obstacles (71). This time, Teresa watches a candle burning out, equating its "sinister brightness" with the passing of her youth. It startles her, however, when "the light sen[ds] out a flash even brighter than the previous ones, but it was the last": left in total darkness, she realizes Sab is hiding in the room with her (90). One might expect that the threat of rape would be Teresa's main concern when Sab jumps out of the shadows to confront her, alone, but she is filled with anticipation. Sab is devising a plan that Teresa knows will disrupt the status quo. She schedules a secret meeting with him, agreeing to support him, although she is not sure what he has planned. At this meeting, Sab declares his love for Carlota and condemns "human society [that] has not imitated the equality of our common mother" (97). Hearing this invocation of natural rights and noting that Sab's eyes "glitter with a sinister fire," Teresa makes a logical assumption. "'Sab,' she sa[ys] with a quivering voice, 'have you perhaps summoned me to this place to reveal some plan of a conspiracy among the blacks? What danger threatens us? Are you one of the—'" (97). But the possibility of rebellion, like the flickering of the candle, extinguishes instantaneously. Before she can finish her sentence, romance intervenes—Teresa recognizes Sab's beautiful soul and falls in love with him, forgetting about rebellion.

Invoking a series of natural law arguments, Sab protests his condition. For a moment, it looks like Sab might unite mind, body, and spirit to assert his manhood. To "tell a slave . . . to forget that he is a man" defies the laws of nature and of God (140). Sab's body comes to life as he seethes against "the iniquitous laws on which one man bases his right to buy and sell another" (142). These racist terms incite Sab's "violent trembling" as much as his hatred for Enrique and his repulsion at the idea that these lies "allow him to desecrate" Carlota (52). Sab reacts in a characteristically scorching and tempestuous manner: "Then a dark rage would constrict [his] breast, and [his] heart's blood coursed like poison through [his] swollen veins" (142). This tumescent imagery is simultaneously insurgent and sexual. Unlike the numerous writers who equated black masculinity with threatening predictions of rebellion and sexual desire for white women, though, Avellaneda's narrator—not to mention the onlooker, Teresa—finds the possibility of rebellion exciting and hopeful. But Sab is even more oblivious to his potential for subversion than he is to Teresa's love. His great plan is to intervene in the marriage plot by luring Enrique into marrying Teresa. Instead of an insurrection, he has planned a buyout. Amazingly, Sab has won forty thousand pesos in the lottery. He knows that if he gives Teresa his forty thousand, the gold-digging Enrique will marry her rather than Carlota. He forfeits the chance to use his lottery money to build his own fortune and perhaps win Carlota's recognition and love. Instead, he sacrifices all to save Carlota from Enrique's insincere embrace. According to Sibylle Fischer, "the particularism of romantic love trumps the universality of the desire for liberty" (116). The plan falls apart when Teresa tells Sab that Carlota will not survive if Enrique leaves her. Sab is afraid that a rejected Carlota will die of a broken heart. His obsession with Carlota and his inability to imagine the world without her leave him with but one alternative: he gives Carlota his money. Enrique marries her immediately. Notably, Sab sells out in a number of ways: he fails to avenge his copper-colored brothers, he plots, literally, to buy Enrique's heart to keep him from Carlota, and he forecloses any opportunity for his own freedom, choosing to remain emotionally subservient to Carlota. The social system that he has so vehemently condemned remains perfectly intact.

While readers might initially have hoped that Sab's passionate love for Carlota would fire his passion for equality, transforming him into a revolutionary leader, the opposite happens. Sab is "doubly enslaved to his mistress Carlota—first as a legal slave then as a lover" (Fischer 116). He is unable to act upon his own desires, either for freedom and justice among the black and copper-colored or for Carlota's reciprocal love. "Since as a slave and a mulatto he knows that he will never be the object of his mistress's desire," Fischer notes, "he takes up the position of the intermediary through whom her desires will be realized" (116). Sab's problem is twofold. He fails Carlota because he cannot assume the masculine position of desiring subject. If he declared his love to her and exhorted her, in return, to recognize his superior soul, he would save her from Enrique's greed and insincerity. He also fails Martina. He is far too brokenhearted over his inability to win or even protect Carlota from Enrique to become an insurgent. He thus cannot express his sexual desire or his political desire. He has no chance for freedom. In his dying letter to Teresa, Sab describes how his "heart . . . of fire" reacts to the "devastating reminder" that "[he is] a mulatto and a slave" (141, 142).

The flow of blood, either as a result of passionate love or of violent insurrection, has a potentially transformative effect on the social system that denies women and slaves desire or agency. For Avellaneda, the flow of blood and the idea of amalgamation are liberating rather than destructive (as is the case for Broca and Nott). The fear and threat of "blood" likewise governs the standards that the ruling elite create to protect their privileged position. Yet Sab's submission to Carlota is also inseparable from his submission to slavery because the dynamic of their relationship mirrors the social relations necessary to maintain Creole control of Cuba. As Fischer says, "the possibility of Cuban autonomy and independence from Spain and its military protection depends on the suppression of black insurrection and the substitution of affective, voluntary submission for submission through brutal force" (117).

The transitional moment that Avellaneda sensed as she wrote *Sab*, nonetheless, was very complex and conflicted because ruptures in the social order appeared imminent at a variety of levels. The emergent middle class, comprised in part of free people of color, exceeded the Creole elite in acquiring wealth. This insurgent capitalism is another aspect of Sab's obvious superiority to Enrique and Don Carlos. In addition to Sab's "superior soul," he has a superior economic mind because his fiscal success is not just a function of luck. Even if he did not win the lottery, his managerial and brokering abilities would suit him for a variety of lucrative positions and make him, as a worker and capitalist, more competent than Enrique or Don Carlos. Aristocratic planters like Don Carlos, whom Avellaneda characterizes as "indolent," eschewed work. The sugar boom, as Fischer points out, citing Pedro Deschamps Chapeaux, brought on an "economic upswing [that] disproportionately benefited the free population of color" because Creoles considered work an activity for slaves, not gentlemen. The possibility that Sab could take his forty thousand and become a wealthy merchant threatens the social hierarchy as much as the possibility that he could marry Carlota, or that he could organize a conspiracy among the slaves. His imminent economic power suggests that he is superior in intellect as well as in the soul, yet his heart—literally and figuratively—negates all this potential. After he exerts himself to secure Carlota's fortune and ensure her marriage to Enrique, Sab collapses and literally dies of a ruptured heart.

If at first it seems that Carlota will inspire Sab, the former slave, to rise up against the status quo and rebel against Cuban society, she instead appropriates Sab's and Martina's heroic qualities. While the novel initially poses Sab as the heroic figure, offering him conjugal, insurgent, and capitalist means through which to transcend the earthly fetters that enslave him, his liberation is a lost cause. Amazingly, Carlota acquires the potential for heroism by finally recognizing the deceased Sab's love for her and by assuming Martina's position as the prophet of freedom. Carlota returns to Cubitas long after Sab and Martina both pass away. The villagers tell her of Martina's great loyalty to Sab, evidenced by her nightly walks to Sab's grave to cry for her lost son. Carlota stays in Cubitas, but the villagers soon forget her because they are distracted by a "miraculous event . . . the old Indian woman, after having been buried for half a year, returned nightly for her habitual walk and could be seen kneeling by the wooden cross that marked Sab's grave" (147).

Although it is obvious that Carlota is the one now visiting Sab's grave, the villagers believed they were in the presence of another indigenous spirit "because in Cubitas it had always been thought that Martina was different from other human beings. The most hardened unbelievers wanted a glimpse of the alleged spirit" (147). Even when Carlota leaves Cubitas and the apparition stops, the villagers continue to believe that Martina's ghost, transformed into a beautiful young woman, was visiting Sab's grave. This belief undoubtedly is influenced by the legend of La Malinche, the Mayan woman who married Cortés and, when he abandoned her, murdered their twin sons rather than allow them to go back to Spain with their father. Anna Brickhouse notes that Martina resurrects Marina, "the indigenous woman and mistress of Cortés who initiates the same interracial genealogies" (179). Throughout Latin America, La Malinche is transformed into the most terrifying of ghosts—La Llorona—the crying woman who visits graves at night and laments the destruction of her indigenous family.

It seems that this substitution of Carlota for Martina and both for La Malinche invests Carlota with great power. Not only has she been wronged as a woman, but she appropriates the wrongs of her fallen lover, Sab, a black slave, and of Martina, who represents La Malinche and virtually all of pre-Spanish Latin America. She has quite a score to settle with the white men of the world. The fact that a white woman ends up in this position, as sole survivor and living embodiment of the spirit of subversion, more or less erases Sab and Martina from the radical picture; they never have any kind of power. As is the case with many nineteenth-century white women's stories of reform, Avellaneda's white female character winds up as the only one with any chance of changing the world. That she must appropriate the experience of the African and the indigenous woman to do so is, perhaps, what makes this story most tragic. Sab's suicide and Martina's passing—undramatic because she practically vanishes, like North American Indians would in the literary imagination of white authors in decades to come—displace the flickering potential of an embodied subaltern subject who can simultaneously challenge racial and gender hierarchies. The fleshly incarnation of black and indigenous bodies capable of laboring, desiring, asserting their will, and refuting the social and juridical constraints upon their rights disappears.

Nonetheless, their spiritual presence within Carlota, the only surviving protagonist, does create a semantic open-endedness rather than foreclosing the possibility of what each represents. *Sab* is almost prescient because the demise of Avellaneda's romantic hero results from the inefficacy of just one of the avenues available to him—the conjugal—while the novel leaves one wondering if the capitalist or insurgent strategies might have worked. The history of the Aponte rebellion in 1812 echoes in the novel, and the radical potential of mulatto citizenship reappears three years after the publication of *Sab* with the conspiracy known as La Escalera. Each exemplifies the forms of martyrdom that Sab might have endured had he fulfilled Martina's and Teresa's wishes as an insurgent. As a different man of action, one whose desire for equality was not subsumed in unrequited love, Sab might have experienced the revolutionary martyrdom of the mulatto poet Plácido. Alternately, Sab could have manifested the capitalist desires of the free black population in Cuba that resisted the encroachment of the ever-expanding U.S. empire. In *Sab*, the sugar plantation is not a viable site of economic success for an independent Cuba; perhaps the planters who supported U.S. annexation symbolized, for Avellaneda, an equally unviable model of Cubanness. In contrast to Sab's ingenuity and productivity, Avellaneda's Creoles are indolent; Sab characterizes the decline in Bellavista's productivity by omission, stating "the principal cause of Bellavista's decline is not the death of the slaves" and implying that, although Don Carlos Bellavista is not a cruel master, he is not a good businessman or capable manager, either (30).

But the real tragedy of Sab's failure is his inability to forge a new world that would suit Carlota's superior soul. Enrique and his father, on the other hand, represent a particularly Anglo-Saxon (and, by extension, U.S.) manifestation of productivity and modern fiscal responsibility. Avellaneda associates this business sense with self-serving greed and spiritual vapidity, instead valorizing Sab's self-effacing and modest economic practices. Capitalism, particularly the Anglo-American kind, threatens beautiful souls like Carlota's, "a poor poetic soul thrown in among a thousand materialistic lives. Gifted with a fertile and active imagination, ignorant of life, at an age when life is no more than feelings, she found herself obliged to live calculatingly, by reflection and by measuring advantage. That mercantile and profit-oriented atmosphere, those unceasing preoccupations with interests of a material nature withered the lovely illusions of her youthful heart" (135). The real problem is not racism, indigenous extinction, or even slavery. Rather, it is the lack of options that Creole or U.S. culture offers to women.

Beautiful Souls, Alienated Bodies

Cuba, of course, was a Spanish colony in the 1840s, one that came very close to being annexed to the United States. The similarity in the way that Avellaneda imagines women's rights in a colony and the way Fuller imagines the relationship between race, gender, and rights in the United States suggests that the idea of nation was somewhat inconsequential to their theories. The romance between men and women, black and white, that promises a degree of liberation from white patriarchal authority indicates that both women considered their relationship to the power structure to be a somewhat colonial one. In *Woman in the Nineteenth Century* (1845), the rights of the "negro" and of "woman" are virtually inseparable. Fuller's appeal for social and political transformation, which relies on the individual right to cultivate his or her soul, challenges the tenets of racial and sexual difference as it challenges the practice of controlling a woman or slave's body: "As the friend of the negro assumes, that one man cannot by right, hold another in bondage, so should the friend of woman assume that man cannot, by right, lay even well-meant restrictions on woman" (20). These bodies are integrally connected to souls, and "if the negro be a soul, if the woman be a soul, appareled in flesh, to one Master only are they accountable. There is but one law for souls, and if there is to be an interpreter of it, he must come, not as man, or son of man, but as son of God" (20).

Metaphors of nature and the soul suffuse Avellaneda's novel; the soul's power vacillates between two forces: the beloved and the landscape. The idea of having a master to whose laws one must submit might be construed as a metaphor of slavery, but the invocation of law also suggests the model of a colony in relation to a nation. The nation, in Fuller's context, had certainly violated natural law. The "law for souls," in this context, rejects the fundamental tenets of liberal democracy and the Enlightenment legacy of contractually negotiated, rationally dispensed freedom. Immersed in the "newness" of transcendentalism, which was in many ways the rebirth and renewal of romanticism, Avellaneda, Fuller, and some of their contemporaries turned to natural law— to the concept of an inalienable and sovereign self—to imagine social transformation beyond the cold rationality of Enlightenment political theory. Philosophers including Rousseau and Locke imagined women in a liminal space between the state of nature and civil society, which left women ill-equipped to participate in politics or submit to the social contract. What had become conventional and institutional structures of power in the United States were irreparably flawed by such myths of race and gender, but Fuller imaginatively returns to that liminal space to channel its creative force. Rather than submit to a flawed model of equality, Avellaneda and Fuller preceded many Americans in the middle of the nineteenth century who would imagine transcending these bodily boundaries to negotiate between self and other, nature and civil society, colony and nation.

Essentially, Fuller envisioned the radical transformation of society as the lifting of racial and gender boundaries. As David M. Robinson points out, *Woman* "stands as a translation of transcendental idealism into social and political realm and as an exemplary bridge between romantic philosophy and social reform" (84). Drawing from William Ellery Channing's metaphor of the soul as a perfectible and constantly expanding source of divine energy, Fuller envisions a society wherein women can cultivate their souls, unhindered, and thus hear whisperings of equality "in their full free sense," the "simple words" that "God is living" and "all are his children" (9). This spiritual transformation yields profound secular results: "Yet then and only then," she continues, "will mankind be ripe for this, when inward and outward freedom for woman as much as for man shall be acknowledged as a right, not yielded as a concession" (20). On the simple condition that "we would have every path laid open to woman as freely as to man," Fuller's treatise promises to have "every arbitrary barrier thrown down" between men and women and to attain "a ravishing harmony of the spheres" (20).

Although Avellaneda's *Sab* is a novel and generically not as polemical as Fuller's *Woman*, her romance delves into the possibility of breaking down the barriers that Fuller says limit the expansion of the soul and the attainment of a romantic vision of social equality. Indeed, if the slave was a soul "appareled in [the] flesh" of a black male body, and the woman was but another soul clothed in the flesh of the female body, unleashing these two souls might lead to a more corporeal form of rebellion. Their freedom from prohibitions based on race and sex could lead to an encounter between their two souls, to love, and to the obsolescence of the earthly (white male) master. If Avellaneda's white heroine and mulatto hero fail to overcome the prohibitions set upon them, it is because the patriarchal capitalist system perpetually alienates them from their own bodies. For women, the alienation is primarily sexual and, obviously, for men and women who are enslaved, labor is also alienated. In *Sab*, material conditions outweigh the rebellious and transcendentalist impulses of the heroic characters, but their grasp for freedom still manages a poetic challenge to those material constraints.

Superior Souls

Although it veils the undercurrent of insurrection that flows through the plot, Avellaneda's romantic ideology also supplants the more biologically deterministic views on race that justified the actions of her conquering ancestors. As Malcolm K. Read suggests, the substantialist ideology that characterized premodern Cuba and its mother country, Spain, "still mired in a delayed transition from feudalism to capitalism," had its roots in Aristotelian notions of natural slavery: one's "blood" indelibly marked one's inherent nobility, serfdom, or servitude (63). A person's identity flowed through his veins, a "genetic endowment" that naturally pulled him toward his appropriate social station (66).

Avellaneda champions what Read calls an "alternative tradition," animism, in which the flow of identity comes, not from the blood, but from the soul (65). Hence Carlota and Sab both display animism's "beautiful soul," the repository of a different kind of superiority than the lineage of the aristocrat (71). Carlota and Sab are the hero and heroine "by virtue of their sensibility or capacity to love," and the novel tragically emphasizes the material constraints that drive apart the "force of attraction" between their beautiful souls (71). Although I contend that she foregrounds women's rights over black or indigenous rights, she still manages to rearrange social hierarchies in a manner that rebels against both Cuban Creole and Anglo-American male claims to superiority. Implicitly, this reordering also makes claims about whether Cuba should remain the white space of Creoles, become an Anglo-American extension of white space, or cease to be white space altogether.

As I mentioned earlier, the "flow" of souls that takes place between Carlota and Sab mirrors a similar synergy between Sab and the natural world. Read in terms of Sab's attempts to resist Enrique's encroachment on the landscape of Cuba, this synergy has political implications that refute the idea of Cuba as an extension of the United States' "white space." At the same time, this romanticized ideal of a black man's almost primordial connection to the landscape is something akin to primitivism and certainly derivative of a "noble savage" stereotype. Yet alienation from the landscape and the material world, or from one's body and the sensations of nature and the environment, prove to be signs of weakness and subordination at other points in the novel. Although Sab never champions the memory of Cuba's first occupants, the Taino, Avellaneda describes him in a way that clearly authorizes his entitlement to the landscape.

Thus a material connection to the world, in this novel, amounts to more than romantic racialism. Avellaneda challenges the states of exception that the likes of Don Carlos or Enrique have created, replacing them with Sab's ingenuity and ability to convert the Cuban landscape into a productive space. Rightful access to Carlota's body and rightful access to the modern Cuba that Avellaneda imagines are interchangeable. In this way, Carlota stands in for the true Cuba. To meet her full potential, she longs for something tangible, a body that has strength relative to her "weakness," and that is "great" in relation to her diminutiveness. Yet this imaginary body has no material corollary in Enrique—it is Sab whom Carlota really desires. Enrique's Anglo-Saxon shape cannot fulfill what the narrator describes as "all the illusions of a first love . . . and the passion of a heart formed under a tropical sky" (37). Descriptions of Sab, alternately, fulfill Carlota's longings perfectly even though she has no idea (due to her virginal naivete) that the object of her desire is usually within reach and that Sab loves her, too.[5] Carlota's future, like Cuba's future, relies on her ability to resist Anglo-American occupation and, alternately, recognize the legitimate power of the free black population. Thus an imagined cross-racial romance signifies the potential for a modern Cuba and a radically egalitarian political future.

Enrique's Anglo-Saxon "characteristics," which include a penchant for business and profit but a lack of physical prominence, feminize him, especially in comparison to Sab, whose protection he requires and who, ironically, will create the financial conditions that precipitate Enrique and Carlota's marriage. Early in the novel, when Enrique foolishly sets forth in a dangerous hurricane to travel overnight because one of his ships has arrived in the port, Carlota sends Sab to protect him. Clearly, the masculine ideal of protector, "all that nature shows is great and beautiful," is Sab: he can reckon with the power of the storm. When a tree branch falls on Enrique's head, Sab is tempted to finish the job by smothering the unconscious and compromised Anglo-Saxon. As Sab deliberates on whether to kill Enrique, he reveals the contours of his own soul, which are "superior to [Enrique's] own, capable of loving, capable of hating" (51). Even more interesting is the contrast between the two men's bodies: "Sab gnashed his teeth and with a powerful arm he lifted up the young Englishman's slender and delicate body as though it were a weightless piece of straw" (51).

Carlota's earlier fantasy of love, of a "protector who will sustain her in weakness," is clearly Sab, whose single arm is "powerful" enough to lift Enrique's entire body, which is "slender and delicate" and in need of Sab's protection (40, 51). Sab wants to kill Enrique, and probably could do so easily—with one "powerful arm"—even if the latter was not unconscious, but an invisible spirit "murmer[s] Carlota's parting words in his ear" and reminds him that she has asked him to be Enrique's protector (51). He rages at the idea that permitting Enrique to live will "allow him to desecrate" Carlota, but despite his display of masculine force and passion, trembling and violently "shaken by a tempest more awful than that of nature," he saves Enrique's life (51).

Just as Sab represents the unmet potential for a new world, Carlota represents the suffocating social ideal of true womanhood that upholds the norms of the old world. As Catherine Davies points out, "it is essential for an elite to control the reproductive capacity of its women in order to preserve its social pre-eminence" (315). Carlota is pure and virginal; she loves Enrique like a true woman. As the narrator illustrates, "Carlota loved Enrique, or perhaps we should say that she loved in Enrique the ideal object of her imagination" (40). Lacking embodied desire and without any knowledge of the two bodies that must be united in an ideal union of souls, Carlota is easily deceived. Although Sab has a body and the narrator attends to the wonders of his embodiment extensively, Carlota's body is not her property. Because she fits the angelic and pure restrictions of asexual womanhood, her love is not centered within herself; even her imagination is consumed with delusions about Enrique. Rather than attend to the force of nature that Sab embodies, Carlota fixates on illusions of courtly love that she projects on Enrique. When, after the storm, she sees Enrique's horse gallop back to the plantation without a rider, Carlota faints. When she finds out, moments later, that he is still alive, she faints again. Any extreme feeling she has about him, whether fear or relief, makes her swoon. In contrast, when Sab kisses her hand in acknowledgment that she has just manumitted him for saving Enrique's life, she "shiver[s], for the slaves lips had burned on her hand like coals" (53). Cold and corpselike or unconscious in response to Enrique, Carlota's body responds very viscerally to Sab.

Carlota's illusory beliefs about love are tragically disembodied and lack material grounding because she fails to recognize the fulfillment and manifestation of her ideal love in Sab's person. If both are alienated from their bodies by contract law, they are disembodied souls to a certain extent. The narrator, however, channels Carlota's love for Sab through another physical medium, the natural world. As she daydreams about taking a trip with her "chosen man," she appears "enraptured by the prospect of the next few days" because "she might be able to enjoy her beloved's presence"; but Carlota has no idea that Enrique has no connection to the feelings stirring within her. The narrator situates the experience of enthrallment in the landscape; it is "embellished by nature" and creates "some inexplicable, magical harmony between the cherished voice, the whispering of trees, the current of the stream, and the murmuring of the breeze" (59). Notably, an invisible spirit murmurs Carlota's words in Sab's ear to make him rescue Enrique, rather than finish him off, earlier in the story. All the magical spiritedness of nature flows between Carlota and Sab; Enrique has no attachment to the Cuban landscape and participates, rather foolishly, in the proverbial man-versus-nature battle that he loses when he nearly dies in the storm. Enrique is just the object through which Carlota and Sab's desire for one another travels. The spirit of nature animates and connects their superior souls; tellingly, the "cherished voice" that narrates and interprets the natural history of the Cuban countryside on the trip is Sab's. Enrique remains relatively silent—mute in the setting of the "immense, powerful vitality" that infuses Cuba's landscape (59).

Like Carlota, Sab is perpetually objectified, absent from his body, incapable of integrating mind, body, and soul into full personhood. Denied full manhood because of his blackness, he loves Carlota only spiritually and lacks the ability to imagine self-ownership of his own body, which makes it easy for him to sacrifice his body in a suicidal attempt to make Carlota happy. Carlota, as a woman, also lacks sovereignty over her own body. The disjuncture between mind, body, and soul that racism and sexism inflict on Sab and Carlota leaves them unable to imagine themselves as "whole." The ability to imagine oneself as "whole" and to define the boundaries of one's own body is integral to having agency. Sab finally dies in a strange form of suicide: he so exhausts himself in heroic efforts to fulfill what he thinks are Carlota's desires that his own heart bursts. He sacrifices his body to Carlota and ultimately alienates his body and soul irrevocably in death. Avellaneda demonstrates, through tragedy, that people who cannot integrate the needs of their mind, body, and soul fail as social agents. They lack the power to narrate their own stories and determine their own destinies.

The visceral quality of Avellaneda's descriptions and the way she merges abstract ideals of freedom and equality with attention to the very real material conditions that can either limit or uphold freedom give her writing an embodied, sensual quality.[6] The novel's argument, then, asserts the need to integrate the corporeal, spiritual, and intellectual self, a radically romantic theme that reappears among the authors discussed in the upcoming chapters. To make the word into flesh, one must extract new examples of selfhood from the imaginative realm and put them into practice in the social world. Figured, either sexually or soulfully, as a cross-racial romance, this kind of realignment of social power could break down the artificial social barriers that Fuller descried. Such a collision of abolitionist and women's rights issues, rather than the "crystallization" of "divine energy" that she anticipated, signaled an assault on the very structure of Anglo-American republican society (20).[7]

Expressions of longing for freedom expressed through metaphors of black male embodiment also did not reflect the realities that black men faced. Nor did these desires reflect very real fears that circulated in Avellaneda's contemporary culture. Among those who enjoyed, and maintained, the hierarchies of privilege that protected patriarchy and slavery, female sexuality and black masculinity were equally frightening. In contrast to Avellaneda's depiction of Sab, a long-standing cultural tradition throughout the Atlantic world cast the mulatto male as hypersexualized and an insurgent threat to the order not only of the slaveholder's world, but to whatever sphere he infiltrated. The eugenicist Josiah Nott asserted that, though more intelligent than the black, the mulatto was also more vengeful and bitter.

Anxieties about retribution for slavery and racism were reflected in the textbooks, novels, and dramas of both English and American men of science and letters. As Hazel Waters points out, the "monstrous evil" and "overwhelming lust" of black figures, usually Moors in seventeenth-century plays, carried through to the Victorian period in representations of the devastatingly wicked "mixed-race villain" who sought to destroy

Christian civilization (8, 147). Lust and vengeance often overlapped as plot motivators in English drama, mirroring scientific racism's theories about the hereditary character of the mulatto and echoing, in a sort of half-truth, the events of New World slave insurrections. British and American authors confused black male political and sexual power, as did James Trecothick Austin when he predicted an amalgamated world where "our fair and beauteous females should give birth to the thick-lipped, woolly-headed children of African fathers" (45). In the final section of this chapter, I emphasize the uniqueness of Avellaneda's representation of black or mulatto masculinity in *Sab* by contrasting it with *Lugarto the Mulatto*, a play about a Brazilian mulatto who preys on white women.

Fear of a Black Planet

Avellaneda was by no means the only author to mix metaphors of blood with images of passionate love and violent insurrection. Mythologies about "mixed blood" produced all kinds of social hysteria and paranoia in the 1840s and 1850s. As Judith Berzon illustrates, these myths suggested that the combination of disproportionately large reproductive organs (less threatening in the blood of the full African who was represented as docile and submissive) and the ambition to dominate inherited from a white father made the "mulatto" a sexual and militant threat (28). Avellaneda's sympathetic portrayal of a mulatto contrasts with many white men's imaginings of the figure. One such example appears in England; first performed in 1850, Charles O'Bryan's play *Lugarto the Mulatto* presents an almost demonic and hypersexual Brazilian villain, Lugarto, who inherits his father's millions when his legitimate half brother dies. The play is set in Paris, where the wealthy and influential attend a ball at the home of the charismatic count, whom other characters compare to Mephistopheles.[8]

Lugarto contaminates Paris with his "black blood" and the taint of the slave trade. His material greed parallels his sexual desires, thus his body creates trouble in all sorts of ways. The romantic relationships in the play are all tainted, even ruined, by Lugarto's influence, the only antidote for which is the uncompromising purity and virtue of white womanhood. In the prehistory of the drama, Lugarto has used his mesmeric powers to broker an illicit affair between an unvirtuous woman, Ursula, who is married to Monsieur Lecherin, and Gontran de Lancry, the future husband of the play's heroine, Mathilde. To "loosen [Gontran's] affection" for Mathilde, Ursula meets him, "one fatal night,"

for an "imprudent rendevous" at a farmhouse near their "aunt's cha-
taeau" (31). When Ursula goes to Abbeville to repent, Gontran marries
Mathilde. Lugarto, however, is privy to the affair and uses his knowledge
of it, combined with mesmeric powers, to control Gontran and manipulate Ursula. Lugarto's greatest worldly desire is to possess Mathilde,
whose "principles, virtue, [and] honor" he recognizes as redemptive (17).
He thinks that she, unlike all the other women he has defiled, can give
him "the happiness . . . I feel is wanting"; the "true woman" Mathilde,
who is pure and chaste, is the only person who will not "sell" herself;
thus Lugarto thinks she can cleanse his soul, perhaps even decontami-
nate his "mixed blood" (10).

In stark contrast to the equality of souls that Avellaneda negotiates between Sab and Carlota, the relationship between Mathilde and
Lugarto accentuates every racial stereotype and anxiety about the
proximity of black men to white women. For O'Bryan, the materialism of the slave economy infects the homes of wealthy whites, prey-
ing upon defenseless and pure white womanhood. The ominous black
male character seems to have no soul; he entrances people as though he
were a vampire and can only negotiate friendship through encourag-
ing illicit relationships, then threatening to blackmail the illicit lovers,
or through luring people into his lavish mansion to enjoy his decadent
parties. Mathilde's protector and "knight errant," Monsieur de Rochegune, describes him as "a kind of Mephistopheles of this world, con-
taminating the very air he breathes!" because of his ability to "defile"
and "dishonor" women and men (11). Rochegune also calls Lugarto
a "fiend," as does Gontran, and Mathilde shrinks in horror when she
sees his "fiend like glance" (11, 33, 23). When Lugarto kidnaps her
and imprisons her in his chateau, then drugs her with a potion, she
first wishes for death and refuses, like a true woman, to submit. As she
begins to lose consciousness from the potion, Lugarto sneers "in five
minutes you are mine" (25). In response, Mathilde "seizes a knife" and
raises it to "stab herself," crying "Never, villain!—never! Rather than
that, Heaven receive my soul!" (25).

Contrasting with Mathilde's purity of soul, the other characters have
unruly bodies that are marred with materialism, sensual desire, and the
pretensions of social status. Lugarto has purchased the title of count,
and he mocks the indulgence and artifice of "high society," as he leers at
the wealthy, fashionable Paris set who frequent his mansion. "This fete,
this luxury, beauty, pleasure, all for me!" he chides, well aware that his
fortunes erase, in his associates' eyes, his ignominious beginnings (17).

He almost elicits sympathy in his only monologue when he contrasts the fanfare his wealth, acquired title, and social position garner with his "other" birthright: "What a crowd! what a noise! and all this for me—a Mulatto! the son of a *slave*!" (17). The artifice of his title and of the people who pretend to befriend him seems to indict the hypocrisy of the wealthy who, although their wealth may come from the slave economy, still associate with Lugarto. When he reasons, "and yet, in their hearts, they laugh at—and *despise* me! Why, then, should not I, in return, hate this vile race?" he seems to have a legitimate point (17). Extending the immorality of the slave economy worldwide, he declares: "Everywhere people *sell* themselves! Bazaars, markets, slaves, everywhere, only here the chain is gold, and it is harder!" (17). "I wished to be noble," he scoffs, recollecting his immersion in European society, "I purchased a name and a title; I am the 'Count de Lugarto,' a noble black! Ha, ha ha!" (17). The contradiction of his dual existence would deessentialize his character from stereotypes of indolence were it not for the stereotypes of lasciviousness that take their place.

In *Sab*, the truly noble mulatto has the option of taking a fortune and becoming, like Lugarto, a wealthy capitalist. Love for a white woman gets in Sab's way; in contrast, a prurient penchant for white women motivates Lugarto. Don Carlos, like Lugarto's father, manumits Sab, but freedom does little to improve the conditions of either character because of the racist societies in which they live. Sab has more dignity than Lugarto and claims descent from a mother who was "born free and a princess" and a father whose name he never knew (31). The erasure of paternity permits Sab to attribute his passion to his mother, who he says loved his father because "a deep and powerful passion was kindled in her African heart" (31). Lugarto, alternately, has little self-respect or passionate love because he lost his mother and was left only with a South American merchant for a father. He claims that his mother "died under the blows of her master . . . who was my father" (17). There is clearly no love lost between Lugarto and his father, but in the interest of preserving his fortune, when he "lost his legitimate son, and remembered his natural child, who was his slave; he was compelled to acknowledge me, before he died; to leave me his name and fortune—" (17). Lugarto does not take his father's name, but he does take the money and attempt (unsuccessfully) to find a home where he can be respected as a human being: "disgusted with my colonial life," he complains, "I visited the great cities of the world, to see liberal men, that I might learn something more; but old Europe and young America are alike!" (17).

Although, to a certain extent, Lugarto recognizes the moral bank-
ruptcy around him, he makes no contribution to the already degenerate, profit-motivated, ignoble white society that he enters. He seems not
to see any civic virtue or dignity in any of the high-society cultures he
visits, whether American, British, or Continental. Despite his criticism
of materialistic lifestyles, he cannot transcend that world without, he
believes, the purifying influence of Mathilde. Controlling women's sexual bodies and reproductive capacity is the only way that the privileged
sector of society can maintain its "purity" and power. O'Bryan ultimately produces a white heroine who resists Lugarto's sexual advances.
In her repeated scenes of chastity, she rejects Lugarto even though her
husband's corrupt loyalty to Lugarto's money has already ruined their
marriage. O'Bryan thus places a white "true woman" as the bastion of
hope and social purity in his drama, and it is her resistance to greed
among social elites as well as sexual depravity emanating from "Lugarto
the Mulatto" that transcends the social pollution surrounding her.

It is precisely this type of "true woman," Carlota, around whom all
of the narrator's frustration and dismay circulates in *Sab*. Avellaneda's
narrator makes the reader sympathize with Sab and pity Carlota. Her
chastity and purity lead her to disappointment and objectification, certainly nowhere near the idealized love and adoration that her type of
virtue is supposed to engender in men. The economy of virtue in *Sab*
critiques the classical republican image of the gentry (the indolent Creole planter) and the individualism of the ambitious foreign merchant.
It also reverses the mark of contamination that surrounds blackness in
plays like O'Bryan's because Sab is entirely capable of recognizing Carlota's virtue and matching up to it, whereas Anglo-Saxon Enrique is not.
Unlike Lugarto, Sab does not participate in the corruption and disorder
of early capitalist society; rather, he represents a successful transition
from an aristocratic to a merit-based understanding of civic virtue and
public benevolence. Sab has the brains and work ethic to become a successful free black member of Cuban society, yet his beautiful soul and
romantic heroism are far more attractive to the narrator, and the author,
than any such banal and realistic conclusions. Avellaneda's main crite-
rion for radical equality resided in the soul, just as women in the United
States would begin to demand their rights and equality based upon the
superiority of their own souls.

Avellaneda's metaphorical language of souls resonates in the writing
of many U.S. transcendentalists, yet the history of the Americas resonates as well. Like Fuller, whose *Summer on the Lakes* is haunted by the

ethereal presence of the Native American brave who was displaced or erased to make the landscape accessible to her, Avellaneda's work is also haunted by the ghostly presence of an indigenous spirit—Camagüey—with whom she would like to make peace. Avellaneda's appropriation of the figure of La Llorona, the spectral weeping woman who mourns her conquered culture and murdered children throughout Latin America, attempts to reconcile her position as a woman with the traumatic memory of conquest and the contemporary reality of slavery. This reconciliation, however, also invokes the image of the cross-racial romance between La Malinche and Cortés, as erotic in its incorporation of otherness as it was disastrous in its ultimate destruction of the other. Still, in *Sab*'s conclusion, the reader finds the beautiful Creole Carlota mourning a loss of opportunity: the possibility that Sab's love for her put her on an equal plane with a man, and that a society could be refashioned to recognize racial and gender difference without subordinating one or the other—that love could supplant inequality and introduce radical egalitarianism to social relations.

4 Republicanism and Soul Philosophy in Elizabeth Livermore's *Zoë*

> She thought over the principal characters among her tribe, who had made their mark upon the world, Toussaint L'Ouverture, Payenga, Placido, and Dumas, besides others known in history and the present times.
>
> —Elizabeth Livermore

IN THE MID-1850S, the wife of a prominent pacifist Unitarian minister moved into Harriet Beecher Stowe's old haunts in Cincinnati, Ohio. This preacher's wife also had authorial aspirations and antislavery inclinations, but rather than write a novel about a nation that had been morally polluted by slavery, she wrote a novel that is not really about any particular nation, or even the idea of nation. Instead, she invented a multiracial West Indian heroine who attends boarding school in Denmark, then departs on a circum-Atlantic journey. In the course of this journey, the quadroon heroine visits England and the West Indies as well as the United States. She ends up at home in St. Croix, where she reads a sermon by William Ellery Channing and decides to ascend into heaven rather than await the "real Christian Republic" she had hoped to inspire on earth. This republic would incorporate the United States, but the heroine and her best friend first travel by ship throughout the Americas, spreading their vision of millennial freedom. As interesting as their destinations, however, are the conversations that take place on the way, in the oceanic space of possibility and open-endedness, between the young West Indian woman, her English schoolmate, the husband of a prominent U.S. feminist, some dreary Calvinists, and an almost jingoistic and prejudiced Anglo-American adventurer who believes it is his "destiny" to settle the West. His name, of course, is Young America. That conversations and even debates among these seemingly factional representatives of U.S. culture could have taken place with any presumed degree of equality seems counterfactual. Yet this scenario is precisely what takes place in Elizabeth Livermore's novel, *Zoë; or, The Quadroon's Triumph* (1855).

Livermore was related by marriage to the Abbots, many of whom were well-known Unitarian ministers, and also to the reformer Mary Livermore. Reviewing *Zoë* in the *Frederick Douglass Paper*, Douglass attributed Livermore's narrative material and creation of a quadroon heroine to her "residence of some time in the Danish West India Isles" (n.p.). Although she invests incredible power in the figure of her quadroon heroine, all evidence affirms that Livermore was a white woman. Born in Windham, New Hampshire, she married her cousin, Abiel Abbot Livermore, who held a pulpit in the First Congregational Unitarian Church in Cincinnati from 1850 to 1856. She enjoyed a literary career during her stay in Ohio, contributing to midwestern literary journals and starting her own publication, the *Independent Highway*. Her husband became the editor of the *Christian Inquirer* the following year, and she discontinued her weekly magazine when they moved to New York (Coyle 387). Abiel was an ardent pacifist and won an award from the American Peace Society for his book *The War with Mexico Reviewed* (1850); this pacifism may have left him in a moral dilemma, unable to articulate a concrete political strategy for ending slavery that would not bring about violence. While church historians characterize Abiel as "not eager to take part in" the abolition of slavery because his primary concern was to keep the church unified and to establish a denominational structure for western Unitarians, his wife Elizabeth's outspokenness disrupted the Livermore family's façade of nonpartisanship and may have precipitated their move to New York (Burns-Watson 7). Although Elizabeth would live for two more decades, the move also marked the end of her known literary career.[1]

With the exception of brief mention in a few journal essays, Livermore has been virtually lost to literary history. Although Livermore's popularity or critical reception in her historical moment in no way rival Stowe's, her work can tell us things about the chaos and uncertainty of the mid-1850s, particularly regarding the narratives of race, gender, and nation in which she attempted to intervene. She illustrates what Robert Levine calls a disruption in the "certitude of traditional arcs in American literary nationalism" and "reminds us that alternative histories are always immanent in particular historical moments" (*Dislocating* 13, 12).

Zoë's plot focuses mainly on the heroine's conversations with people of various nationalities (first as a boarding-school student in Denmark, then in a transatlantic voyage back to St. Croix) but also includes a slave rebellion. People of African descent, as well as Jews, Creoles, Danes, Anglo-Saxons, and Young America, negotiate the meaning of

Christian republicanism in this series of encounters, which set every negative quality of racial Anglo-Saxondom in relief with the romanticized racial attributes of other "races." While Livermore engages in the rhetoric of romantic racialism that self-described Anglo-Americans used to substantiate American exceptionalism, she makes a clear distinction between the present situation, wherein race defines social relations, and a millennial future wherein racial and sexual differences seem to dissolve. Most importantly to the argument of this book, her rebellious desire to amalgamate nations, islands, or people in a metaphorical loving embrace that would usher in revolutionary equality indexes her connection to her better-known transcendentalist and abolitionist contemporaries.

Livermore believed a real "Christian Republic" could only be created through a coalition between black and women's rights as well as the amalgamation of American cultures in a hemispheric sense. While *Zoë* is somewhat remarkable in its attempt to reimagine human categories in a way that erases the idea of embodied racial or sexual difference, Livermore's magazine writing is also remarkable because it connects the political discourse of "Higher Law" to an explicit demand for women's bodily integrity. For example, in 1856, only weeks after Margaret Garner's tragic attempts to avoid apprehension, she wrote a play that retold Garner's story and published it in her literary magazine, the *Independent Highway* (1856). Published 130 years before Toni Morrison's *Beloved*, Livermore's play *The Fugitives* might be the first literary interpretation of Garner's homicidal desire for freedom. The play about Garner takes place largely in the Cincinnati courthouse. Yet Livermore's vision for radical equality in a "Christian Republic" that respects the sacred body and the individual soul of each person is not restricted to any local or national legal system. In fact, the location of her "Christian Republic" seems closest as Zoë sails the Atlantic, in the interstitial space between nations and colonies that would otherwise define the racialized and gendered subject.

Higher Law and Bodily Integrity

Both *Zoë* and the *Independent Highway* make strident antislavery claims based in the political discourse of "higher law," the term coined by William H. Seward in the U.S. Senate in his maiden speech on March 11, 1850. As a political term that relied on moral suasion, "higher law" upheld Douglass's belief in the unconstitutionality of slavery. According to Gregg Crane: "Seward threw down a gauntlet on the issue most sharply dividing the country. He flatly denied 'that the Constitution recognizes property in man' and asserted, in a phrase that became infamous, that the nation's charter must heed 'a higher law.' Seward cannily recognized both that a society's moral consensus delimits the scope and effect of its laws and that that consensus is mutable" (*Race* 12–13).[2] Livermore believed that women's literature could sway moral consensus just as she believed women would take a leadership role in Christian republicanism, her term for Bible politics. She also believed that a person's body was her own property—that the Bible and the Constitution recognized "property in man" insofar as each person was the exclusive owner of his or her sovereign self and the steward of a sacred body.

Both Livermore and Seward used the term "higher law" to demand social transformation, but for Livermore the political term is explicitly connected to one's right to what we now call bodily integrity. In her literary imagination, women both usher in the future where a "higher order of beings" might exist and stand to benefit from the implementation of "higher law" in their contemporary world because it guarantees the sacred sovereignty of self, or corporeal Christianity, that Jacobs also demands (1:120). The idea of "higher law" was entrenched in U.S. political debates by the time Livermore commenced her publishing flurry. While it guided the nation toward Christian republican principles, higher law was also a governing principle that reckoned with issues of territorial expansion. Seward first articulated "higher law" politics in the speech "Freedom in the New Territories (Appeal to a Higher Law)."[3]

The speech was also typically transatlantic in its intellectual influences. It drew from *The Federalist Papers*, Machiavelli, and Montesquieu but perhaps most directly from Edmund Burke's 1794 speech on the impeachment of Warren Hastings, which condemned the governor of Bengal's alleged tyranny toward colonial subjects: "there is but one law for all—namely, that law which governs all law—the law of our Creator—the law of humanity, justice, equity—the law of nature and of nations. So far as any laws fortify this primeval law, and give it more precision, more energy, more effect, by their declarations, such laws enter into the sanctuary and participate in the sacredness of the character" (Seward 303). Like the authors in this study, Seward seems to recognize sacredness of self as a fundamental characteristic of citizenship. Another soft undercurrent of his rhetoric, via its references to Burke's 1794 speech, is a recognition that oppressed and colonized peoples might rightfully rebel against their oppressors, as the Bengali people did. The claim of righteous rebellion and anticolonial sentiment is not so soft in Livermore's rhetoric, but both harken to the millennial revolutionary belief that "the American Revolution heralded the millennial reign of Christ on Earth" (Foner 113).

In a sense continuing the unfinished business of the American Revolution, higher law addressed the nonpersonhood of enslaved Americans. To fulfill the revolutionary promise of equality, Seward advocated Burke's ideals, particularly his assertion that laws that "fortify" natural law "enter into the sanctuary" of "the law of our Creator" and mirror the law of nations. Notably, this law of nations seems to apply transnationally, not just to the "exceptional" United States. Seward's antislavery arguments upheld the sovereignty of the Constitution and read it, as did Frederick Douglass and the Radical Abolitionist Party in 1855, as a document that should be interpreted through "higher law," a concept that Livermore enthusiastically endorsed. Burke's conceptual "sacredness of character" likewise reappears in Livermore's definition of citizenship in her ideal "Christian Republic" (Seward 283). For Seward (and for Livermore), personal liberty was essential to maintaining the "sacredness of the character" and the sacredness of the nation (Seward 302). For Seward, the absence of personal liberty for the slave and for the "free citizen" prosecuted under the Fugitive Slave Law constituted a violation of natural law due to the degrading premise that slaves are "property and chattels" (302). For Livermore, personal liberty was a God-given right that all humans shared. Whatever affected the sovereignty of the individual affected not only the nation, but the world— a cosmopolitan contingency God created "by making of one blood all the nations and families of the earth" (Zoë 1:197). In Livermore's Christian republic, individual nationhood dispersed in favor of world peace. Livermore's version of higher law, unlike that of her pacifist husband, however, justified rebellion and violent retribution.

Her most passionate invocation of Seward's higher law comes in defense of Margaret Garner, the inspiration for Morrison's main character, Sethe, in *Beloved*. Less than a month after Garner attempted to murder her children rather than have them taken back to slavery, Livermore published the first installation of her play *The Fugitive: A Tragedy in Six Scenes*. The play begins with a parlor conversation between the newly escaped Garner and her parents regarding their reason for fleeing the South—because they want to protect Margaret from further sexual objectification. In the next scene, they are duped into recapture. The majority of the remaining scenes reenact the events in the courtroom, which are largely debates couched in the language of higher law. A note below the cast of characters indicates that "this little drama purports to give the true expression of the *deepest soul* of the Negroes, which their conduct manifests, and which Slavery, with its consequent ignorance, denies them" (6, original emphasis). Like a true romanticist and transcendentalist, Livermore locates radical equality in the soul.

Yet Livermore, like Jacobs, is equally concerned with the integrity of the body. *The Fugitive* opens with a critique of black women's lack of sexual rights voiced through Garner's parents. Because a pure body is so integral to the expression of a beautiful soul in Livermore's philosophy, sexual assault is one of slavery's most despicable practices. Garner's mother explains that she ran because she refused to "stay to see the lewd young Massa exult over the ruin of our youngest darling's purity" (6). The tie between personhood and bodily integrity emerges in *The Fugitive,* particularly because the Garner family sees the threat of rape by the lustful son of their master as slavery's greatest crime. One "true expression" of the woman's "deepest soul" is her commitment to protecting the sanctity of her child's body (6). Like Seward, who asserts that "the Constitution designedly mentions slaves, not as slaves, much less as chattels, but as *persons*," Livermore asserts Margaret Garner's personhood, defined as the right to protect one's own body (306, original emphasis). Garner's violent impulses are never questioned, or even mentioned.

Interspersed with allusions to the defilement and sexual degradation of the slave woman's body are references to her superior soul. The characters in *The Fugitive* are duped by a capturer who pretends to follow Christ's teachings and act as a neighbor; they naively permit him to usher them into a room in his house (where he promptly locks the door) because "he is a pious man. . . . Wicked men don't pray" (13). The fact that the fugitives withhold judgment on the man and believe him when he asks them to join him in "family prayers" indicates their pure sentiments; they embody the "tender spirituality and angelic self-sacrifice of the Son of God" in their refusal to judge, condemn, or even distrust the white man without empirical evidence that he is a sinner (13). Like Zoë, they demonstrate what Mia Bay calls "the religious racialism of nineteenth-century black ethnology" (20). While the family does not display the demeaning attributes of romantic racialism—its assertion of childlike lightheartedness or subservience—they embody the core values of a "peculiarly Christian and 'feminine' civilization" that abolitionists imagined in the 1840s and colonizationists promoted in the 1850s (Fredrickson 115).[4] Livermore is no colonizationist, but her writing provides great insight into this peculiar feminine, millennial vision of civilization.

The religious character of the Garner family exemplifies what an essay in the *Independent Highway* titled "The Education of the Body" calls "Soul-Philosophy." Because Jesus Christ exemplifies the potential for a *"completed life"* (original emphasis), the magazine encourages its reader to "go to his precepts, his parables, and the expression of his most heartfelt sentiments. Those are the data, by which to judge how he arrived at his sublime manhood" (Livermore, *Independent* 12). The Garners, who refuse to pass judgment on their persecutors, are Christ-like in this sense. But this "Soul-Philosophy" is not just spiritual; it has a material character because its practitioners "observe[s] the facts of Nature" and employ them "in human action and improvement (12). Drawing from health reform and physical education rhetoric, she connects the physical self to the spiritual self. The sanctity and health of the body prove integral to one's ability to act in accord with the laws of nature; "human action" requires a mobile body. The essay offers a locomotive means for arriving at "sublime manhood" (12). "When we walk abroad, we can gain not merely bodily strength," it explains; "every nerve of the healthy, physical system can be an inlet of more than pleasurable sensation, even a portal for the ever-present Holy Spirit to flow into the soul" (10). Thus an active, locomotive body provides the vessel for a superior soul. The kinesthetic imagery of Livermore's insistence on mobility and movement contrasts with Jacobs's accounts of immobilization and restriction, hiding in swamps or garrets. But the possibility that the holy spirit could flow into such a mobile body to enact divine retribution—or rebel violently against oppression—is there.

Because the feature of religiosity or Christian zeal is often a facet of romantic racialism, it is easy to overlook Livermore's radical Christian and perfectionist beliefs. Connecting the radical Enlightenment to the idea of Christian republicanism suggests that Livermore's political agenda might be more interesting than what Suzanne Bost describes as a "literary product" that "confine[s] biracial characters within restrictive, one-dimensional roles that fail to leave room for agency, escape, or subversion" (62). When the Spinozian idea of a human being as matter in motion meets Livermore's perfectionist insistence on the radical equality of souls, the mobility of both the Garner family and her eponymous heroine takes on a new dimension. While Spinoza, as Nick Nesbitt explains, proposes that "movement and the capacity for self-determination is inherent in matter itself (natura naturans), not instilled by an external First Mover" (22), Livermore persistently tries to wed materialism (the materiality of the body) and motion with the soul.

The connection between body and soul is integral to Livermore's concept of a corporeal Christianity in which the soul manifests through the integrity of the sexual and laboring body. Romantic and rebellious demands for equality are divinely sanctioned yet performed in physical acts of intimacy or resistance to oppression. The fugitives also enact the Soul-Philosophy as they seek liberty, both because they are using their bodies to move toward freedom and because they are protecting Margaret's sexual body.[5] The morally depraved lawyer who represents their owner uses the antithesis of "Soul-Philosophy" to argue for remand. He says: "these prisoners, forgetful of the allegiance due to their legal masters, have dared to use the power of motion invested in them for *their owner's good*, to flee from him" (20). Directly contradicting Livermore's and Seward's stated principles, he goes on to say, "they were under the delusion that they had a right to their bodies and souls, and the liberty to use them. I deny them such liberty" (20).

The opposing counsel in the drama counters with perfectionist rhetoric: "the Fugitive Slave Law commands you to treat these people as slaves; the Bible, as men. As slaves, they are condemned to a brutish life,—bereft of hope, affection, and the soul's right to full expansion. The Bible commands all men to be perfect as He is perfect. Do you not see that the Bible and this law are at fearful variance?" (21). Concluding that "there is a 'higher law,' aye, it mounts upwards farther than the eagle ever flew. Obey that law," the counsel echoes Seward's claim in "Freedom in the Territories" (21). This somewhat bizarre connection between Christ-like spirituality and an expanding, migratory, even soaring mode of embodiment emphasizes the connection between body and soul that Livermore finds so integral to Christian republicanism. Immediately following scene 3 of *The Fugitive,* she quotes Jane Swisshelm's essay titled "Women's Rights": "Every man and woman has a right to do that which he or she is best fitted to perform, as his or her share of the world's work, and *to be protected in his or her person*, and the enjoyment of the proceeds of his or her labor" (14, emphasis added).[6] The placement of this quote right below "The Fugitive" suggests that women's demands for the integrity of the laboring body should align with demands for the integrity of the sexual body. It also echoes Spinoza's argument, per Nesbitt, that "natural right must protect and cultivate not only biological life but also any being's fullest, unrealized possibilities" (22).

Through Livermore's literary imagination, Seward's well-known political discourse becomes enmeshed in a story of a black woman's right to the integrity of her body. She stretches Seward's meaning, adding revolutionary and romantic nuances to his definition of "higher law." She substitutes her own ideas for Seward's and pushes the boundaries of his political convictions, just as *Zoë* pushes the borders and boundaries of belonging for people of African and indigenous descent throughout the Americas. *Zoë* expands the migratory, ambulatory corporeal Christianity of the Garner family well beyond the borders of the United States. As a woman, *Zoë* is a member of the tribe most numerous and powerful; she uses that position of relative authority to invoke the rights of the various races in the Americas as well. *Zoë* is unique because it celebrates the presence and voice of a black woman representing republican values that have been redefined according to the demands of bodily integrity and an accompanying freedom of movement.

Zoë never faces sexual assault or even seduction, as do most of the quadroon heroines in the writing of Lydia Child, Harriet Beecher Stowe, or William Wells Brown. Yet the violent manifestation of cross-racial sex is a prominent concern. Part of the reason that men are ill-suited to leadership stems from their particularly exploitative and sexual oppression of women during slavery. Anyone who dominates others sexually or through other forms of sexual exploitation is what Livermore calls an "Ani-MAL" and has not integrated body and soul in the way that Margaret Garner or Zoë do.

One quintessential example of "Ani-MAL" behavior plays out on Zoë's home island of St. Croix. A slaveholder and colonial official on the island, General Rutgard, is also the father of a mulatto son. A conversation among women on the island subverts Rutgard's public authority by making him the object of ridicule and scrutiny regarding his past sexual transgressions. As elite white Creole women and men discuss the outcome of the recent peaceful insurrection that emancipated the island, even the Creole women find humor in General Rutgard's hypocritical Anglo-Saxon pretensions. The women mock and laugh at Rutgard's complaint that "the impudence of these colored rascals is insufferable. . . . [T]hat scoundrel Bill had the impertinence to nod to me with a twinkle in his eye, as if I were his equal" (2:30). The narrator summarily reveals that "Bill" is Rutgard's illegitimate son.

The other Creoles find Rutgard's complaint amusing because "so striking was the resemblance between [Rutgard and Bill] that among both slaves and freemen of all colors [Bill] bore the sportive appellation of Gen. Rutgard, Jr." (2:30). General Rutgard, then, represents the "old regime" in politics as he, like many French Creoles in Haiti, refuses to acknowledge his son (2:33). Yet this scandalous family drama ceases to be amusing or titillating when the leaders of the insurrection are executed. Bill, the disenfranchised mulatto son, begins to resemble Vincent Ogé; with Bill's brutal murder, the scene recalls the events of the Haitian Revolution.

In contrast to the corrupt and low-souled Anglo-Saxon man or the Creole women who laugh at amalgamation, Livermore depicts members of Zoë's multiracial St. Croix family, particularly her mother Sophia, as theorists of a rebellious and romantic political philosophy. As Sophia muses on the events of St. Croix's peaceful insurrection (which ceased in its peacefulness when Danish officials executed the leaders of the insurgency), the narrator ponders the necessity of individual freedom and exercise of natural rights, for "we must guard with delicate care against the absorption of ourselves in the general mass" (2:33). Like Margaret Garner, Sophia sees an end to sexual violence—forced amalgamation—as a fundamental right.

Yet to guard against "absorption of ourselves in the general mass" seems to assert that this new, amalgamated race needs to remain distinct from other races, and women's right to self-defense is the first step. She analyzes the situation leading up to emancipation and anticipates the insurrection itself, calmly accepting the civil disobedience practiced by the blacks and finding it morally sound. Her allegiance to the blacks (although she is "colored" and the daughter of a rich Martinique planter, she lived as a slave for her first twenty years) comes to voice as the narrator states: "It is time to understand that we belong to the great Father, not to each other in any servile or arbitrary sense. To him we look for communion; his universal spirit influences without enslaving; his enlightening voice speaks, when we will let it" (2:33). A universal spirit, of course, transcends national and racial boundaries, but it also supports insurgents and rebels. The cross-racial contours that Livermore saw manifest in "God's moral laws" also read divine providence in amalgamation of the races. As Sophia points out, however, amalgamation does not mean assimilation. It is critical to retain the different contributions that different cultures bring to the table in order to make something new.

The Conversion of Young America

In contrast to the masculinist narrative of nation and literary production propounded by "Young America," a character Livermore creates to lambaste the cadre of authors associated with John O'Sullivan's *United States Magazine and Democratic Review*, characters like Zoë and the ubiquitous Mrs. Pumpkin disrupt and contest male authority, white supremacy, and Manifest Destiny.[7] One of Livermore's idiosyncrasies is that characters in the literary magazine talk about Zoë as if she were a real person. Similarly, Zoë reads the *Independent Highway* during her transatlantic voyage. Both fictional realms—novel and magazine—overlap and interweave as they discuss race, sex, and rights. Mrs. Pumpkin, a character who appears in both texts, is just one of "a great mob of women who were assailing the printing presses, eager to have their works published"; her radical views of humanity are as "globular," "ripe," and "round" as Mrs. Pumpkin herself (2:176, 185). This roundness signifies a very whole and inclusive view of the world—or of the globe—that Mrs. Pumpkin shares with her sister-authors in the book. It points toward a cosmopolitan millennialism, one that eschews national boundaries. The female literati of the novel are also highly critical of contemporary notions of racial and gender difference. Mrs. Pumpkin explains the reclassification of humanity that undergirds womens' literary project:

> There are four great divisions of humanity at the present time. They are the *Feminines*, which include the very choicest portion of both sexes of all races, conditions, classes and color. Over against these are the *Ani-MALS*, or animated evils, just as you please to call them. Then there are the *Big-eyes*, which mean those who are always on the look-out for something wonderful, and who, at the present day, are mastered by the exciting subjects of Magnetism, Spiritualism, Psychology, etc., etc. The fourth are the *Commons*, who have not much character or principles of any kind, but are moulded [*sic*] by the influences around them. (*Zoë* 2:177)

Livermore creates four categories that transcend race and gender to disturb a hierarchy that places Anglo-American men at the top. The great differences among people yield from the degree to which each individual displays moral sentiment, spiritual openness, benevolence, rational intelligence, faith, and self-reliance. The Feminines are superior, but because they "include the very choicest portion of both sexes of all races, conditions, classes and color," their superiority is not rooted in biological sex or race (*Zoë* 2:177). Although they are superior in moral sentiment and spiritual depth, which are "female" and "African" qualities in a sentimentalist or romantic racialist context, they reject embodied notions of identity and pursue a spiritual realm. They recognize equality in the souls of all people, and their power comes from divine sources. The Ani-MALS (who seem very much like Anglo-Saxons) can assert physical and economic power, but, because animal nature rather than divine sentiment guides their desires, they tend to exploit others and create hierarchies based on wealth and strength rather than govern with the benevolence that the feminines promise. The Big-eyes cast common sense aside and become distracted by any utopian fad or trend that spiritualist charlatans or free-love advocates conjure up. The Commons lack self-reliance and faith; they accept the status quo and lack imagination.

This recategorization of human nature is remarkable because it does not rely on biological classifications of identity. While Livermore sees the superior souls of the Feminines primarily among women, she also lists Ralph Waldo Emerson as one of them. According to Livermore, men in politics, particularly those invested in Calvinist beliefs about the sinfulness of the soul and Anglo-American racial ideologies, lack "public spirit" as well as "private benevolence" (2:118). Her philosophy has much in common with Margaret Fuller and women's rights advocates who defined a distinctly female "feminine" nature that built upon emotional depth and spiritual expansiveness. Fuller contrasted women's spiritual power with men's "low materialist tendency" (65). Fuller did not argue that these qualities were essential and immutable; she said it is "no more the order of nature" that women should be "incarnated pure" as feminine than that "masculine energy should exist unmingled" with feminine in a man (68). Livermore's system makes similarly nonessentialist claims, but it is interesting that, whereas Fuller retains the "twofold" system of gender difference—masculine and feminine—Livermore disposes with masculinity and offers, in its stead, an inferior class of Ani-MALS. Race also disappears entirely from the lexicon, although the implicit message that "amalgamated" people like Zoë and Sophia prevail among the Feminines invokes some of the tenets of romantic racialism. Still, the signal difference between individuals is based more on imagination, morals, faith, and intellect than physically identifiable characteristics.

Livermore anticipates the reorganization of society and the moment when the "*Feminines*" reign over the "*Ani-MALS*" and the other two less powerful of the "four great divisions of humanity" (*Zoë* 2:177). In this millennial future, an ideal of cross-racial love that might perpetuate Zoë's "amalgamated" race can ameliorate the base tendencies of the Ani-MALS. She is also aware that recent history and contemporary reality fall far short of this ideal. While her characters recognize that white slave owners "for a time violated with impunity" the natural laws of personhood by raping black women, the result of this practice will ultimately chastise these "waste products of the earth"— "Ani-MALS," who very often appear to the rest of the world as slaveholding white men—for "the wicked indulgence of their beastly appetites" (*Zoë* 2:212; 1:iv; 2:177, 212). Even if the rapists "tread the souls of their victims down," the "stronger races" emerge because of amalgamation, "from the marriage of the whites with the Africans" (*Zoë* 2:212). Notably, the "stronger races" are the multiracial and diverse *"Feminines"* in Livermore's lexicon—a bold rewriting of the medical and legal genres that defined race through biology. Livermore rewrites the history of amalgamation by acknowledging that slavery and sexual violence precipitated the blending of the races, then prophesies along the lines of Psalms 68:31—"Ethiopia shall stretch forth her hands unto God"—that people of African descent will become major contributors to the creation of God's kingdom on earth. This looks something like Charles Emerson's premonition that whites will covet alliances with the descendants of the Ethiopian.

Although bodies are somewhat irrelevant to one's membership in each of Livermore's four main categories of humanity, and social identity is based on nonessential characteristics, she still develops the personal identity and self-worth of her characters by asserting their own sense of self-ownership of the body. Like many of the reformers of her day, she had a theory of the soul that substantiated human freedom. What distinguishes her from many others is her belief that immanence was not a distraction from the work of the soul, but rather that the body and its well-being were integral to the expansion of the soul. She connects the body to the soul, in Zoë's case particularly, in a manner that exalts womanhood and interprets her color as a marker of the "African" qualities she imagines in her heroine's soul rather than as a biological marker of inferiority. Whereas race science, the law, and dominant social perceptions would interpret Zoë's "color" and her identity as "quadroon," as well as her gender, as negations of her personhood and of her citizenship, Livermore locates great potential in her hybrid identity: she is a quadroon, thus embodying the qualities of the European and the African; she is the daughter of former slaves, thus representing the "condition" of servitude; she is an author, but also labors with her mother in a bakery, evidence of her connection to two "classes"; and, finally, her "color" marks her, not as an inferior being, but as the quintessential *"Feminine."* When a Calvinist minister complains that "feminine" philosophy would put the likes of Zoë "on equal footing with the Anglo Saxon race," it becomes clear that this is Livermore's precise objective (2:228).

This revolutionary philosophy, although it invokes some of the millennial tenets of American revolutionary thought, does not emerge exclusively from the United States. An international cadre of women writers that includes Lisbet Liebenhoff, Mrs. Lindsey, Mrs. Applebutter, and the eponymous Zoë philosophize and make "Feminine" political proclamations throughout the novel. Notably, these women are from different nations or colonial places, including Europe and the Caribbean. This cosmopolitan cohort, which often convenes in a parlor for conversations not unlike those that Margaret Fuller led, provides Zoë and Hilda with a much better education than they receive in their boarding school. For example, Zoë and Hilda have to learn how to resist their Anglo-Saxon headmistress's attempts to make them into a particular kind of "lady." Like Livermore's literary target, the Young Americans, the headmistress has the "physical courage, energy, self-reliance, and practical power of that predominant race. She believed in its 'manifest destiny' which by the majority is supposed to involve a superiority over the rest of the world" (1:98). This passage echoes the sentiments of "The Great Nation of Futurity" as well as some of the thoughts expressed by Stowe's Augustine St. Claire.

The title of the chapter about the headmistress (whose disdain and contempt for Zoë are obvious) is not so subtle: "Anglo-Saxons Do Not Know Everything." Under the aegis of what might be a "civilizing mission," the headmistress attempts to make Zoë assimilate by refusing to let her spend time alone in her room or, generally, to daydream. Refusing to participate in the kind of vigorous physical activity or rigorously rational academic interests that the headmistress espouses, "Zoë, finding in her teacher's staid, bare practical world no home for her glowing fancies . . . and enkindled hopes . . . buried herself in her chamber to call about her the spirits of a clearer ether and intenser being" (1:99). Notably, Zoë is not imitative, as is supposedly the characteristic of her "race"; instead, she cultivates her own distinct form of genius. She also finds refuge in Mrs. Liebenhoff's parlor. As a woman of African descent, Zoë brings a special contribution to those conversations; she is a visionary, fragile and creative as a spider that "spins itself a world according to the beautiful laws with which its Creator has inspired it" (1:98). The passage echoes both an abolitionist discourse of freedom through natural law and a romantic racialist characterization of African spirituality.

The amalgamation of two disparate cultures—African and Anglo-Saxon—underlies the "romantic friendship" that Zoë and Hilda develop in their Danish boarding school (1:37). Surprisingly, Hilda's family made their fortune as slaveholders on the same island where Zoë's family was enslaved. Initially, Hilda possesses the qualities of "a real Anglo-Saxon in character and mind, as well as in descent; energetic, expressive in action as well as in word; inventive, decided and managing" (1:38). Yet without Zoë's calming influence, Hilda might become a *"tyrant"* like the headmistress of the school (1:39, original emphasis). In Livermore's closest earthly approximation to an ideal world—the female space of the boarding school and its extension, the women's parlor—the essential gifts that Zoë and Hilda bring to the world can coalesce. Hilda's inherent "physical courage, energy, self-reliance, and practical power" meet Zoë's "fiery temperament, imagination, strong affections, and religious aspiration (1:98–99). Like the "black hearts of men" that united radical abolitionists, the love between Zoë and Hilda is a platonic form of romance based on mutual recognition and an idealized belief in the power of the "black heart" to ameliorate the excesses of Anglo-America.

Livermore's "romantic racialism" has much in common with that of Unitarian minister Theodore Parker, mentioned in the first chapter, for its antipathy toward "Anglo Saxons." Zoë's qualities fall in line with those attributed, through romantic racialism, to Africans. Her face is "pure and intellectual," with the "mysterious pensiveness quite common to her caste, and visible even in the face of the full African" (1:20). As a woman of mixed race, her "difference of expression" is a "prophecy of the fulfillment of the bitter struggle of the spirit which in all of them is to be wrought out by groans and tears" (1:20). Zoë's ultimate triumph, her struggle of the spirit, is to imagine the glorious potential of hemispheric American democracy when it is infused with the "intellect and poetry" of the African as well as the impulse toward inclusion that characterizes the noble and intelligent females in the novel. In addition to the contrast between "African" Zoë and "Anglo-Saxon" Hilda, Livermore contrasts several other nationalities including Jews, Hungarians, Germans, American Indians, and Danes. Her classification of nationalities, however, does not branch into a hierarchy; rather, it is like a web of nations, each with its own strengths, weaknesses, distinct contributions, and possible liabilities—another example of romantic racialism. Although liberals advocate this view in the twenty-first century under the aegis of progressive multiculturalism, scholars of the nineteenth century often criticize romantic racialism's idea of "contributions" because its differences are based on seemingly inherent characteristics rather than shared history and experience.

This catalogue of romantic racialist traits, however, is only a provisional scheme for characterization. Livermore begins to dismantle romantic racialism as Hilda, also an Anglo-Saxon, breaks from the pattern of her "race" and begins to take on some of Zoë's more pensive traits. Zoë, likewise, begins to speak publicly rather than remain pensive and withdrawn. Thus the specific qualities of the Anglo-Saxon or the African are by no means immutable, and in this equation, the African reforms the Anglo-Saxon—certainly not the agenda of manifest destiny. To overcome the limitations of racial difference, particularly in Hilda's case, Livermore prescribes becoming "one with every tribe, nation, and kingdom under heaven," a task that "no broad sweep of sympathies" could complete (1:100). Hilda has to go beyond sentimental identification with others, particularly African Americans. She has to engage in a corporeal Christianity, one that encourages her to travel and proselytize as an activist. By the end of the novel, she declares her intention to work for equality and recognize her oneness with God and thus with all people, regardless of their Anglo, African, or Indian ancestry or nationality. The ability to transcend racial identity is a sign of the expansiveness of the soul, a quality that will "lift her to companionship with the realms above" (1:100).

After Zoë transforms Hilda, the latter is ready to engage in a reformative romance with George Stephenson, or "Young America," whom she converts from a rugged frontiersman into a republican gentleman. In the second volume of the novel, Zoë also develops a relationship with America that is based on a different kind of romance than Hilda's relationship with Young America. She begins writing her own treatise on equality, which she hopes might usher in a "real Christian Republic" in the United States. As a romance of the imagination that rewrites and improves upon reality, her writing becomes "a legacy to my poor people . . . who, like Tantalus, are nearly immersed to the brim in the liberty they pant for, and cannot quaff of the stream" (2:303). Zoë's intellectual vision develops into a love affair with the very idea of America and its concomitant female, negro, and American Indian "declaration[s] of Independence" (the labels by which the character Young America characterizes progressive reformers) (2:191). This renewed "declaration of Independence" engages the three tribes that John Adams mentioned in the well-known letter to his wife. This time, there are no states of exception.

It is also crucial that Zoë and Hilda define the parameters of their racially inclusive, feminine, and Christian civilization while at sea, sailing from London to the Bahamas; Mobile, Alabama; Cuba; Jamaica; and Barbados to reach the final destination of their "home" island, St. Croix. The constant mobility of their maritime voyage, which takes up the trajectory of the original civilizing mission, but this time incorporates an "African" influence, fosters the expansion of ideas that takes place aboard ship. Separated from the influence of their beloved "Mrs. Lieben-hoff," they begin a dialogue-at-sea with a group of American men. The fluidity of their conversations seems to be nourished by the fact that they are all removed from the white space of the United States. The Atlan-tic and the Caribbean Sea provide interstitial spaces for the idea of free-dom to expand in, beyond the suffocating borders of Anglo-American law. Mr. Lindsey, a Unitarian Congregationalist minister, is little more than a mouthpiece for his wife's feminist letters. Mrs. Lindsey's letters, combined with Zoë and Hilda's influence, convert a cadre of American "types" to their "feminine" philosophy of republicanism. Most nota-bly, this feminine trio negotiates the differences between "Young Amer-ica," a rugged individualist, and "Mr. Pierson," a blue-blooded Boston pseudo-aristocrat and Calvinist minister. The women's combined efforts result in a pedagogy of citizenship that converts Young America's racism and sexism as well as Pierson's elitism. As Young America becomes Hil-da's suitor, she and Zoë surmise "all that he seemed to need was a firm and rational Christian faith . . . and the softening, refining influence of feminine society" (2:200).

The pedagogy of citizenship enacted upon Young America carries within it a particularly nuanced definition of "feminine society." As Hilda schools Young America on women's rights and Zoë introduces him to a more filial acceptance of Africans within the Americas, Young America becomes, like his nation, "the future of this world for the next age" as Zoë and Hilda see it (2:174). Particularly germane to the lessons that make Young America a suitable suitor as well as representative of the nation's future is a conversation he has with Mr. Lindsey (who acts as a mouthpiece for Mrs. Lindsey) about amalgamation. Young America has proven himself in great need of instruction when he exclaims, after listening to a woman suffrage treatise in the company of Zoë and Hilda, that he "expect[s] they [the women] are concocting a second declaration of independence with the niggers to back them" (2:191). This reference to revolution, of course, is immediately associated with amalgamation schemes. When Mr. Lindsey takes him aside to explain that "each of God's children comes from His hand with the germ of immortal pow-ers, differing, it is true, in combination and character, so as to make up a beautiful variety," Young America accuses him of espousing amalga-mationist theories (2:210, 211). Lindsey, however, retorts that "from the marriage of the whites with the Africans, has sprung up a race in our midst, who, by the development, in every direction, required by physical, intellectual, and spiritual laws, are equal to the duties of a complete manhood and womanhood. This class is, in the future, to be a power, no less mighty than subtle, to help carry on our country to its magnificent destiny" (2:211–12). As a pun on "manifest destiny," magnificent destiny reverses the trajectory of the civilizing mission that Anglo-Saxons assumed.

Like Harriet Jacobs, who worked hard in her narrative to take the scene of cross-racial sexual encounter beyond a victimology of black womanhood, Livermore tries to recast the history of amalgamation in a different light. Mr. Lindsey's use of the term "marriage" refers to the reality of amalgamation through slavery. He compares the birth of illegitimate mulatto children to Christ's first incarnation, thereby spiritually marrying enslaved women to God rather than acknowledging their rapists. He says "if an immortal spirit has descended from on high, it is the fruit of *marriage*, though no priest may have pronounced the bans nor ritual joined the hands nor human laws proclaimed its sanction!" (2:212). The essential equality of souls, black and white, sanctifies these bonds. Similarly, Young America learns to look from his soul into the souls of others as he overcomes his previously virulent racist tendencies. He concedes that he can only fulfill his destiny as he learns that "the want is in my own soul, and if that is about the right," God will meet his other needs as they come along (2:215). To be in "right relations with God," as Mr. Lindsey defines them, necessitates a profound respect for humanity in all its diversity—particularly as that diversity might manifest in "feminine" or "African" qualities.

The conversion and education of Young America provide an explicit and specific pedagogy of citizenship that will release "the spirit of the age" and bring about the new era Livermore envisions. In this interest, Zoë proceeds to write her own contribution to visionary politics. As the heterosexual romance between Young America and Hilda develops, Zoë's romantic quest for a real Christian republic continues; as Young America becomes the individual, George Stephenson, all three voices rebel against the masculinist, racist manifestation of United States nationalism.

In the end, this rebelliousness, which releases the spirit of the age, is inseparable from cross-racial romance. It is not until Zoë reaches her home island, St. Croix, that her prospects for romance develop. Her suitor, Ben Ezra, is a Hungarian Jewish scholar who fell in love with Zoë while he was her German teacher in Denmark. He follows her across the Atlantic and throughout the Americas to declare his love for her. We know that Ezra is a highly evolved man because he is in love with Zoë, and he travels to "the isle of the Holy Cross" to find his beloved (2:297). By the time he finds her, though, she has decided to ascend to a purely spiritual existence, which will allow her soul to expand beyond material limits and effect changes that her embodied form cannot achieve on earth. Assumedly, this is because she has perfected her soul already, before the rest of the world can catch up to her. She leaves her treatise, though, as a prophetic guidebook that Hilda can disperse to help usher in the millennium. As previously mentioned, one of Channing's speeches on the afterlife inspires Zoë's feeling that "her hour of change was approaching" (2:302). By the time Ezra reaches her, she exalts in her proximity to God and is about to leave the earth. (Livermore never calls this fading away "death.") In a bizarre turn of events, he converts to Christianity and relinquishes his "imaginary curse" as the Wandering Jew (2:297). During a "pageant" of affection, Ezra mysteriously appears among Zoë's friends and family, next to her bed: "Ben Ezra stood before her. He laid his hand upon her shoulder, as if he would stay the parting spirit in its flight. 'Nay, my friend!' she said, 'seek not to recall me to the earth, but rather ascend yourself to the glorified spheres, where we will exchange with each other the sign of the soul, which will unite us forever and ever.' She ceased to breathe, and when they looked upon her again, her face was, as it were, the face of an angel. When Hilda arose from her supporting position by Zoë's side, she looked around for Ben Ezra. He had vanished" (2:304). Their union takes place beyond the earthly sphere, and it is truly eternal.

While the politics of conversion in this story verge on anti-Semitism, or at least Jews-for-Jesus fundamentalism, it is notable that Ezra is not a gothic villain as in *The Monk* (1796) or *Melmoth the Wanderer* (1820). He is, perhaps, the most noble of the male characters in the novel and certainly the most soulful. His values and virtues are sufficiently Christian, according to the narrator, and the only step he needs to take toward perfection is to willingly disapparate to a Christian heaven with Zoë. He flashes forth from actual reality into optimal futurity. He embraces evangelical perfectionism in its embodied form, his beloved Zoë, but her transformative power shuttles them both into the heavenly sphere with lightning speed. Knowing that reformers in the 1850s valued truth and authenticity (hence the numerous prologues to slave narratives that validated and endorsed their claims), it is easy to see how this novel was way ahead of its time. The reintroduction of Ben Ezra at the end of the novel is even more strange because Livermore was apparently the friend of a

Cincinnati rabbi, and she also vanished from the earthly sphere, or at least from print culture, when her husband left Cincinnati. One of the last published records to mention Elizabeth Livermore is the Cincinnati city register, which lists her address as the same as the rabbi's. For some reason, after her husband left the city, Livermore remained in the rabbi's home. Given the overlaps between reality and fiction, between Livermore and Lisbet Leibenhoff or the character in the novel who starts a magazine called the *Independent Highway*, one wonders about this relationship between the visionary woman writer and the Jewish man.

Regardless of what happened to Livermore, she concluded her novel on a hopeful note. Hilda and her future husband, the reformed George Stephenson or "Young America," survive to carry out the work of embodied republicanism in the United States. Zoë, who is too pure and spiritual to continue her existence on earth, sends Hilda forth to "upturn every root of oppression" in the United States, work on behalf of Zoë's "people" in "the land of their forced adoption, and make them equal partakers, with us, of each and all of its blessings" (2:304). The potential of a multicultural embodied republicanism seems to fade away, like Zoë, since both she and the Wandering Jew do not return to the United States but rather inspire the activity of the white characters. But this does not negate Livermore's brief moment of literary triumph. Just as a contrast between Ben Ezra and Melmoth or Lewis's monk, Ambrosio, suggests that Livermore has revised the figure of the Wandering Jew in a more tolerant and humanistic light, her rewriting of the "tragic mulatta" story into the "quadroon's triumph" is a truly fascinating and singular literary move.

From Triumph to Revenge

Although Zoë dies at the end of the novel, Livermore's optimism about amalgamation and the future of racial coexistence persists because Hilda has set forth in the world to engender the radical changes that would accommodate souls like Zoë's. Zoë passes to another realm, but her spirit rises and becomes the spirit of a new age to come. Livermore's views on amalgamation and the feminine contours of the soul are even more remarkable because they contrast so dramatically with those of most of her contemporaries. Harriet Beecher Stowe, for instance, did not flirt with the idea of romance, rebellion, or amalgamation when she wrote *Uncle Tom's Cabin*. She demanded no public influence for women (although her novel did command much public attention). Essentially, *Uncle Tom's Cabin* does not meet the main criteria for rebellious romance because Stowe did not create a world wherein, to use Fuller's poetic line, "the perfect two embrace, / Male and female, black and white" (Murray 289). Stowe did not envision African Americans as neighbors or members of the body politic, nor was she interested in championing the black soul or the African's contributions to an amalgamated society. Rather, Stowe would have been satisfied to end slavery and send free blacks "back" to Africa. Of course, the process must be gradual: "To fill up Liberia with an ignorant, inexperienced, half-barbarized race, just escaped from the chains of slavery," explained the narrator of *Uncle Tom's Cabin*, "would be only to prolong, for ages, the period of struggle and conflict which attends the inception of new enterprises" (386).

My point here is not to lambaste Stowe, nor to dismiss the important work Jane Tompkins and others undertook to restore her to her proper place in the American literary canon. Rather, it is to emphasize the plurality of ideas about race relations and geographic amalgamation that circulated in the 1850s and to draw attention the counterfactual imaginings displayed by Charles Emerson, Avellaneda, Jacobs, and Livermore. Stowe may be the most acclaimed abolitionist novelist, yet she was no radical; her vision of a Christian republic in the postslavery United States could only accommodate blacks temporarily. She wanted to "let the church of the north receive these poor sufferers in the spirit of Christ" only until "they have attained to somewhat of a moral and intellectual maturity" (386). Stowe's implication that blacks lack "moral and intellectual maturity" contrasts with Livermore's insistence upon including the perspectives of blacks and women in national politics. Livermore's belief in amalgamation and the embodied nature of a Christian republicanism that respected black contributions distinguishes her from Stowe, who was rather eager to "assist them in their passage to those shores, where they may put in practice the lessons they have learned in America" (386). Instead, Livermore's quadroon heroine travels in the opposite direction, instructing America with lessons brought from the Caribbean.

While Livermore's Africans (particularly those of mixed racial heritage) are indispensable to creating a Christian republic, her contemporaries were less enthusiastic about the African presence in the United States. As an emigrationist, Stowe endorsed the "repatriation" of African Americans to Liberia after a short period during which they could "receive them to the educating advantages of Christian Republican society" (386). Only then would they be free to "put in practice the lessons they have learned in America" (386). This implies that "Christian

Republican society" is an exclusively Anglo-American construct. Some of her imitators shared the belief that the United States should be an exclusive, Anglo-American space; Elizabeth Roe celebrated the day when the United States would "let the oppressed go free to your fatherland, where you may have all the social, civil, political, and religious privileges that we enjoy in our own Christian Republic" (269). Imagining God's perspective on emigration and the necessary separation of the races, Sarah Josepha Hale described a boat in transit to Liberia "laden with emigrants returning, Christianized and civilized, to the land which, two centuries before, their fathers had left degraded and idolatrous savages" (preface). Invoking the language of Bible politics to support the Liberia plan, Hale even assumed Almighty approval by claiming: "Would he not have thought that . . . in thus providing a home for 'the stranger within her gates' our beloved Union was nobly justifying herself" (preface).

Among Stowe and her imitators, the high destiny of the Anglo-Saxon race in the Americas, in addition to introducing "civilization" to a New World and to Africans within it, was to create a racially exclusive "Christian Republic" by sending freed slaves to Africa. A specifically Anglo-American ethnic group excluded "unassimilable" African Americans from the imagined homogeneity of American identity.[8] While Stowe and her counterparts use terms like "maturity" and "strangers" to explain their views on progress and civilization (particularly the idea that African Americans are less suited to republican government because of their close ancestral relation to "savage" cultures), Livermore refuted such hierarchical language and referred to Anglo-American culture as a "half-barbarous civilization" (2:305).

The culture of domesticity and sympathy that Stowe and her imitators upheld eschewed radical abolitionist beliefs about gender, race, and religion, seeking to preserve the social order—replete with its race and gender hierarchies—through a "politics of respectability."[9] Thus while Stowe would have emigrated Africans "put into practice the lessons they have learned in America," Livermore, like Jacobs, found it necessary to create a pedagogy of citizenship directed toward Anglo-American men. Her version of Christian republican society engages with radical abolitionist dialogue to illustrate a more gender-specific evocation of the radical abolitionist language of Bible politics, higher law, and a Christian republic. A corporeal Christianity, one that accounted for women as sexual beings, both offered a radical contrast to what Gillian Brown calls Stowe's "spiritual, bodiless existence" and recognized the amalgamation that created American society (64).

Contrasting *Zoë* with another popular representation of the quadroon's place in the Atlantic world emphasizes the radical nature of Livermore's ideals. The magazine author and editor Maturin Murray Ballou was also a member of a prominent Unitarian family, the son of "Hosea Ballou (April 30, 1771–June 7, 1852)," who, according to the Universalist Unitarian Association, "was the most influential of the preachers in the second generation of the Universalist movement. His book, *A Treatise on Atonement*, radically altered the thinking of his colleagues in the ministry and their congregations" (Cassara). Soon after Hosea's death, his apparently rebellious-preacher's-kid son, Maturin, published "lurid adventure novels" and a series of travel narratives, the best-known of which described Cuba (Cassara). His adventure story "The Sea Witch; or, The African Quadroon" has, like Livermore's novel, a transatlantic and cross-racial theme, but his quadroon antagonist is nothing like the ethereal, angelic Zoë. In fact, Ballou's "quadroon" is as vindictive as O'Bryan's Lugarto, discussed in the previous chapter. Somewhat surprisingly, Echo Library republished an edition of "The Sea Witch" as juvenile fiction in 2000.

Ballou's story revolves around the reformation of Captain Ratlin, an Englishman engaged in the slave trade. On a trip to the coast of Africa, he assists the victims of a shipwreck and coincidentally and fortuitously rescues his childhood sweetheart, who was on a return voyage from her father's colonial post in India. Like Hilda, who reforms "Young America" and impresses a pedagogy of citizenship upon him, the virtuous and pure Englishwoman Helen Huntington convinces her beloved to give up the slave trade in the interest of becoming a respectable husband.

While Ballou claims to take no moral stand on the issue of slavery, claiming in his preface that "'the peculiar institution' which is herein introduced, is brought forward simply as an auxiliary, not as a feature of the story," he participates in a racist discourse of civilization to justify slavery by invoking the paternalistic image of the slave trader. Ballou romanticizes Captain Ratlin's treatment of his "cargo" on the transatlantic voyage: "declaring that he was a father to all the people he took away in his ship, and how kind he was to them; that he always knocked off their shackles at once and made friends of them by real kindness" (36). Mooring his ship off the coast of Sierra Leone, he awaits the delivery of his human cargo while staying in the home of Don Leonardo, a Spanish slave trader who runs a factory there. Ratlin's return voyage is delayed because Don Leonardo must "send his runners inland to the chiefs of the various coast tribes to forward the prisoners of war to his barracoons" (87). Meanwhile, Ratlin renews and intensifies his relationship with Miss Huntington.

The themes of romance and rebellion take on an entirely different cast in Ballou's work. Leonardo's quadroon daughter, Maud, instigates most of the action in the story because she is in love with Ratlin and chooses to destroy him rather than see him choose Helen. Supposedly infused with the passion and fire of her Spanish father, Maud's love almost immediately turns diabolical and fiendish. She then assumes "typical" mixed-race characteristics because "jealousy is an apt teacher, and the spirit of Maud Leonardo was now thoroughly aroused; she sighed for revenge and puzzled her brain how she might gain the longed for end" (88). The "end" Maud desires is the end of Ratlin, including his business enterprises, when he proves incapable of considering a quadroon an appropriate companion or wife. Her jealousy and vindictiveness, much like that of Lugarto, fuel her vendetta against the white race in general, so she capitalizes on her father's vulnerable position in relation to the surrounding local tribes.

Consorting with local chiefs, Maud exacts her revenge by inciting a rebellion among the enslaved captives with enforcements from the neighboring tribes, whom she lets into the slave factory so they can attack and steal Don Leonardo's gold. Maud's vengeful orchestration of the rebellion, which targets her father as much as her former beloved, evokes the American construction of revolution as parricide, but Maud perpetrates her wrath without any delusions of natural rights or divine justice: "Perhaps the fact that some portion of the blood of that despised race ran in her own veins, led her to conceive a plan for revenge which should embrace not only the part who was the grave object of her hate, but even every person of white blood in her father's household, not even excepting her father! No one, save a North American Indian, can hold and nourish a spirit of revenge like a Quadroon. It seems to be an innate trait of their nature, and ever ready to burst forth in a blaze at any moment" (40).

Stepping back to analyze the way Ballou represents Maud, "the African quadroon," it is important to note that Ballou uses practically every stereotype of the dangers of the African uncultivated by the influence and control of a superior race. As Maggie Sale points out, "racialist discourses constructed Africans and their descendents in opposition to this masculine Anglo-Saxon model, figuring them as naturally brutal, savage, even cannibalistic" (41). Ballou's extreme language of jungle savagery depicts Africa as a terrible, amoral, diabolical place. When Maud conspires to murder her father's household, the author suggests that her plot will fail because Don Leonardo "knew full well the treacherous character of the negroes" and armed his house heavily lest "they would have it in their power to revenge themselves for all their past wrongs at [his] hands, fancied or real" (40). Leonardo has no affection for his daughter, and the qualities she has inherited from her violent, selfish, and ruthless father and her savage mother appear distinctly. Her selfishness and eagerness to fight anyone who gets in her way comes from her greedy father, and her vicious bloodlust comes from her mulatto mother. She is barely the product of amalgamation; she is more like a terrible monster with the violent need to conquer grafted from the Spaniard and the savage treachery grafted from the African. Her "negro" blood subsumes her "Spanish" blood, or floats over it like oil on water, and her rage spills over as she targets her own father and her own home.

In fact, the only way that Ballou can imagine the real amalgamation of black and white bodies is through cannibalism. When Ratlin escapes a Sierra Leone jail later in the story (where he ends up due to another of Maud's treacherous plots), he must trek through the jungle to get back to Don Leonardo's compound so he can be with Helen. Like Maud, his African guide has a "most strange and inhuman expression to his countenance" that foreshadows his complicity in a plan among the shore tribes to dispose of Ratlin. The captain learns that "the cannibals intended to lead him, apparently in good faith, to the neighborhood of their village, where he was to be seized, sacrificed to some deity of these poor ignorant creatures' manufacture, and afterwards *be eaten* in council with great ceremony" (69, original emphasis). In alarming contrast to Livermore's idea of amalgamation, where black and white come together in Zoë's body to produce a unified Anglo-African subject, Ballou can only incorporate the white hero within the body of the black savage through cannibalism.

Maud proves so expressly horrible a creature that her jealousy renders her "completely unsexed," as one who "could herself scarcely contain her own anger and passion so far as not to spring, tiger-like, upon the object of her hatred" (40). Ballou emphasizes the sanguine horror of the battle as the local tribesmen prepare to attack the Europeans in a heathen ritual, adding, "they had sacrificed an infant to their deity, to propitiate him and insure success" (80). Like Frances Hammond Pratt's novel about the Haitian Revolution, *La Belle Zoa* (1864), this novella goes to extremes to emphasize black bloodlust, including the iconic image of the slaughtered infant (though not impaled, this baby still dies a death horrific enough to rival Cotton Mather's depiction of Indians or

Thomas Gray's *Nat Turner*). Not only are African women complicit in these vicious attacks, they apparently do not protect their own offspring. Combined with repeated references to cannibalism, the "fiendish expression of the Quadroon's countenance" (48) and the way Mrs. Huntington sees Maud's "bosom heave quickly, and her eye flash with a wild and startling fire that made her tremble" (37) suggests that social contact between black and white is ultimately disastrous. Maud, after all, is the product of African and European bloodlines and proves the most ominous character in the entire novella. Her idea of romance and rebellion exemplifies the dangers of amalgamation—because her unnatural and hideous racial admixture has produced a fiend—and also suggests that cross-racial romance, her love for a white man, verges on cannibalism.

But Ballou does seem to share with Livermore, to a certain extent, a belief in women's chastening and purifying effect on men, as long as the women in question are white. Ballou's English lady, Helen Huntington, also exacts a pledge from slave trader Will Ratlin that he will quit the trade, although her concern is that his "calling, which though it affords fortune and command, can never permit [him] self-respect" (49). Helen simply wants her future husband to participate in legitimate commerce so he can ascend to her elevated social and economic status. Ballou claims that slaves in Don Leonardo's barracoons "were quite indifferent themselves as to their fate, and were very happy, with good food to eat, and plenty of it" (36). Contrasting with Maud's diabolical die, of course, is Helen Huntington's purity and goodness. She clearly does not belong among the likes of Maud Leonardo, for her mother "preferred to make her daughter a true and noble-hearted woman, possessed of intrinsic excellence, . . . sound principles and an excellent education" (26). Helen is so pure and asexual that her mother refuses to "teach her that the chief end and aim of life were to learn how to captivate a husband, . . . to make her marketable for matrimonial sale" (50). While Helen does marry Ratlin and retire to his English countryside estate in the happy ending, her selection of a husband yields from her passivity and purity. The Anglo-Saxon Ratlin is an appropriately noble and aristocratic suitor who recognizes her goodness and wins her hand. Unlike Maud, who repeatedly tramps through the jungle in pursuit of Ratlin, Helen remains safely perched atop her pedestal. Her existence on the slave coast of Africa emphasizes her feminine virtue, as defined by Ruth Bloch: "private benevolence, personal manners, and female sexual propriety" characterize her entire being and contrast her dramatically with Maud (47).

The appearance of both *Zoë* and "The Sea Witch" as well as Herman Melville's *Benito Cereno* in 1855 indexes American anxiety about the intimacy and proximity that blacks share with white masters and employers in the North and South. Clearly, Maud's violence suggests that there is no safe means by which black and white can coexist. Projecting the scene of conflict from the United States to Africa or South America does not override the fact that an American captain witnesses the action and relays it to an American audience within the pages of popular monthly literary magazines. Ballou's 1855 magazine fiction effectively settles the question of peaceful coexistence between the races in terms that oppose Livermore's vision. Aptly projected through the ubiquitous image of slave rebellion and black violence, human capacity for evil, and white American anxiety over emergent black power, the anxieties of cross-racial intimacy—of the potential for romance and rebellion to transform the known world—resonate through texts like "The Sea Witch" and *Zoë*.

Livermore's forays into racial representation sometimes engaged in the abolitionist language of romantic racialism; she idealized Zoë much like other abolitionists idealized Toussaint. She also attempted, however, to challenge romantic racialism by identifying a fundamental, radical equality of souls among all races. Negotiating the boundary, or connection, between these radically equal souls and the bodies that clothed them pushed both authors to consider what differently marked bodies had come to represent in U.S. history and in their own contemporary culture. Livermore remarked very little about the physical vulnerability of white women to the "ani-MALs," yet her defense of black women like Margaret Garner allowed her to demand bodily integrity for all women. Like Avellaneda, however, Livermore could not articulate her own identity without engaging with an alter ego who was black, mulatto, or quadroon. As each seeks to expand her soul and imagine the radical reform of society to better meet her ideals of freedom, she must engage with an idealized racial "other" whose very presence exemplifies the embodied nature of the quest for a sacred self. In the imagined space of narrative, each author can negotiate her own freedom from socially imposed definitions of self by identifying with someone of another race. Much like Avellaneda, who leaves the future in Carlota's hands, Livermore sends Hilda, a white woman, out to transform the world.

Still, I want to push the boundaries of interpretation regarding novels and drama that have been traditionally read as abolitionist literature, positing that some rebelliously romantic texts are both antiracist and antisexist rather than just antislavery. I base the distinction between antiracist and antislavery on the fact that Avellaneda and Livermore analyze the way race and gender shape their characters' destinies and interrogate accepted notions of "natural" inferiority rather than just calling for the abolition of the institution of slavery. Their stories of cross-racial and transnational desire bear little semblance to the likes of Stowe's classic, *Uncle Tom's Cabin*, because they take greater interest in the possibilities for racial coexistence and gender equity in a postcolonial Caribbean or Atlantic world than in eradicating slavery and its subjects from the New World. Livermore's *Zoë* and *Independent Highway*, like Avellaneda's *Sab*, also locate the transformative powers of romance and rebellion in the Caribbean. Although I make no claims about familiarity or influence, a republican ideal of natural rights and human freedom and equality based on romantic notions of the "perfect soul" pervade both it and *Sab*. The signal difference is that Livermore seems to have believed that amalgamation was a form of salvation for civilization, whereas Ballou or proslavery authors saw amalgamation as the destruction of society. Harriet Jacobs, on the other hand, perpetuates an idea that is present in Livermore's romance—that white Americans, white men in particular, have much to learn from women of African descent. Julia Collins, the subject of the next chapter, continues the struggle to insert black women into the language and practice of Christian republicanism and to claim a radical equality that exceeds Avellaneda or Livermore's erasure of race.

5   Reconstruction Optimism in Julia Collins's *The Curse of Caste*

> The institution of slavery is itself accursed, and will yet prove the fatal Nemesis of the South, for do not think that a just God will allow any people so deeply wronged to go unavenged.
>
> —Julia Collins

The Curse of Caste; or the Slave Bride seems like an ominous title, even for a story that begins with a tragic cross-racial affair that took place in the antebellum period and concludes with a happy postwar family reunion. This novel's author, Julia C. Collins, began contributing essays and a serialized novel to the African Methodist Episcopal Church newspaper, the *Christian Recorder,* after the Civil War.[1] Collins lived in Willamsport, Pennsylvania, and sometimes sent correspondence to the *Recorder* from Oswego, New York. She also worked as a schoolteacher, was married, and died of tuberculosis in the autumn of 1865. The serialized novel that she died without finishing, *The Curse of Caste*, features a love affair and forbidden marriage between a Louisiana planter's son, Richard Tracy, and another planter's illegitimate daughter, Lina Hartley, who becomes the slave bride. The novel offers a second plot that takes place eighteen years later. The daughter of the ill-fated Louisiana lovers, Claire Neville, returns to the South to educate the Tracy family. As a governess, one would expect her to teach the children, but her most needful pupil is her own grandfather, Colonel Tracy. No one, even Richard, knows that Claire is a Tracy because Lina died in childbirth while Richard was recuperating from a gunshot wound inflicted by his own father.

A father who would be so brutal as to attempt to murder his only son seems like an abolitionist stereotype of a cruel southern slaveholder—a Simon Legree with sadistic traits. The family mystery that unfolds in the novel has gothic elements and at least two references to revenge; its "curse" overshadows the optimistic theme of reconciliation. But this Louisiana brute is not a Creole; he is a Yankee by birth.[2] That Collins chose Louisiana as the setting for most of the novel seems to signify the desire for a reunion between North and South, but the story's prehistory also reveals that the Tracy family migrated from New England and became absorbed into the seductive New Orleans lifestyle. When their blue blood mixes with Creole stock, the family's New England patriarch brings a curse upon himself—he takes on the guilt and greed of a slaveholding society with roots in the decadent Haitian refugee culture of New Orleans.

Collins's insight into the culture clash between North and South suggests that anxieties about expansion are easily allayed by power and privilege. Nonetheless, Thomas Jefferson's biographer Dumas Malone surmised that many northerners criticized the Louisiana Purchase because its inhabitants were labeled a childlike mass of "Creole ignorance" who were "incapable of self government" and, in many cases, had fled Haiti to take refuge in Louisiana (349–50). Implicit in these condemnations of the Creole population were popular ideas about the attitude toward cross-racial romances in that culture. By 1841, Joseph Ingraham had written one of the first novels to attack the system of plaçage in New Orleans. Entitled *The Quadroone; or, St. Michaels Day*, the novel documents the moral depravity of a society that sanctions illegitimate relationships between wealthy white men and beautiful, exotic quadroon women.

The regional identity of the Northeast, abolitionist or not, was based in a sense of superiority to the aristocratic, decadent, Old World culture of the South, especially the French-influenced Creole culture. But no person of privilege is immune to the contagion of racism and greed that New Orleans represents in the novel. Even the heroic, antiracist Richard Tracy falls prey to Creole culture. While at a party in New Orleans, he meets George Manville, "a gay, good-looking fellow, good-natured and perfectly well acquainted with the city and the circle in which Richard moved" (22). This friendship, and Manville's elite and lascivious nature, bring the curse down on Richard. Although New Orleans became the nation's largest port in the 1840s, offering great opportunities for wealth, abolitionists were fond of propaganda that sensationalized the issue of "white slavery" in Louisiana. A woman like Lina, white-looking and cultivated, could easily be cast into sexual slavery. Therefore, the elite set and social scene that the virtuous Richard encounters in New Orleans has a dark underbelly, and it eventually destroys his pure love for Lina and even infiltrates idyllic New England to bring a tragic end to their marriage. Manville, the new friend Richard meets in New Orleans shortly after he meets Lina, is a "villain" (22). Although he is rich and handsome, "the beautiful casket [was] enshrined in a heart black as the shadows of Hades" (22). The gothic clues here convey another nightmare of the Haitian Revolution—not the fear of black violence, but the specter of Creole excess.

As a holdover of similar sexual practices in prerevolutionary Haiti, Manville's villainous intentions can, and do, make Lina's life Hell. He wants Lina, too, but not to marry honorably. In the New Orleans system of plaçage, it would be socially acceptable for him to keep Lina as his slave and mistress. Like Lydia Maria Child's story "The Quadroons" and Dion Boucicault's play *The Octoroon*—the story of a young man who falls in love with a woman whose "blood" is one-eighth "black"—*The Curse of Caste* dramatizes the dangers faced by beautiful white-looking women in New Orleans. Unlike Boucicault's white male hero, however, the heroic figure in Collins's novel is ultimately Claire. She is the only one who can recuperate her mother Lina's reputation and memory, just as she is the only one who can reconcile her father, Richard, as heir to the Tracy family estate.

It is important to remember at this juncture that *The Curse of Caste* is not an antislavery novel. Emancipation is a done deal by 1865, when the novel appeared. What Collins really attacks is the legacy of racism that persists among whites, North and South. The awful history of cross-racial sexual violence during slavery needs to be rewritten in order to eradicate racism from the nation. The novel's vengeful, gothic elements haunt Colonel Tracy's imagination, and they are connected to the guilt and greed of a Creole culture that was punished with, but did not learn its lesson from, the Haitian Revolution.

Although Richard and Lina's cross-racial romance is doomed, it still plants the seed—literally, Claire—for an optimal future in which Anglo-American and Creole culture are chastened and reformed. Amalgamation, both of families and of geographies, is successful only when women and people of African descent are recognized as equals. While Collins died before she finished the novel, it points toward the Colonel's recognition of amalgamation and black female virtue as important characteristics of his family. As a narrative of nation, one could say that the family reunion that eventually takes place in *The Curse of Caste* reveals Reconstruction optimism, or the belief that the nation can emerge from its most horrific rebellion to achieve a universal ideal of equality among men and women, or black, white, and Indian. At the same time, however, it is a cautionary tale about the consequences of repeating the wrongs of the past.

North/South Intercourse

No Civil War takes place in *The Curse of Caste*, and the commerce between North and South is complicated only when abolitionist ideas of liberty invade New Orleans. Although Richard attempts to rebel against his father on those terms, the effort essentially fails. When he completes his education in the North, and during his return journey by riverboat to New Orleans, Richard falls in love with and pledges to marry a beautiful young woman, also traveling "home" to the South from a northern boarding school. Lina, the young woman, represents the untold family history of the plantation South. She will soon learn that her mother was a slave and that her deceased father, Master Hartley, has neglected to manumit her.

The incompletion of Lina's manumission, then, mirrors the unfinished business of liberation and equality that persists after the Revolution and an unmentioned Civil War. Before she learns of her unfree status, Lina speaks intuitively of her tenuous social standing and her vulnerability to her siblings. She, like the black nurse Juno who will eventually raise her orphan daughter, has a preternatural ability to detect evil. Sensing that her brother and sister plot to disinherit her, she tells Richard, "A presentiment of evil hovers over me" (31).

This memory or impression of evil also flashes back to a jaded Creole past. The novel frequently describes Creole characters as evil, fiendish, or otherwise dastardly. Several references to French items—a clock, a hair-do, and even the nephew of a French count—hint that the Hartleys and Manville could be of French heritage. Hartley also educates his daughters in a Catholic convent in Canada. Although Lina is described as a beauty whose "dark, rich-looking complexion" features "that dark brownish skin which we observe in the Spaniard and half-breed Indians" (18–19), her sister Mary looks nothing like her. Her brother, Ralph, gazes at her "with an expression that is almost fiendish," and this deportment supports her suspicion that she "may be penniless or even worse" (31). Richard responds gallantly to this threat, like a republican gentleman: "Lina, whatever be your fate or fortune, I will never desert you, so help me God! I will make you my own dear wife; my arm shall protect you and all the love of my warm, true heart shall be yours" (20).

Of course, Richard's promise (like the promises of the American Revolution) falls apart when it comes to race and gender difference. Echoing Thomas Jefferson, Richard later prophesies "a just God will [not] allow any people so deeply wronged to go unavenged" (40). Richard, however, will not become the purveyor of this divine justice, nor will he be able to protect Lina's rights. When he first makes the pledge on the riverboat, romantic images of wrathful nature signal that unabashed Creole villains are about to take their next African American victim. "Piles of black clouds," "a loud peel of thunder," and a "vivid flash of lightning" interrupt Lina and Richard's conversation, casting a gothic shade of impending doom over the romance (20). Although Lina claims that she trusts Richard to protect her, she seems much more savvy about the danger that faces them as cross-racial lovers. Lina has very little faith in Richard and reacts in horror, a few chapters later, when the Colonel attempts to "rescue" her from a slave auction.

These gothic elements provide a sense of skepticism about the limits of Anglo-masculine protection and benevolence. Although he confides in his mother, Richard does not announce his engagement to his father when he first arrives home, but rather seeks to refamiliarize himself with the Colonel, who is at once proud of his son's educated demeanor and "horrified and dismayed to hear Richard give expression to many anti-slavery principles, which he had imbibed while at the north" (21). Remembering that he, too, was once a "northerner," Colonel Tracy is confident in "the influence of Southern principles and society, to affect the desired change" (21). But he is not thinking of the enticements of New Orleans. The southern life, according to its most loyal defender and proselyte Colonel Tracy, thrives on gentility, prosperity, and a natural order wherein the good and noble are rewarded by station and honor. But Juno later describes the Colonel rather differently. She "knew much about the character and disposition of Colonel Frank Tracy" and had seen evidence of "his overweening family pride and love of wealth, and position" (29). The only black woman in the novel—Juno—sees Colonel Tracy in a different light, in which "southern principles and society" involve wealth, elitism, and privilege.

Meanwhile, when Richard first tells his mother of his beloved Lina Hartley, it remains unclear whether either of them recognizes Lina's racial heritage. Mrs. Tracy worries, nonetheless, about the Colonel's reaction to the match; her immediate concern is, "you know your father's prejudice against persons marrying with those beneath them in rank and fortune, no matter what their qualities may be" (22). Collins does not make it clear whether Richard understands that Lina is the daughter of a slave woman and must, therefore, follow in the condition of her mother. The literary portrait that she paints of Lina would intimate to her African American readership that Lina is not white; she has the "dark flashing eyes and a profusion of curling black hair" that any darkly beautiful heroine might display (18–19). Just as Richard and his mother might assume that Hartley's Creole "blood" has darkened Lina's skin, they might also think that his dissolute Creole ethics will offend Colonel Tracy. The Colonel thinks he can enjoy all of the privileges of slavery but condemn its attendant evils. Perhaps, as a New Englander, he thinks his purchase on morality is superior to that of Creoles. In fact, Hartley is "formerly a man of considerable wealth, but being of a wild, reckless disposition, has, in a few years, squandered his fortune, and degenerated into a confirmed drunkard and gambler" (23). His plantation is to be auctioned, and Lina is a slave who must be sold as well.

Hartley's drinking and gambling mark him as the type of man who might be sexually dissolute as well. Remand to slavery confirms Lina's racial identity, leaving no room for doubt that Richard understands that he is about to marry a black woman. Lina "believed herself [Hartley's] lawful child" but learns otherwise when the dissolution of her father's estate permits Colonel Tracy to purchase her (23). While the "fancy girl auction" is a recurrent theme in other novels about octoroons and quadroons, Colonel Tracy intervenes to spare Lina this degrading experience. As he reports his new acquisitions to his wife and son, he says, "Her distress was really affecting, and, out of pity for the young thing, I bought her with the lot" (23). He then goes on to describe his buyer's remorse and dissatisfaction with her (and perhaps a subtle chastisement of his Yankee-educated son), for "slaves educated at the North, are not just the thing to be introduced into a southern household. So, I guess I will sell this bit of humanity at the first offer" (23). Having expressed his pity for and even recognition of "this bit of humanity," Tracy goes on to explain his main reason for selling her: "Why, she had the audacity to faint, when, by accident, she learned the name of her future master was Col. Tracy" (23). Ironically, he will learn twenty years later that "slaves educated at the North" such as his granddaughter Claire are the only thing that can save a southern household.

Clearly, the Colonel is in denial about why southern gentlemen routinely purchase beautiful black women. He pays a large sum because he pities Lina, because he perceives her distress as a function of her loss of class status. He attributes her suffering to her northern education and abolitionist propaganda, which has instilled a sense of entitlement that the Colonel finds inappropriate in a slave. He is also quite offended by her fainting spell and apparent lack of gratitude or, at least, confidence in his gentlemanly intentions. He does not know about Lina's relationship with his son and assumes that Lina faints because she expects to become a concubine. The Colonel takes umbrage with Lina's educated and genteel demeanor, but the glimpse he gets of Lina's capacity for virtue is what really disarms him. He is quite offended by her fainting spell—the swoon suggests that she perceives herself as a lady in sexual jeopardy.

The integrity of his image as a southern gentleman, built upon ideals of racial purity and self-control, comes into crisis with even the implication that he would take a slave for a concubine. Faced with the reality of white men's sexual predation upon black women, Tracy's reaction to Lina becomes increasingly absurd. Meanwhile, the reader already questions the social institution of the southern gentleman, which feeds the Colonel's ability to invoke racial myths about Lina, because both Lina's father and grandfather were white men who probably owned her mother and grandmother, respectively. Racism is irrational, and Colonel Tracy's absurd beliefs in the integrity and virtue of the southern gentleman illustrate that irrationality because they conflict with reality—the fact that these men father children with anonymous, and powerless, women who are enslaved.

Colonel Tracy's belief system, which denies and constantly erases white men's hypocritical sexual behavior, substantiates his assumptions about his own superiority and justifies his exclusive purchase on social and political power. A main tenet of the Colonel's belief system, sexual self-restraint, was so important a virtue within the cult of the southern gentleman because, in addition to being a key component of racial purity, it distinguished white men from the racist image they perpetuated of promiscuous blacks. Sexual self-restraint virtually parallels the capacity for self-government in racist discourse; by asserting black promiscuity, the southern gentleman justified his paternalism and denial of rights to his slaves as he alleged their innate inferiority. The spectacle of Master Hartley emphasizes how much the Colonel must deny to uphold his institution, and the contradiction is obvious. As Colonel Tracy faces Lina, he must likewise face the legacy of plaçage and the hypocrisy of the southern slaveholding way.

Lina's very existence calls attention to failed southern gentility because she is the product of an illicit cross-racial sexual relationship.

Rather than face that legacy, however, the Colonel chooses to condemn Lina for attracting the attention of wealthy white men and believing she has the right to be treated like a true woman. Knowing nothing of his son's intentions toward Lina, Colonel Tracy sells her to the diabolical Manville. (One might ask what the Colonel thinks a wealthy, dashing young rake like Manville will do with Lina.) In confidence with his mother, Richard orchestrates Lina's rescue. He takes Lina to New England, a place that touts promises of equality and democratic principles. The romance between Richard and Lina, which becomes "ill-fated" because Colonel Tracy rightly interprets it as an affront to his proslavery stance, emerges first as idyllic. Collins writes: "One beautiful morning, in a quiet New England village, far from their own home, Richard Tracy and the beautiful quadroon, Lina, were united for life" (24).

Colonel Tracy cuts this lifelong union short. When Richard returns home to announce that he has eloped with Lina, Colonel Tracy goes on a tirade. Rather than acknowledge the problem of Hartley's depravity or distinguish it from Richard's sincere belief that Lina is his social equal, Colonel Tracy declares: "Oh! That a son of mine should thus disgrace himself and family, as to marry a negress—a slave—the illegitimate offspring of a spendthrift, a drunkard, and a libertine; a being sunk so low on the scale of humanity as to be unworth the name of man. It's awful! It's abominable!" (39). Because Richard emulates Hartley's assault on racial purity, a key element in the construction of patriarchal power, he disgraces his family and lowers himself to the level of a libertine in his father's eyes. Colonel Tracy cannot, and will not, separate masculine honor and racial purity. One function of masculine honor and the foundation of patriarchy is that the father, because he provides for the family financially and protects its "helpless" members (women and children), is entitled to govern not only the family but the entire nation. Richard's indiscretion and Lina's very existence emphasize the frequency with which white men fail to protect their own children, thus undermining the Colonel's central justifications for patriarchal power.

Colonel Tracy indicts himself, in the reader's eyes, by rehearsing an absurd and reprehensible set of social prejudices; he reacts viciously when Richard and Lina challenge his hypocritical and exclusive definition of slaveholding freedom. While he previously described Lina as a "bit of humanity" regardless of her black blood, she becomes the sexual predator as his rage escalates (23). He accuses Richard: "Fool that you are, you allowed yourself to be thus entrapped by a pretty face; and, no doubt, by this time you have wearied of your toy" (39).

Although the Colonel never mentions her, Lina's black mother presents an even greater problem than her profligate father because the Colonel assumes that sexual excess is an inheritable trait passed on through the black mother. He resorts to stereotypes of black female sexuality to blame Lina for ruining his son. She becomes the scapegoat for all sexual indiscretions that undermine patriarchy because her mother was a slave and, according to the Colonel's beliefs, not only the condition of slavery but also the tendency toward hypersexual behavior is inherited from the mother. The phrenologist Orson Fowler and others emphasized the imperative duty of parents, mothers in particular, to mold their children's moral natures. By this point, the Colonel nearly forgets that Lina's father is a "libertine." He cannot fathom the presence of feminine virtue within the system of slavery. Lina's race poses a greater social threat than her father's ungentlemanly behavior; Colonel Tracy concludes by saying, "our society is getting into a pretty state, when the sons of the best families stoop to marry their father's slaves" (*Curse* 39).

In short, Colonel Tracy is thoroughly immersed in a racist discourse that justifies the sexual exploitation of black women by accusing those women of lascivious, immoral character. His solution for this problem, of course, is his recourse to the law that protects elite gentlemen like him from contact with individuals whose race and class mark them as inferior to him. He demands that Richard seek a divorce, expecting Richard to have lost interest in his sexual toy: "'If you have, it will be well, for as you are under age, your marriage is illegal, and with the assistance of a trusty lawyer, its validity may be annulled. You can visit Europe a year or two, until the memory of this disgraceful affair has died out. I will settle an annuity on your--' he could not add the word *wife*, it would have choked him" (39). The Colonel cannot refer to a slave as a member of his family or social equal; he chokes on the word "wife," so he corrects himself by saying "on the girl, which will be sufficient to support her decently; and that is much better than she deserves, the artful wench, to palm herself off for a lady" (39). Although Lina is an "artful wench" who has only enough sexual agency "to palm herself off for a lady" upon his gullible young son, it is the "northern demagogue," the abolitionist, who truly threatens Colonel Tracy's claims to power and has "encompassed the ruin" of his son (39). He goes on to say, "What is to become of our institution if we take our slaves on an equality with ourselves?" (39). Richard's belief in racial equality shakes the very foundations of his father's white patriarchal world.

Richard, alternately, represents northern republican principles and the heart of a reformer. He begins to spout a revolutionary language of radical equality to challenge his father, who now represents the aristocratic, loyalist South. Richard promises another rebellion, or at least vengeance. Although the Colonel plans to solve the problem of race and inheritance through legal recourse, Richard refuses to divorce Lina. He says, "Those pernicious sentiments, as you are pleased to term them, which I have imbibed at the north only teach me to respect the rights of my *fellow citizens*" (40, emphasis added). Richard calls the institution "accursed" and reminds his father not to "think that a just God will allow any people so deeply wronged to go unavenged" (40). Richard attacks the institution of southern gentlemanhood, invoking God as the ultimate patriarchal power and suggesting that a righteous rebellion is imminent. Richard sacrifices his family ties and patriarchal inheritance in a futile attempt to protect his wife, and perhaps his radical claim that Lina is his "fellow citizen" pushes his father over the edge. The image of citizenship and equality for the freed people that Richard imagines through his relationship with Lina proves irreconcilable with the institution of the southern gentleman as Colonel Tracy knows it. Richard's principles connect the explosive issue of amalgamation with the expansion of citizenship rights for African Americans.[3]

Richard upholds the reformer's most glorified image of the cross-racial relationship—a marriage between black and white wherein complete equality can be negotiated. Given an ultimatum by his father, who threatens to disinherit and disown him, Richard merely says, "I cannot forsake my wife" (41). His insistence that Lina is his social equal, using the word "wife" that his father could not even say, legitimizes amalgamation and reasserts African American claims to the inheritance of citizenship. Unlike her American literary predecessors Child, Stowe, Brown, and Jacobs, Collins imagines a miscegenation story in which the white male tries to do right by his slave bride; Richard Tracy is the only U.S. male figure in a "tragic mulatta" story to marry his enslaved beloved legally by removing her to a place where slavery is not the law of the land. He is the only one to assert, as he does when he refers to blacks as citizens, that she is his equal. Yet he still fails to protect her.

That Richard Tracy has the courage to marry Lina in spite of his father's imminent curse—the dramatic challenge that Richard Tracy poses to his father and to all of southern genteel life—is perhaps the most subversive aspect of his rebellious romance. While he espouses abolitionist views acquired during his education in the North, the reader never witnesses him asking his father to manumit all the slaves; it is only when he learns that his beloved is a black woman that Richard is inspired to *act* on behalf of universal justice. Romance, in this case, inspires his attempt at rebellion. The cult of true white gentlemanhood is permanently altered to include a moral responsibility toward slaves, one that makes southern principles and society inconsistent with the noble and seemingly upstanding civic virtue of the republican citizen. Yet Richard's activism is not enough to resolve the problem of racism, and at this point it is useful to think of the story as a national allegory. The aristocratic South bullies the triumphant North into submission, or the Colonel attacks Richard and renders his abolitionist, revolutionary rhetoric meaningless. This mirrors the situation in the aftermath of the Civil War, when the North slowly began to accommodate southern views. The solution for the problem is not only in Richard's idea of equality. To reform the nation, a black woman's voice must come to the fore.

Virtuous Voters

The Colonel's antebellum rant, tied up in a hypocritical Anglo-supremacist logic and doused in shame for a decadent Creole past, was not actually a thing of the past in 1865—that kind of prejudice survived the Civil War completely intact. The Colonel's attack on Lina's sexual virtue represents the racist, antisuffrage view of amalgamation that also pervaded debates over black citizenship in 1865. Collins's attention to these topics addresses key political issues; by recasting amalgamation and black female virtue, she enters the national debate over black citizenship. Opponents of black citizenship could not separate the concepts of civic and sexual virtue; they argued that black men in particular would use political enfranchisement to pursue white women. The recurrent image of the cross-racial sexual relationship continued to occupy the American political imagination. To connect the issue of sexual virtue to citizenship and voting rights, I turn to some of the articles about suffrage that appeared adjacent to installations of *The Curse of Caste* in the *Christian Recorder*. Notably, almost every issue of the newspaper that prints a chapter of the novel precedes or follows that chapter with an essay about voting and citizenship rights.

Many essays in the *Recorder* focused on asserting black claims to citizenship while addressing the challenges of Reconstruction. To assert black men's entitlement to the inheritance of freedom, for example, the *Recorder* reported on the patriotism of the Fifty-Fourth Massachusetts Regiment. Their valor in battle and their commitment to the Union cause despite the federal government's attempt to swindle them out of wages substantiated the regiment's, and by association all black men's, demand for equal rights ("Fifty Fourth"). The Fifty-Fourth earned their rightful place in America through their patriotism, a central tenet of republican citizenship. They deserved, therefore, to be amalgamated into the national family.

Because black women's sexual virtue was as important an issue as black men's military loyalty in arguments for racial equality, the topic appears frequently throughout the newspaper and certainly in suffrage discourse. Lina represents a model of feminine virtue that Richard recognizes but cannot protect due to Manville's Creole predilections and his father's bullying. Collins's rewriting of feminine virtue—black womanhood—as a counterpart to the masculine virtue displayed by black men conveys an implicit demand for political rights. Women like Lina need full voting rights to protect themselves from further exploitation. As appropriately gendered members of the national family, African Americans could enter into the political arena. Immediately following the first chapter of the novel, a reprint of an article from the *Evening Bulletin* appears.[4] Responding to an "opprobrious" essay in the *Inquirer* authored by an opponent to black suffrage who takes the pen name "American," the reprint in the *Christian Recorder* has been penned by "Another American." Responding to "American's" series of irrational arguments against black suffrage, "Another American," as the editors put it, "handles the author . . . without gloves" to refute racism in a manner that "our readers will all take delight in" ("Negro Suffrage" n.p.). Of course, the issue of political equality is once again inextricable from images of a cross-racial relationship.

Objecting to "American's" claim that a "scheme now on foot for giving social and political equality to the negro" is opprobrious, "Another American" asserts that the movement strives to "grant political equality to individuals irrespective of the race to which they belong, the only qualification necessary, being the enlightenment which would fit them for the exercise of the right of suffrage" (n.p.). For example, Collins's first essay, "Mental Improvement," appeared in the *Recorder* on April 16, 1864. In it, she urged her readers to apply their "well-cultivated" minds to reading and not only to reflect upon "all the most important circumstances connected with the improvement of human society" but also to "combine anew the items of knowledge" that would lead to that improvement (*Curse of Caste* 122). The idea of combining knowledge anew suggests that her primarily African American readership has a distinct intellectual contribution to make to the United States during Reconstruction. As Elizabeth McHenry illustrates, literature and reading groups constituted a form of social activism grounded in divine sanction: "to break down the strong barrier of prejudice, and raise ourselves in equality with those of our fellow beings who differ from us in complexion, but who are, with ourselves, children of the eternal parent" (58). Literacy and religious devotion evidenced African American suitability for citizenship and equality, so the appearance of a novel in the *Christian Recorder* might be construed as its own form of activism (125).

This calls to mind Harriet Jacobs's recollections of her mind beginning to expand in the North and argues for a quick transition from the mentality of slavery to the outlook of a virtuous citizen. Enlightenment is measured by the collective virtue of a community—it is both a function of the "Mental Improvement" that Collins advocates and a function of the way a community's members respect one another's rights. "Another American" also finds inclusive democracy integral to the nation's future, noting that "an opposite course violates the first principle of Democracy, for that principle asserts that the powers of government are derived from the governed" (n.p.).

"Another American's" points are grounded in republican principles and make his opponent seem somewhat mad. His counterarguments mock the way that the antireformer, "American," conflates political rights with the persistent anxiety about intermarriage. In this sense, "American" sounds not unlike James Trecothick Austin or John Fletcher, mentioned in chapter 1. For example, "American" claims that desegregation in railroad cars would eradicate "the instinctive repugnance that counteracts the suggestion of passion, and keeps the races apart in marriage" (n.p.). "American" goes on to assert that "what is now called prejudice is the instinct that made the Anglo-Saxon the only successful colonist, and enabled him to carry religious liberty and civilization around the globe" (n.p.). Unlike the French, the Spaniard, and the Portuguese, who have taken "the negress or the squaw to his home as a wife," the Anglo-Saxon has instinctively kept the font of his racial greatness pure (n.p.).

"Another American's" response to this ridiculous myth of racial purity is priceless. He counters that French, Portugese, and Spanish settlers intermarried with black and Native American women because "they preferred a virtuous black woman to a vicious white one" (n.p.). "Another American" explains that miscegenation takes place because black women are more virtuous than white women (n.p.). Contrary to social myths about black women's lack of virtue, "Another American" upholds black women as the epitome of virtue. He then criticizes "the present concubinage in the South" as a result of the moral failure of white men. Redefining black women's role in relation to white men, for black writers like Collins and "Another American," asserted fundamental equality between black and white, sometimes even elevating black women above white men in their morals and virtue.

"Avenging" the Mother's Race

Even in the aftermath of the Civil War, Julia Collins's novel was haunted, as were the pages of the *Christian Recorder*, with remnants of a racist past. Fulfilling Richard's prediction, Lina's vengeful spirit becomes an invisible presence in the Tracy household as her daughter Claire disproves the southern gentry's prejudices and myths about black female sexuality. Yet the "avenging spirit" that haunts the Colonel does not look like Lina; it is in Claire's face, which looks so much like Richard's (now assumed dead), that he recognizes the full horror of his actions (59). While Claire engenders the Colonel's change of conscience, Lina's spirit also forces the southern gentleman to revisit his class pretensions and racial prejudices because his memories of shooting Richard become "retribution" for the sin of slavery (59). Claire, as living proof that her mother was a true woman because she has inherited her mother's grace rather than her grandfather's shame, proves Colonel Tracy's assumptions about Lina entirely wrong. Claire picks up where her mother left off; she assumes an active textual role in transforming the Colonel's belief system just as Lina solidified Richard's radically egalitarian beliefs.

Claire, like Jacobs, takes on the task of instructing and converting members of the national family who are reluctant to accept radical equality. In this manner, Collins's narrator steps in to create a pedagogy of citizenship for her white male characters to follow. I find Ross Chambers's distinction between *narrator* and *narratee* helpful. While both Lina and Claire are narrators who have a particular story of racial equality to impart upon the Tracy family, various members of that family provisionally take on the role of narratee. The Tracy men are molded and transformed through their encounters with Lina and Claire, although in the final analysis they have ultimate power over both women because of the socially structured dynamics of race and gender. Power does not circulate on a one-way street between black woman and white man, however, as the influence of narrator over narratee attests. While Colonel Tracy has the power to buy Lina from a slave trader and Richard can choose to free her or even marry her, thus elevating her to a legitimate social station, both Lina and Claire have the narrative power to elicit changes in either man's acceptance of dominant ideology, particularly the doctrines of racial inferiority and social purity that the Colonel uses to condemn Lina. Claire succeeds; the southern demagogue Colonel Tracy comes to accept his son's beliefs and his octoroon granddaughter.

Collins has set the stage for the resolution of racial conflict by imagining the intimate and transformative contact between black women and the white men who have political, social, and economic power over them. Despite his position of power, Richard, the eldest son, is incapable of changing his father's mind about slavery, intermarriage, or family authority. He crumbles under the weight of racism. His father guns him down in response to his feeble attempts to defy racist definitions of black womanhood. Richard's daughter, on the other hand, actually engenders a transformation in the patriarch, Colonel Tracy, and her presence renegotiates his authority over the rest of the family. In this dramatic performance between black woman and white man, Collins also situates the reader as spectator and interpreter of events through narrative disclosures that are withheld from the actors in the drama, the narrator and narratee. As the reader occupies what Chambers calls "the third position . . . in a triangulated relationship," one that "coincide[s] fully with neither [narrator] nor with [narratee]," the reader himself or herself enjoys and profits from the scene unfolding and is, in his or her interpretation, contributing to the production of the text (24). As Chambers argues, "the text becomes 'text' only through interpretive reading" (17). The imaginary domain that Collins creates, I would add, only materializes within a textual space when that third position of interpretive pleasure and participation emerges through the act of reading—it is her audience whom she intends to civilize, cultivate, and instruct as they identify with the characters in the story.

Collins has thus demonstrated how reading can lead to "the improvement of human society"; her novel demonstrates an ability to "combine anew the items of knowledge" that will lead to that improvement by creating a narrative space wherein those whose "caste and misfortune" was previously defined in racist Anglo-masculine terms takes on new definitions and the black female voice reigns (122). Collins's depiction of Richard reflects her desire for power and influence that crosses lines of gender and race. It is significant and strategic to devise a pedagogy of citizenship through which the black woman heroine instructs the white man; to imagine and write into existence a prescriptive model of citizenship and civility for empowered, influential whites affords struggling and still disenfranchised black women a measure of power over their oppressors. Richard's vision depends on his daughter Claire—before the Tracy family can learn to accept Richard's views, the truth in his beliefs about his wife must be substantiated through the virtue of his daughter.

Haunted Portraits

All of this requires a remedy for the mistakes of the past, one that can uproot the toxic imagery of race and caste that cursed the American Revolution and became a gothic nightmare in many renderings of the Haitian Revolution. The narrator of *The Curse of Caste* begins to hint, by chapter 2, that Claire has connections to the "accursed" race (40). In the conventional lexicon of mid-nineteenth-century America, the "accursed" race would be African Americans, yet in Collins's lexicon, slavery is an "accursed institution" that precipitates the Tracy family's "curse of caste"—the Colonel's racism—which incites him to curse his own son and banish him from the family. The very title of the novel inverts the dominant logic of race, much as the characterization of women inverts portraits of virtue.

Returning to the point that the Tracy family's New Orleans lifestyle is tainted by the decadent practices of prerevolutionary Creole Haiti, I want to consider Claire's "double," her aunt Isabelle. Born on the same day, Isabelle is Claire's double with the exception that the former has no black female ancestry and is the product, apparently, of "pure" bloodlines. At the same time, Isabelle has the penetrating eyes and bewitching, almost malevolent demeanor of a gothic villainess. Isabelle is as beautiful as Claire but selfish, vain, and cold, and her womanly disgraces accentuate Claire's goodness—the indispensable quality of virtue Claire acquires from her contact with the black community via Juno. Although Isabelle's mother, Mrs. Tracy, is as virtuous as Claire's mother, and although Isabelle very likely had black nurses as well, her conditioning as a privileged planter's daughter—her environment and upbringing—result in her diabolical qualities.

Isabelle and Claire are almost visually identical to one another; the distinction emerges in Claire's moral nature. Child-rearing experts in the mid-nineteenth century argued that the protean nature of heredity includes both biological and environmental traits, so the fact that Claire enjoys Lina's influence in utero, then grows up with a black surrogate mother, Juno, suggests that black womanhood has a salutary effect on a child's character. Yet Isabelle, who is "a child of wealth and position,"

lacks Claire's virtue. Unfortunately, chapter 3, in which Collins introduces Isabelle, is lost, but the beginning of the fourth chapter suggests
that she has the same enchanting and mesmerizing influence on suitors
as any gothic villainess. Count Sayford, Isabelle's love interest, finds her
"the most fascinating woman he ever met," yet Collins suggests that
vain, gorgeous, spoiled southern belles are not as beautiful on the inside
as out: "thus far," she writes, "the Count had failed in reading her true
character" (10–11). Claire perceives Isabelle's character more readily;
she "shuddered as she encountered the piercing glance which seemed
to read her very soul" (12). Claire immediately sees through Isabelle's
veneer of beauty. Claire's presence, meanwhile, serves as a positive contrast that helps Sayford "read [Isabelle's] true character" (11). Not only
does Claire understand character, but she also teaches the white men
around her to better judge it.

Signaling her own self-absorption, Isabelle takes her place "before
the faithful mirror, which reflected a fair face, striking in its singular
beauty" (51). As "singular" as her reflection might be, it also reflects
Claire: her "almond-shaped black eyes, with curving black brows and
sweeping silken lashes" resemble Claire's "eyes of midnight blackness,
overshadowed by lightly arching brows of the same jetty hue"; Isabelle's
"small mouth, which rivaled a half-blown rose in its dewy loveliness, dis-
playing rows of even, pearl-white teeth" is barely distinct from Claire's
"perfect mouth, disclosing rows of even, pearl-white teeth;" Isabelle's
"crowning attraction, a wealth of beautiful black hair, which rippled
in curling waves to her slender waist" seems much like Claire's "wealth
of purple black hair, which in its natural loveliness enveloped her like a
cloud" (51, 4, 51, 4, 51,4). Each resembles a typical dark heroine—the
type who often has "mesmeric" powers and lacks feminine virtue. Bor-
rowing the trope of the double from great historical romances like *Ivanhoe*, Collins emphasizes that virtue is not skin deep.

Very significantly, Claire does not stand in front of a mirror to admire
herself; she actually gazes upon the portrait of a man who looks just like
her, ascertaining her lineage "by a re-tracing of recognized traits from
other faces, signally from portraits" (Sedgwick 261). The first concrete
evidence of her identity is her father's portrait; in order to view it, she
and her grandmother sneak into the deserted library where the Colonel
shot Richard eighteen years earlier. As Deidre Lynch says about the long-
standing gothic tradition, to enter the old library "is to be recruited into
a genealogical plot. . . . [W]hile surrounded by books, ink, and paper
the protagonists of Gothic fiction embark on their projects of memory

and mourning. These projects establish the terms on which the generations will be linked and on which the living will relate to the family dead" (29).[5]

Rather than turn to written evidence in the Tracy library that has been left by lawyers or patriarchs, however, Collins relies on the gothic trope of the portrait to establish Claire's lineage. The undeniable evidence of amalgamation, of the deep interconnectedness between black and white Americans, appears in the dual images of Richard Tracy's portrait and Claire's face. The connection between Richard and Claire also reminds the family of Lina's existence and of the love affair that made the Tracy family reckon with the legacy of slavery.

While the social assumptions and stereotypes that the Colonel uses to vilify and destroy Lina certainly would have resonated with African Americans in 1865, so too would the search for family identity that characterizes Claire's narrative. The search for family identity, although it invokes the legacy of slavery, also meshes with the tradition of the gothic family mystery. A somewhat haunted portrait of Claire's father provides the imaginative side of the story.

As the story's ghost and "avenging spirit," Lina's memory and presence saturates the story shortly after Claire confides in Mrs. Tracy that she is an orphan and knows nothing of her parents (59). Mrs. Tracy responds: "Claire, dear, you remind me in a thousand ways of my poor son" (55–56). Mrs. Tracy then tells Claire the history of her family's downfall, saying: "I could not confide my life history to an indifferent person, but with your kind sensitive heart, I know you will sympathize with me" (56).

The emotional connection between Claire and the Tracy family, and the fact that she can "sympathize" with their history of family fragmentation, connects the world of the freed people to the southern gentry. By establishing her familial relationship with the Tracy clan, Claire also establishes that she "belongs" in the reunified family of North and South. Her past, the history of exclusion from the inheritance of freedom, connects her to the freed people as well as to the Tracy family. As she listens to the story of "Richard and his slave bride," she becomes aware of this racial connection, and her "blood thrill[s] through her veins" (55). The sensational aspect of the novel, the "thrill" that Claire experiences, is even more pronounced in her grandfather's visceral response to the memory of his son.

Meanwhile, Colonel Tracy, avowed slaveholder and defender of "the Southern way," is haunted and puzzled by the resemblance of their new governess to his son Richard (59). The Colonel cannot think of Richard or Claire without remembering Lina; he complains that "the pale face of Claire Neville haunts my sleeping and waking hours, follows me like an avenging spirit! Her voice and smile madden me. Fool that I am to allow myself to be thus imprisoned" (59). Collins parodies the male bravery of the most politically powerful character in the novel, making him look rather foolish. As a colonel, he should be brave. (Military bravery is integral to republican masculinity.)

The only way that the Colonel and, unbeknownst to him, Claire and Mrs. Tracy can undo their haunting is to visit the old library, which has been locked and forbidden because it is the scene of Richard's attempted murder and the place where his portrait has been hidden away. As the Colonel enters the haunted library, his stature and power are significantly reduced by his own admission of his guilt: "Oh Richard, my son! My son! My punishment is indeed greater than I can bear" (59). He then names the curse that has befallen his family, proclaiming: "A thousand times have I bitterly execrated that deed. My curse has recoiled upon my own head" (59). The "dark epoch" and the "canker worm" affecting the Colonel's memory and heart parallel the epoch of slavery in American history (58). When he realizes that his curse has recoiled on his own head, he must be aware that his complicity in slavery and the selling of other humans has fragmented his own family, just as the sale of slaves fragments African American families, and the institution of slavery has torn the nation apart. By adopting the ways of Louisiana Creoles, the Colonel has ushered the phantoms of the Haitian Revolution into his own house.

Certainly, his descriptions of a canker worm gnawing at his heart, the dark epoch of his life's history, and the curse recoiled upon his head would suggest to newly emancipated and free black readers that the guilty and penitent Colonel realizes he has enslaved himself. That a plantation master so obliviously laments his situation using the language of slavery subverts and supplants his privilege as a slave owner; presumably scenes of subjection self-inflicted by elite whites may have been rather humorous to a black readership.

When Claire and Mrs. Tracy enter the library, Mrs. Tracy draws back a heavy veil that covers the portrait. Practically speaking, the veil protects the stored painting, yet Collins implies a double meaning. Richard's face is veiled because of his forbidden romance; the metaphor of the veil conveys the unspeakable fact of Richard's marriage and, for the Colonel Tracy, a mark of shame. Richard's portrait is veiled because of the prohibitions and stigma attached to amalgamation, which likewise serve as a major legal and cultural symbol of inequality. Hiding the portrait from view and concealing the history of a forbidden marriage, the veil marks "a system of prohibitions by which sexual desire is enhanced and specified" (Sedgwick 256). The shadow or shade over their romance is like the dark cloud of imminent gothic doom that Lina perceives early on in their relationship. These images of shadows, which are metaphors for slavery, are also metaphorical veils. The literal veil overlays Richard's image because, as Sedgwick says, social institutions construct racial identity and social status; they are "social and relational rather than original and private" (256).

Mrs. Tracy, however, pulls this veil aside for Claire's benefit. By making amalgamation honorable through her clearly virtuous characterization of Richard, Lina, and Claire, Collins challenges a social taboo. While Colonel Tracy's initial insistence that intermarriage is a legal impossibility dishonors and degrades Lina, the narrator makes it eminently clear how wrong the Colonel is. Lina's drop of "black blood" is not shameful, but the Colonel's belief in racial purity and black inferiority bring about *his* shame and the attendant need to hide his son's face with a veil. That this veil can be drawn back and the shame execrated reveals that racial inferiority is a personal belief rather than an innate characteristic. Drawing back the veil exposes the family's connection to slavery and to Lina as well as Claire. By drawing back the veil, Claire and Mrs. Tracy open up a future in which racial myths, particularly myths about Lina's sexuality, can be undone.

As he looks at his son in Claire's face, the Colonel's racial stereotypes begin to crumble. Shocked when he finds his wife and Claire already viewing the portrait, he gazes "alternately, with staring eyes, upon the portrait of Richard and the pale trembling girl" (60). Claire's identity, signally, traces through her white father—certainly a novel idea and demand for recognition in contrast to slavery's norm, a system in which the child always follows the condition of the mother. "Claire's eyes were riveted by the striking face" as she recognizes her long-lost father (57). Only when the Colonel begins to recognize and perhaps embrace a filial relationship with Claire does he witness the horror of slavery as a curse within his own home.

When Mrs. Tracy reveals Richard's portrait to Claire, she exclaims: "Mrs. Tracy, who am I? Oh, that face has haunted my dreams since my earliest recollection!" (57). Her ensuing search for identity, inspired by a portrait, invokes the gothic trope of portraiture as proseopopeia. To ascertain one's sense of self through the "fiction of an apostrophe to an absent, deceased, or voiceless entity," as de Man suggests, "confers upon it the power of speech" (75–76). Richard's portrait gives voice to Claire's identity as a Tracy; the moment of recognition that solidifies their genealogy, furthermore, voices the unspoken interrelationship between the Haitian and American Revolutions. Claire's resemblance to Richard's picture brings to the fore the attendant memory of his radical political position regarding the interrelatedness of black and white. Couched in Jeffersonian language, Richard's revolutionary claims of equality have more in common with Haitian ideals of freedom than his forefathers'. The portrait reminds the Colonel of the sacrifice Richard made for his stated fellow citizens—his picture and memory might even serve as proxy for an image of the freed people as equal American citizens.

Because Collins emphasizes the similarities between Richard's and Claire's countenances, she challenges racist beliefs in hereditary differences between black and white; she also provides an alternative image to the pervasive racial caricatures that represented the freed people as grotesque. While political cartoons portrayed the freed people by exaggerating and contorting their facial figures to make them as unlike white people as possible, Collins renders the difference invisible. Claire's visible resemblance to her father, rather than her mother, bespeaks a different social status than that of a slave. She is Richard's fellow citizen. As she wrestles with her own sense of belonging and lineage, she not only enlists the support of Colonel and Mrs. Tracy but also brings them closer to their long-lost son. Eventually, Claire and a family friend deliver Richard from exile and excommunication. As Claire gives a new voice to the family history of silence and shame, she restores him to his place in the household. By endowing her father with access to his home and inheritance, Claire effectively rescues him.

Claire's resemblance to Richard also destabilizes the legal power of white male identity because her image replaces, and even improves upon, his. As Cheryl Harris argues: "The state's official recognition of a racial identity that subordinated Blacks and of privileged rights in property based on race elevated whiteness from a passive attribute to an object of law and a resource deployable at the social, political, and institutional level to maintain control. . . . Whiteness as the embodiment of white privilege transcended mere belief or preference; it became usable property, the subject of law's regard and protection" (1734).[6] Divested of whiteness, Collins's heroines assume their own system of value by enacting virtue, the property of their individual character. Given the shortcomings of white masculinity, they demand protection and regard on their own merits. Claire's gaze upon the portrait of white patriarchy interrogates the value of whiteness, reducing it to a physical attribute, prioritizing action and speech as true markers of virtue.

Collins's contemporaries also emphasized action and speech in the pages of the *Christian Recorder* as they strived toward asserting racial equality and the rights of the freed people. Collins, likewise, devoted herself to literary activism, creating a new literature that reflected a brief era of Reconstruction optimism. The potential power of a novel to impact political reform suggests several reasons that Collins would turn to a story of romance and rebellion to enact social change. A novel like *The Curse of Caste* gave cultural credibility to claims of social equality between black and white by demonstrating the intellectual and artistic potential of its author. The emergence of African Americans as equal citizens in the reunited states also required cultural representations of this potential citizenry that refuted the caricatures and racist stereotypes about the freed people that pervaded public discourse, which Collins provided. Most importantly, as Collins resurrected Lina's memory, and restored life to all black women victimized through slavery, she challenged the powerful social institutions that worked against black citizenship and equality. To gain power in the cultural milieu and make political statements, as Orlando Patterson tells us, one must "control (or at least be in a position to manipulate) appropriate symbolic instruments" (37). One must ask, then, whether nineteenth-century romance novels in the United States constituted a form of cultural production authorized to transform political ideas and social values. It seems that, to Julia Collins, they most certainly did.

6 The End of Romance in Frances Watkins Harper's *Minnie's Sacrifice*

Le Croix was the only son of a Spanish lady, and a French gentle-man, who were married in Hayti a few months before the revolu-tion, which gave freedom to the island, and made Hayti an inde-pendent nation.

. . . Le Grange, like Le Croix, was of French and Spanish descent, and his father had also been a Haytian refugee. . . . [H]e had grown up a gay and reckless young man, fond of sports and living an aim-less life.

—Frances Watkins Harper

SHORTLY AFTER JULIA COLLINS passed away, her Reconstruc-tion optimism—the hope that the end of slavery would signal a new era of citizenship and radical equality—died away too. Readers might imagine that her heroine, Claire Neville—the offspring of a union between a Loui-siana Creole and a blue-blooded Yankee—could symbolize an amalgam-ated and reunified nation, one that could incorporate the vast geography and attendant cultural differences of the ever-expanding United States in its definition of citizenship. That Claire brings a particularly feminine form of virtue and influence to the fractured family she reunites suggests, too, that women might play an integral role in the reunification of the nation. Yet only four years after Collins died, leaving the uncompleted manu-script of *The Curse of Caste* and the unfinished project of Reconstruction behind her, it became clear to her contemporary Frances Watkins Harper that the longing for union—whether between black and white, North and South, or men and women—would not result in political recognition based on the radical equality of souls or the metaphor of a loving, amal-gamated national family. Nor would the nation move beyond a moment of violent rebellion, symbolized through family violence in *The Curse of*

Caste or abolitionist enthusiasm for John Brown's and Toussaint Louver-ture's uprisings, to ameliorate the racial and gender inequities of the past. Rather, as Harper's postbellum speeches, letters, and 1869 novel *Min-nie's Sacrifice* attest, the language of racialized sexuality and the threat of political and social upheaval signal the end of romance in the various emancipatory and radically egalitarian shapes that reformers understood it. Like "Hayti, an independent nation," black writers and activists in the United States would have to rebuild the nation without the "reckless" and sometimes "aimless" influence of white bourgeois reformers.

Both *The Curse of Caste* and *Minnie's Sacrifice* intervene in popular representations of black and white womanhood, Creole or Caribbean influ-ence, and gendered virtue that their white contemporaries produced. Harper both rebels against the rhetoric of black womanhood that emerged in suf-frage debates and publications after 1865 and revises novelistic ones, such as best-selling author E.D.E.N. Southworth's first novel, *Retribution*, which precedes both Collins's and Harper's novels by more than a decade. Com-paring Southworth to the two illustrates Collins's and Harper's challenge to assumptions about race, gender, and sexuality that shaped contemporary discourses of citizenship. Collins's and Harper's work rebels against the lit-erary romances of their predecessors; they therefore create a new meaning and a new use for the tropes of romance and rebellion by reinventing Creole heroines and redefining their relationship to elite white women.

Retribution, for example, replicates a pattern of female friendship common to nineteenth-century women's novels. Its heroine, Hester Grey, meets the antiheroine, Juliette Summers, in boarding school. Hes-ter marries a handsome Virginian, Colonel Dent, but dies prematurely. When Dent fails to fulfill Hester's dying wish that her slaves be eman-cipated, he endures retribution for his actions. The retribution comes in the form of his second wife, the "mesmeric . . . sinister and inviting coquette"—Juliette (31). The new Mrs. Dent's penchant for jewels and her general avarice bring about her husband's ruin (and the dissolution of her late friend's plantation). Juliette, furthermore, is a refugee from the Haitian Revolution—a decadent Creole whose excessive desires and demands contaminate the home, and the Virginia estate, of her pure and angelic predecessor, Hester Grey.

In contrast to the innocence of frail, gray-eyed Hester, Juliette's almost tropical beauty presents a clear sense of danger to the wholesome and Christian values upon which Hester builds her home. The contami-nating force of Creole culture, like Juliette's dark beauty, leads an oth-erwise respectable Virginian (Colonel Dent) to forsake his wife's dying wish and preserve the institution of slavery. While Southworth does not explicitly suggest that Juliette's corruption and overt sexual appeal come from possible "African" ancestry (which many Anglo-Americans believed infiltrated Creole bloodlines), her beauty is described in signs that often mark beautiful octoroons and "tragic mulatta" characters in other novels of the period, including those by Collins and Harper. Her "richness of complexion could only come from Italy," and her "shining black hair" dropped in "large, smooth, glossy ringlets" to frame "black eyes, with their long black fringes, so dusky and brooding one instant, so melting and suffused the next, and suddenly so resplendent with light and soul, and upon occasion, so fierce and flaming in anger" (31). The dualisms within her appearance, "dusky and brooding" yet "resplendent with light," seem to symbolize her dual nature, perhaps her dual ancestry. Most remarkable are the "occasions" when her eyes are "fierce and flaming in anger," a mirror of the fires and violence she recounts when she describes fleeing the violence and destruction of black revolutionaries in insurgent Haiti.

Juliette is also rebellious; she refuses to assume the angelic and humble role of a good Virginia matron and must instead dazzle the courts of Europe with her magnificence (again, ruining her husband's inherited Virginia estate through the practice of Creole absenteeism). The lesson seems quite clear: sexually desirable and desiring women, particularly Creoles, sully the fabric of old Virginia values. The lost and forgotten purity and virtue of the pious Hester Grey symbolize a republican tradition that offers the only peaceful means toward ending slavery—voluntary emancipation—and idealizes the role of white womanhood in upholding the moral values of the nation.

Both Collins and Harper respond to the imagery, contexts, and codes of *Retribution* in rather obvious ways. Collins's ravishingly beautiful Creole—Lina Hartley Tracy—actually embodies the purity and sweetness of Hester Grey rather than the tainted sensuality of Juliette Summers. When Lina's daughter enters the Tracy household, she restores it and reunites the family rather than destroys it, as Juliette did when she entered the Dent household. This seems to refute the racial logic of "tropical loveliness" (Collins 4) as a danger to the Anglo-American family. Collins and Harper acknowledge the "African" blood of their Creole characters and make it a strength rather than a contaminant. The "black blood" of the mothers in their novels seems to endow the daughters with an ability to stand up for themselves as well as an ability to see beyond the racist viewpoints they encounter; they instead advocate a shared humanity.

Harper's apparent response to *Retribution* in her own 1869 novel is particularly interesting not only because she borrows the name of Southworth's "tragic mulatta" character, Minnie, for her eponymous heroine, but also because she refutes the assertions of benevolent white womanhood as a virtuous antislavery force (Hester's dying wish) and refuses to endow the fair, blue-eyed blond women with greater virtue than their darker, glossy-ringletted, black-eyed counterparts.[1] While Southworth's "Minnie" is beautiful and musically talented yet helpless and vulnerable, very much like Lydia Maria Child's octoroon characters in *Romance of the Republic*, both white authors assume that the cross-racial women benefit from and are uplifted by the culture and sophistication of their white fathers (decadent Creoles) and husbands. Harper's hero and heroine, also the cross-racial children of Creole fathers, can pass for white but choose not to. Unlike Child's characters, they vocally critique their fathers' weakness. The extent to which Harper's hero and heroine feel betrayed by the South, the nation, their parents, or their white friends sheds light on the bourgeois reform culture that Harper rebels against in her fiction.

Like Southworth's Juliette and Collins's Claire, Harper's Minnie leaves her northern school days, and white school friends, behind to travel south. Most striking, however, is the way Harper reshapes the incidents of betrayal. While Juliette betrays Hester's dying wish by marrying her husband and making it impossible to manumit Hester's slaves, Harper's Minnie is betrayed by Carrie Wise, a white northern woman who was her school friend, when Minnie's formerly enslaved mother appears. In response to the negative reactions she experiences from white women, Minnie pivots away from the company of her white friends, adoptive family, and sister-in-law, adopting the freed women of the South as her new people. This chapter discusses the background of Harper's sense of betrayal—the conflict over the Fifteenth Amendment that led to the "great schism" in the woman suffrage movement, her insistence on black woman suffrage as the only means to prevent the sexual violence and betrayals of the past, and her focus on forming ties among educated black women from the North and the freed women of the South as they work toward building a self-sufficient place of freedom beyond the racial and gender limitations of national politics.

Notably, in addition to being involved in Reconstruction political activism regarding the Fifteenth Amendment, Harper's protagonists Minnie and Louis are the descendants of Haitian Creoles. They differ from these white ancestors, however, because they choose to collaborate with the newly freed black population rather than flee the scene of violent upheaval. As they engender a project of reform for the decadent (and defeated) South, their vision for the future of the republic seems to have more in common with the self-sufficient postcolonial nation of Haiti than the South they once knew. As Carla Peterson illustrates: "In Harper's literary imagination, Southern slaveholding culture has its origins in the foreign Creole culture of pre-revolutionary Haiti and is characterized by ostentatious displays of wealth and moral self-indulgence. As such, it stands in negative contrast to both the many accounts of the independent black Republic of Haiti published in the *Recorder* and to Harper's vision of the North as a site of industrious free labor" (*Reconstructing the Nation* 314).

Yet Harper also gestures to the silent aspect of that Creole culture—the black mothers who brought African or Caribbean influence to it. The contributions that working black women bring to *Minnie's Sacrifice* (or that Juno brings to *The Curse of Caste*) reaffirm the black ancestry within decadent Creole culture, an ancestry that gave birth to the free republic of Haiti. Harper's contemporaries, such as Theodore Holley, also turned to Haitian history because, as John Ernest points out, "Haiti played a significant role in this vision of destiny—sometimes representing the promise of those of African heritage in the United States, and sometimes serving as both the ideological and the symbolic site for a rising black nation (88).

Like the black people of Haiti, Louis and Minnie must create a new republic. Bourgeois precepts of civilization (the self-indulgence and wealth of her white past) do not inform Minnie's political project; in fact, Harper finds impoverished former slaves more honorable than their masters. They work to distance themselves from white bourgeois society and its artificial "civility"; labor and black self-sufficiency remedy Louis and Minnie's decadent Creole background. In turning away from wealth, they also turn away from the moral depravity they see in white slaveholding society. Similarly, they pivot away from political alliances with white abolitionists and suffragists as they remove themselves from the liberal North to the black South and engage in community-building projects with the freed people. The next section describes the historical circumstances of the scene of political betrayal that underlies Harper's choice to dissociate from the white woman suffrage movement after the great schism of 1869, which occurred as she was in the process of writing and publishing *Minnie's Sacrifice* serially. The second section reads *Minnie's Sacrifice* as a call for black woman suffrage; the third explores

Harper's critique of white women's complicity in creating a hypersex-ualized image of the freed women; and the final section describes the work ethic and labor ideology of Harper's creolized version of black womanhood.

The Racist *Revolution*

Frances Harper's involvement with white women activists became increasingly strained due to debates over the Fifteenth Amendment. The failures of Reconstruction and the "great schism" in the women's rights and antislavery movement make it seem even more tragic that, for a brief period immediately after the Civil War, American reformers optimistically imagined a reconstructed republic that would incorporate woman suffrage and abolitionist interests. An 1865 pamphlet entitled *Equal Rights Convention for New York State* conveys this optimism nobly, imagining reforms in the state that would translate seamlessly to a national political level. It endorses "the right of suffrage to all citizens, without distinction of race or sex" and envisions the "reconstruction of this Union [as] a broader, deeper work than the restoration of the rebel States. It is the lifting of the entire nation into the practical realiza-tion of our Republican Idea." Below this appeal to make New York a "genuine republic," the pamphlet also advertises a group of convention speakers—including Henry Blackwell, Frederick Douglass, Harper, and Elizabeth Cady Stanton. This list of men and women, black and white, epitomizes the alliance between abolition and suffrage that could, but never did, further a radically romantic ideal of equality.

By the end of the decade, the cross-racial unity among these reform-ers would disappear; men and women, black and white, would excori-ate one another's views on race, gender, and class in debates over the Fifteenth Amendment. For example, Frances Harper's 1866 speech "We Are All Bound up Together" declared, "I tell you that if there is any class of people who need to be lifted out of their airy nothings and selfishness, it is the white women of America" (Sklar 198).[2] Harper's 1866 speech did not dismiss white women's concerns entirely; instead, she suggested that suffrage for white women was not the most compelling need of the hour. She seems, however, to have lost her patience with white women at the 1869 meeting of the American Equal Rights Association (AERA). By that point, she and many other reformers had also lost faith in the ideal of a productive engagement between abolition and woman suf-frage. The meeting, led by Stanton and Susan B. Anthony, is often called the "great schism" in the woman suffrage movement.[3] Divorce became a more salient metaphor than romance as woman suffrage clashed with the interests of black suffrage, and a cohort of reformers who had previously collaborated fought bitter public battles over whether black men should attain voting rights before women.

The sexually charged nature of a heated exchange between Paulina Davis, Stanton, Frederick Douglass, and Harper at the annual meeting of the AERA exemplifies the demolition of their republican ideal. Ironically, the same fear of black male proximity to white women that led to the burning of Freedom Hall in Philadelphia became the justification for Stanton to abandon black civil rights and "unfurl a new banner to the breeze" ("To Our Radical Friends"). Fletcher described the dangerous and obscene "circumstance which filled to overflowing this cup of abolitionist wickedness. . . . [C]ertain young women of anti-slavery faith were seen to walk the streets with colored young men!" (214). At the 1869 AERA meeting, the idea of white women in proximity to black men took on a similarly sinister cast. Specifically, the argument at the annual meeting echoed many articles in the *Revolution* that had cast the freedmen as tyrants. The term "tyrant" had a specifically sexual connotation in AERA rhetoric; white men, too, could act as tyrants by controlling female sexuality.[4] Such an equation of political and sexual rights for women reflects a foundational feminist concern still relevant in the twenty-first century. Yet the converse assumption that black men's political desire was indistinct from sexual desire—particularly desire for white women—as well as the conspicuous erasure of black women's sexual exploitation during slavery and pervasive lack of marriage rights reflects the sordid underbelly of sexual politics that also pervades the twenty-first century.[5]

Paulina Davis incited the clash over sex at the annual meeting by arguing that enfranchised black men would use their political power to pursue helpless white women, claiming that "that sort of men should not have the makings of the laws for the governance of women throughout the land" ("Annual Meeting"). Her speech depicted black men as brutes and attributed the freedwomen's relatively more developed intellect to their contact with the white women who had owned them. She went on to suggest that denying black men the franchise and giving educated, white, middle-class women the vote would also protect black women from tyrannical black men. AERA members who claimed that black men were sexual predators, however, did not go unchallenged.[6]

When Frederick Douglass took the floor, he garnered immediate crowd approval by declaring: "This Equal Rights meeting has been pre-eminently a Woman's Rights meeting" ("Annual Meeting"). Dismissing Davis's indictment of "that sort of men," he went on to make a sexually charged quip: "Here is a woman who, since the day the snake talked with our mother in the garden . . . has been divested of her rights." This reference to Eve mounted a personal attack on Davis, bringing loud laughter, applause, and apparent mayhem from the crowd. Douglass's statement had such an effect because it played into a specifically sexualized reference; the story of Adam and Eve represented sexual desire in the vernacular of the mid-nineteenth century. Davis's sexual stereotyping of African Americans had provoked Douglass, who in turn insulted her with a distinctly antireform slur.

As I explained in the first chapter, referring to Mason Stokes, proslavery and antisuffrage lecturers and propagandists promulgated a version of the Eden story in which the snake was a black man and Eve an unruly activist woman who transgressed race and gender boundaries through her illicit relationship with the snake.[7] Stanton, however, interpreted the Eden myth as an allegory of women's quest for knowledge, so the fact that Douglass invoked the antisuffragist version of the story may have been particularly aggravating to her.[8] According to *Revolution* logic, black men wanted the vote to fulfill their desire for white women, but Douglass's slur implied that white women wanted the vote to fulfill their desire for black men.

Douglass paused as the crowd reacted to the Adam and Eve reference, giving Anthony a moment to jump up and respond to him. More laughter, applause, and general mayhem drowned out Anthony's words to Douglass. When silence was restored, Douglass continued: "You see when women get into trouble how they act. Miss Anthony comes to the rescue—(laughter)—and these good people have not yet learned to hear people through." Shifting the focus of the vernacular Adam and Eve reference by indicating that the women speaking about black male sexuality would "get into trouble," Douglass's ribald stereotype averted his listeners' attention from the image of black "tyrants" to a spectacle of unruly and rebellious white women. Douglass's comment implicitly dismissed the idea that white women needed the vote to protect themselves from black men, instead asserting that political and sexual desire were related, much like the *Revolution* made political and sexual rights codependent. He concluded by asserting, "I do not believe the story that the slaves who are enfranchised become the worst of tyrants."

Stanton retaliated, couching her response in racially charged language and reaffirming Davis's previous comment that she would not "have a race of tyrants raised above her in the South," and that "she did not believe in allowing ignorant negroes and ignorant and debased Chinamen to make laws for her to obey." Stanton's reference to "ignorant negroes" governing her and its attendant implication of sexual depravity again mark a racialized conflation of political and sexual power. That she would make such a comment to Douglass's face suggests that she was as unconcerned about insulting him as he was with her when he made the "Eve" comment. Douglass's suggestion that "Miss Anthony comes to the rescue" also echoes, in a bizarre way, a story that Stanton would recount in *The History of Woman Suffrage*. Stanton reflected on a March 3, 1869, meeting with Douglass, two months before the AERA convention:

> On the way from Galena to Toledo we met Frederick Douglass, dressed in a cap and a great circular cape of wolf-skins. He really presented a most formidable and ferocious aspect. . . . As I had been talking against the pending amendment of manhood suffrage, I trembled in my shoes and was almost as paralyzed as Little Red Riding Hood in a similar encounter. But unlike the little maiden, I had a friend at hand, and, as usual in the hour of danger, I fell back in the shadow of Miss Anthony, who stepped forward bravely and took the wolf by the hand. (377)

Stanton seems not to have been "tremb[ling] in [her] shoes" as she contradicts Douglass at the meeting two months later, but it is interesting that, in both cases, Anthony "step[s] forward" and tries to control Douglass (377). Stanton is most likely being playful when she refers to Douglass as "ferocious" and to their meeting as an "hour of danger," but there is a great deal of sexual tension in her fantasy that she is Little Red Riding Hood and he a big, bad wolf. Since it is the wolf's goal, furthermore, to eat Little Red Riding Hood, comparing herself and Douglass to the two characters harkens the cannibalistic metaphor of amalgamation that made radical romance seem dangerous and disgusting.

The battle that took place over race, gender, and rights in 1869 was waged in the language of racialized sexuality and emphasized the failure of the ideal of romance and rebellion to construct an alternative to Anglo-American nationalism. Antimiscegenation rhetoric in the *Revolution* during the year leading up to the annual meeting, which looked not unlike the writings by Austin, Broca, or Nott described in previous chapters, had set the stage for a major conflict over AERA representations of cross-racial sexual desire.

When Harper first intervened in the sexually charged exchange among Davis, Stanton, and Douglass at the meeting, it appears that she tried to diffuse the situation. Caught at the crossroads of a debate that had grown ugly, Harper called on Henry Blackwell (who, with Lucy Stone, had attempted to negotiate between Stanton and Douglass's positions regarding the Fifteenth Amendment earlier in the meeting).[9] Harper's compromise would have been to support the spirit of Blackwell's resolution, stating, "that while we heartily approve of the Fifteenth Amendment . . . we nevertheless feel profound regret that Congress has not submitted a parallel amendment for the enfranchisement of women" ("Equal Rights" 5). Blackwell could not reread the resolution, though, because Anthony tried to override Harper's control of the floor. Douglass objected to Anthony's interruption, cutting her off to say, "Oh! No, you cannot do that while the floor is occupied" ("Annual Meeting"). Interestingly, despite the fact that she nearly steamrolled Harper's contributions to the discussion, Anthony asserted later on that "attempts at gagging discussion would not be countenanced" ("Annual Meeting"). Both Stanton and Anthony's *History of Woman Suffrage* and the report of the meeting in their newspaper, the *Revolution*, go on to devote but a few lines to Harper: "Mrs. Harper then proceeded with her remarks, saying that when it was a question of race she would let the lesser question of sex go. But the white women all go for sex, letting race occupy a minor position" ("Annual Meeting"). As she joined Douglass in dissent, her multivalent reference to sex signified comparable sarcasm and disdain for AERA sexual politics.

Harper's somewhat infamous statement at the convention, that "when it was a question of race she let the lesser question of sex go," seems to make a transparent choice of racial loyalty over her commitment to woman suffrage ("Annual Meeting"). If her comment was accurately recorded—which is not certain—it seems to conflict with the more balanced arguments for black *women's* rights in her letters, speeches, and fiction. These sources tell us a great deal more about Harper's views during this critical historical moment than a brief AERA transcript can, and they also shed light on her distinct vision of political activism. Harper's AERA comment named two major points—race and sex—that coincide with two major problems she had with the AERA: first, it reveals her frustration with the sexual politics that white women engaged to attack the Fifteenth Amendment and that antireformers had used persistently to deny African American citizenship; second, it indicates that, although both African Americans and women were under scrutiny as potential citizens, women's rights offered her nothing if they did not acknowledge her rights as a black woman.

While one might infer that Harper's "lesser question of sex" merely refers to gender and woman suffrage, the tone of the debate over the Fifteenth Amendment and the novel that Harper was writing at the same time, *Minnie's Sacrifice*, indicate that this question of sex also had to do with sexuality. Sexual politics, in this context, had much to do with stereotypes about sexual behavior rather than the mere difference between men and women. In light of Douglass's preceding comments about Adam and Eve, it is possible to read Harper's reference to white women and sex in terms of Mae Henderson's definition of heteroglossia. Harper meant, literally, that white women like Stanton and Anthony were more interested in an amendment that would enfranchise their sex—women—than they were in the Fifteenth Amendment. Yet she also implied that they were invoking the long-standing, pejorative image of a white woman in a black man's embrace that had motivated antiblack violence throughout the century and originated, in part, in gothic reports of the Haitian Revolution.

Given the sexually charged nature and rape-panic language that women like Stanton and Davis were using to attack black men, both at the AERA meeting and in their newspaper, the *Revolution*, one might also assume that Harper's reference to "sex" indicated her disgust with the way the racist sexual politics of Reconstruction had infiltrated the AERA.[10] Similarly, when Stanton and Davis insisted that the Fifteenth Amendment would place them in sexual jeopardy at the hands of black "tyrants," the argument was primarily about sex, but not merely biological sex ("Annual Meeting"). The argument was sexual; it claimed that black men desired the vote so they could control white female sexuality; it thus catapulted the language of women's rights into the arena of racist stereotypes of black men that justified lynching.[11] Many white women thereby participated in a dominant logic that veiled African American political or economic power in a pathological sexual mythology. As Martha Hode points out, this logic was widespread: Klansmen and their supporters "conflated the newly won political and economic power of black men with alleged sexual liaisons with white women" (407). Sexual power was inextricable from discussions of political or economic power in the terms that many suffragists, northern reformers, and former confederates alike used to describe the future of racial coexistence.

Harper explores different plans for attaining race and gender equality in the letters and stories she wrote in 1869. Jean Lee Cole and Leslie Lewis have argued that *Minnie's Sacrifice* engages a vision for black civil rights that eschews white influence in favor of coalition building between educated free blacks like Harper and the freed people. *Minnie's Sacrifice*, however, is also very much about woman suffrage and Harper's experience with the AERA. Thus the novel asks readers to reconsider her comments at the 1869 meeting and critiques the ideal of cross-racial coalitions. As an activist who had seen the conditions in the South and who recognized both the danger of persistent sexual stereotypes and the integral role that black women had to play in order to rebuild the South, she doubted white woman suffragists' strategies, or any national strategies, for attaining equality. While abolitionist rhetoric had decried and, arguably, sensationalized the sexual exploitation of black women, suffrage rhetoric after 1865 began to exploit stereotypes of black sexuality to assert white women's greater suitability for Anglo-American citizenship. The romantic quest for equality in which white women and African American activists had engaged for a half century was essentially over.

Harper let "the lesser question of sex go" after Anthony interrupted her a second time, not to forego her rights as a woman, but to get beyond the rivalry between black men and white women and its attendant hypersexualized language of black tyrants and vulnerable white ladies that was derailing the issue of suffrage. Harper's writing suggests that the question of sex—both in terms of women's rights and in terms of safety from sexual exploitation—was profoundly important to her. Yet the idea that black women would learn to be equal citizens from white "mistresses" like Davis must have been alarming.[12] In terms of greater safety from white vigilantes in the South and in terms of economic opportunity, delaying black men's suffrage would also hurt black women. She concluded: "If the nation could only handle one question, she would not have the black women *put a single straw in the way* if only the race of men could obtain what they wanted. (Great applause)" ("Annual Meeting," original emphasis).

This allegiance to black men does not forego woman suffrage indefinitely; it merely indicates that black women stand a better chance of attaining equality by casting their lot with black men than by working with white women. Stanton and Davis were trying to stand in the way of the Fifteenth Amendment, and to support their position would jeopardize black men and women's safety from the racist sexual politics of Reconstruction, just as it would do nothing to further black women's voting rights.[13] As *Minnie's Sacrifice* reveals, however, that the nation cannot "handle [even] one question," the conditional nature of Harper's comments on black men's rights suggest that the politics of race and gender are far too complicated to be resolved within the context of an

Anglo-masculine nation at all. Rather, *Minnie's Sacrifice* will illustrate the impossibility for the nation to accommodate, much less to protect, the rights of black people—particularly women.

"Some Power to Defend Herself from Oppression"

Both *Minnie's Sacrifice* and the letters Harper wrote about her own experience in the South clarify Harper's views on black suffrage. Minnie makes recurring political statements that echo Harper's, such as when she says: "I cannot recognize the claim that the negro man is the only one who has pressing claims at this hour. To-day our government needs women's conscience as well as man's judgment. And while *I would not throw a straw in the way* of the colored man, even though I know he would vote against me as soon as he gets his vote, yet I do think that woman should have some power to defend herself from oppression, and equal laws as if she were a man" (78, emphasis added). Minnie's comment thus revises and expands Harper's truncated and somewhat cryptic statement at the meeting; women need the vote for self-defense, but in Harper's example, *black* women must protect themselves from *white* men. In a radical (and more historically accurate) reversal of the "mistress narrative," Harper's novel shows that black women must also distance themselves from white women in order to succeed economically.

Situated between sex and race, Minnie's statement invokes women's moral authority and demands that "woman should have some power to defend herself," suggesting that sexual immorality and oppression threaten black women as much, if not more than, white women (78). Yet Minnie is in the proverbial double bind because she identifies as African American and as a woman—doubly disenfranchised—and forced, by the Fifteenth Amendment, to prioritize one-half of her rights over the other. She regrets that men "would vote against me," presumably because she thinks the majority of black men will not support woman suffrage. Minnie debates her husband about universal suffrage and refuses to concede that "the negro hour" could upstage the "negro woman's hour" (78). This comment explicitly rejects Douglass's claim for the Fifteenth Amendment. He had said repeatedly that it was the "negro hour" rather than the "woman's hour"; Harper's use of the new term "negro woman's hour" suggests that her chosen "side" of the suffrage debate cannot be delineated in terms of black and white, or male and female. Simply put, she argues that enfranchisement does not engender sexual tyranny; rather, it ameliorates it. Yet the novel does not prioritize black men's rights over women's rights; it makes an argument for black women's rights as the most pressing concern of the era.

As a window to Harper's thinking on citizenship, race, and the promise of the American republic, her fiction provides a rich field from which to reap the full breadth of her ideas. Both at the convention and in the novel she was writing at the time, Harper and her heroine refuse to put a "straw in the way" of black male suffrage. As southern legislatures virtually reinstalled slavery by passing black codes, and white supremacists raped and murdered black republicans, activists like Harper, Sojourner Truth, and Wendell Phillips "saw black suffrage as necessary to sustain emancipation" (Painter, "Voices" 45). Of course, *Minnie's Sacrifice* is a novel published in a reform-oriented church newspaper, the *Christian Recorder*, which regularly and unequivocally demanded full citizenship rights and social equality for African Americans. In the context of this periodical, which assumed the urgency of black male, and sometimes female, voting rights with the same fervor that the *Revolution* assumed the urgency of white female suffrage, Harper emphasized the rights of black women, expanding the position she took on race during the AERA Fifteenth Amendment debate. Yet the ultimate murder of her heroine illustrates that black male suffrage is ultimately not enough to protect the interests of all.

The AERA emphasis on "tyrannical" black male sexuality erased the sexual exploitation of African American women during slavery, so one of the first goals of Harper's serialized novel is to restore black women to a position of respect, both as a historical presence and as integral contributors to the future. The way that the novel casts cross-racial sexual relationships is arresting, particularly because the moment of the heroine's conception and of her death exemplify African American women's distinct need for citizenship rights in order to combat a history of sexual abuse. Any hope for cross-racial union that Collins had retained in her novel five years earlier was gone. The novel opens with another reference to the history of abuse, a description of her hero Louis's mother, a woman who "had been a slave, with no power to protect herself from the highest insults that brutality could offer to innocence . . . a victim to the wiles and power of her master" (3). Setting up a rhetorical equation wherein sex equals power, Harper deflects the question of sexuality away from blacks and back toward white men who have the power to exploit women sexually.

Minnie's Sacrifice envisions the end of this sexual history. The novel, which is about Minnie working alongside her husband, Louis, in the

South, also unveils the second issue Harper voiced at the AERA meeting—work. She had little faith in the AERA's commitment to what she saw as one of the most compelling goals of Reconstruction—economic uplift through property ownership and greater employment opportunities for African Americans. Like Harper, Minnie spends her time in the aftermath of the war in the South among the freed people rather than among her elite northern white friends. She and Louis at first believe they are rightful, white heirs of New Orleans planters but learn as the Civil War erupts that they are both illegitimate children of slave women. They immediately break from their adoptive white families and, when the war ends, immerse themselves among the freed people, just as Harper was doing at that time, to work for racial and gender equality by endorsing economic self-reliance. Their major obstacle, however, is the danger they face from white rebels who use sexual allegations to justify the murder of economically successful African Americans.

In the end, Minnie's sacrifice is not to defer her voting rights to her husband: her sacrifice is her life itself. Although the chapter describing her death has been lost, the subsequent chapter indicts the Ku Klux Klan because Minnie has "no power to defend herself," a power that she identifies early in the novel as the right to vote (78). Minnie's murder has great personal resonance for Harper; although she apparently avoided the Klan during her time in the South, her letters tell us that they were a constant threat to her own safety. The Ku Klux Klan activity in 1869 was at epidemic proportions. Harper repeatedly reassured her friend William Still in letters she wrote from the South that she was not afraid, but she clearly made an excellent target for Klansmen terrorizing blacks who dared to vote or make economic advancements toward community self-sufficiency. In one letter to Still, she writes: "when will we have a government strong enough to make human life safe? . . . Last summer a Mr. Luke was hung, and several other men also, I heard" (Foster, *Brighter* 131).

Harper asserts the urgency of women's rights by illustrating the inextricable racial and sexual violence that results from African American disenfranchisement, a threat that affects black women as much as men. In one example of a scene from *Minnie's Sacrifice* drawn directly from Harper's experience, a black mother describes the reason for her daughter's murder by white rebels. In her happiness at seeing the Union troops, the woman's daughter had said, "I'm gwine to marry a Linkum soger" (87). This woman's daughter challenged southern white male supremacy; her crime involved a challenge to the color line and the insinuation that she could attain the legal right of marriage. The murder of a young black woman for talking about intermarriage directly reflects Harper's experience of southern brutality. In a letter dated May 13, 1867, she writes: "About two years ago, a girl was hung for making a childish and indiscreet speech. . . . Our army had been through, and this poor, ill-fated girl . . . rejoicing over the event, said that she was going to marry a Yankee and set up housekeeping. She was reported as having made an incendiary speech and arrested, cruelly scourged, and then brutally hung" (Foster, *Brighter* 123). Many of Harper's letters, such as the one describing this young girl, describe sexual crimes and lynchings committed against African Americans (123). She writes of a man in Eufala, Alabama, who "had a son who married a white woman, or girl, and was shot down, and there was, as I understand, no investigation by the jury; and a number of cases have occurred of murders, for which the punishment has been very lax, or not at all" (128).[14]

Minnie's choice of the freed people over her privileged white family is also a choice to reverse the trajectory of miscegenation. Whereas white men previously had the power to violate the black community through rape, Minnie inserts herself into that community in a radically different way—by relinquishing the power and privilege of her whiteness. Threatening the southern way of life, particularly when women cross the racial lines drawn in the sand by white southern men, has lethal consequences. Sandra Gunning interprets the failure of Reconstruction and scenes of racial violence in terms of white male anxiety: "This translation of the freed people's impulse toward democracy into ultimately a threat against the most personal, most sacred aspect of white life meant that what might have begun in the late 1860s and 1870s as a political struggle was increasingly characterized by the 1890s as a social rape, an encroachment on the sacred Anglo-Saxon male right to everything in American society and civilization" (*Race* 7). Thus white racists envisioned black women, not just black male rapists, as the desecraters of their "civilization"; Minnie's choice to transgress the color line, though she passes from whiteness into blackness, is a perceived threat to white supremacy.

That the two most significant scenes of murder in *Minnie's Sacrifice* involve black female victims redirects the reader's attention toward the intersection of race, women's rights, and sexual politics. White male supremacists perceive these two martyrs as a major threat because they encroach upon the personal and sacred definitions of domesticity as the exclusive purchase of white civilization; their choice to live beyond the control of white male fathers or masters, furthermore, challenges the "sacred Anglo-Saxon male right" to his property, whether black, female, or both (Gunning, *Race* 7). As tragic heroines, Minnie and the young woman die in the face of a formidable power, inextricably white and male, thus defining the intersection of race and gender as the nexus of political change. The novel condemns white slaveholders as traitors and defends the honor and dignity of the freed people. Political virtue and valor parallel sexual virtue as well because the white men who commit sexual violence are likewise traitors and rebels.

Minnie's hope that women like her mother might gain "power to defend herself from oppression, and equal laws as if she were a man" is informed by a long history of sexual abuse and oppression (*Minnie* 78). Like Louis's mother, Agnes, Minnie's mother, Ellen, was the mistress of a wealthy planter. Both mothers are "quadroons," which means they are the second generation of enslaved women born to a black mother and a white father. This history of interracial sex, which continues through Minnie and Louis's generation but ends there, provides Harper's evidence of the sexual depravity of white slaveholding men and of black women's compelling need to defend themselves with the vote that Minnie demands. With the vote, black women can let the question of past sexual abuse go, move forward, and build a future through work.

Despite their fate at the hands of white men, the black mothers in the novel do not take the role of victims but rather engender critical transformations in the civic identity of the main characters. Minnie and Louis believe they are white for the first few installments of the novel, but the pivotal moment in their development as activists comes when they recognize their black mothers. Minnie, schooled in the North, knows nothing of her mother's background until she meets her mother on the street. Her white school friends ostracize her, but Minnie remains loyal to her mother. Louis, likewise, does not know his mother's identity until the Civil War begins. When Louis goes to his grandmother to tell her that he is joining the Confederate army, she reveals to him that he cannot fight for the "secesh" because to do so would be "to raise your hand [against] your own race" (58). Louis deserts the Confederate troops, fights for the Union, and finally breaks ties with his white past and family to marry Minnie and work among the freed people in the South. The couple turns away from any association with white America, choosing to collaborate with the freed people in the South and build a society independent from white influence. Louis asks only that "American people will take their Christless, Godless prejudices out of the way, and give us a chance to grow, an opportunity to accept life" (73).

Louis repeatedly asserts that the miscegenation that produced him and Minnie must stop. Despite the fact that his father raised him like a legitimate heir, endowing him with all the educational and social privileges of whiteness, and that Louis himself secured an officer's position in the Confederate army, he refuses to forgive his father's sexual transgressions: "I have heard some colored persons boasting of the white blood, but I always feel like blushing for mine. Much as my father did for me he could never atone for giving me life under the conditions he did" (80). Louis's language of sin dismisses the possibility that his father could atone for his irresponsible and indulgent sexual practices. Instead, Louis wants to focus on "how we can make life secure in the South," meaning that blacks should become self-sufficient and free from the sexual violence, or violence justified through sexual mythology, perpetrated by white "citizens" (81). Louis's priorities mirror Harper's; both look to the northern black community to rebuild the South rather than appealing to white northerners or former slaveholders to repent and atone for the national sin of slavery.

Through personal experience, Louis extends his father's sexual behavior, a betrayal of the domestic sphere of his Creole and enslaved families, to a national political level—the Republican Party itself.[15] He brings Minnie a copy of the *New York Tribune* as proof that northern Republicans have let "negro suffrage" slip away in their own states, telling her: "I have been trying to persuade our people to vote the Republican ticket, but to-day, I feel like blushing for the party. They are weakening our hands and strengthening those of the rebels" (75). Like his father, who left him vulnerable to slavery, the Republican Party leaves him vulnerable to the rebels. In each case, white irresponsibility and the hypocritical discourse of race and sexual politics endanger black efforts toward securing freedom and nation building. That he blushes for his father and for the Republicans suggests that personal and political levels of betrayal equate. Despite the fact that his father raised him like a legitimate heir, sparing no expense in education or lifestyle, Louis places all of the sin, stigma, and moral pollution of miscegenation on his father.

Miscegenation, too, is a metaphor for the paternalistic past; African Americans no longer need white Americans. When discussing the intermarriage between an Englishman and a former slave, Louis says: "I do not think under the present condition of things there will be any general intermarrying of the races" (80). His reason for doubting that miscegenation will become common, referenced as "the present condition of things," suggests that rampant racism and ideas about racial difference (which to him are all "moonshine") and the failure among slaveholders and white society in general to repent for their collective sin maintain the "prejudices" and "customs" that uphold racial difference. Hence the only way to combat the customary racism of the white South is to vote down its practices. Louis's reluctance to believe that white Americans can repent for their racist past distinguishes his political position from Stanton and Anthony.

The renaming of amalgamation also marked a shift in racial politics. Miscegenation, defined by the journalist David Croly in 1864 as the "mingling of diverse races" leading to "legitimate unions between whites and blacks," was a heated political and social issue deployed by politicians and journalists to cause panic about African American demands for equality (65).[16] The panic over miscegenation infiltrated the official AERA newspaper, the *Revolution*—which was funded by a wealthy Kansas Democrat, George Train, infamous for his racism. Very different from Harper's "glorious revolution" of color-blindness, the AERA *Revolution*'s references to black male tyrants became a major symbol in the assertion of white women's rights. As Stanton explains in her missive "To Our Radical Friends," "Republicans and abolitionists were alike determined that woman's claim should be held in abeyance to that of the negro." It becomes clear that "woman" is implicitly white and under assault by the implicitly male "negro." Stanton defends her choice of white women's rights over the Fifteenth Amendment by suggesting that white women, unprotected by the vote, will become victims of enfranchised "negroes": "seeing that the women of virtue, wealth, and character in this country were to be made the subjects of every vicious, ignorant, degraded type of manhood, we unfurled the new banner to the breeze, 'immediate and unconditional enfranchisement for the women of the republic.'"

Stanton thus helped to create a dividing line between herself and black men as she ignored the concerns—or existence—of black women. Harper seems to have been equally disinterested in white women's rights. In both Harper and Stanton's 1869 writings, cross-racial relationships are dangerous and divisive. Just as references to the threat of miscegenation that results from white women's vulnerability to the "negro" pervade AERA rhetoric in the *Revolution*, Harper's writings in a black-owned newspaper, the *Christian Recorder*, also emphasize the evils of miscegenation. In Harper's case, however, this miscegenation was a continuation of the sexual depravity of slavery. White men, in Harper's examples, were the rapists, and black women the victims. This converse equation is also a demand for the vote; Harper demanded votes for black women so they could protect themselves from white male predators.

"I Will Help You Pay It"

For the most part, *Minnie's Sacrifice* tries to envision a new culture and move beyond the crimes of the past. Black mothers play a very important role in this cultural development, and their contributions to the upbuilding of the nation do not go unnoticed in the novel. Minnie and Louis discuss their indebtedness to their mothers, which parallels a national debt owed to the freed people for their labor. Descriptions of the freed people in the novel and in Harper's letters locate humanity and a very concrete, powerful understanding of freedom among former slaves. Similarly, Minnie learns how to become a black woman rather than imposing her white bourgeois background on her newfound family or the people she works among in the South. As both Minnie and Louis redirect their loyalty and commitment away from northern Republicans and white men, they are inspired, in many ways, by their black foremothers. Black women are the central characters in Harper's vision of the hope and danger offered by the Reconstruction South. The benefits of white society mean nothing to Minnie when compared to her loyalty to her mother and her moral conviction that society should judge all people equally, by character, regardless of poverty or their color. Her vision of an egalitarian society, one that Minnie enacts by her "resolution . . . to join the fortunes of my mother's race," cannot come to fruition if "I left her [my mother] unrecognized" (72).

Recognition for Minnie's mother has added significance in the decade when the United States finally recognized the independent nation of Haiti. Minnie's rejection of a decadent U.S. reform culture in the North in favor of a working black women's culture in the South recasts the Haitian influence that Carla Peterson notes in the novel. Cultivation, wealth, and refinement are critical terms in Minnie's statement; her dismissive gesture toward a society that is "cultivated, wealthy, or refined" calls to mind her father's Creole culture and also dismisses Stanton's cohort, who were very much part of that world and who claimed that identity very proudly in the *Revolution* (*Minnie's Sacrifice* 72).[17] But to emphasize that previously unrecognized aspect of the Creole character—the black woman who stood in the shadow of the decadent French or Spanish "gentleman"—is to redefine the place of unfree laborers of African descent in the New World. Looking at the other side of the Creole, a virtuous black citizen appears.

Recasting the image of the free people was no easy task. Like Harper, Parker Pillsbury traveled the Reconstruction South and wrote letters to his friends in the North, many of which the *Revolution* published. According to Stacey Robertson, Pillsbury's rhetoric (not unlike Louis's) reflected his perfectionism and anger with the Republican Party; since Republicans conceded to "compromise" with Andrew Johnson, Pillsbury felt they had effectively sold the prospect of equality and justice for blacks and women down the river (134–56). His proclaimed sympathy for the freed people's cause, however, did not prevent him from promulgating racist stereotypes to challenge the Fifteenth Amendment. The transformative relationship between a black male abolitionist and a white female suffragist had disintegrated into stereotypes of black male hypersexuality, and a mistress narrative of white feminism alienated black women. To add to this bleak picture, representations of the freed women published in the *Revolution* illustrate the dissonance between black and white reformers, another sign that their attempted union was a catastrophic failure.

Pillsbury's letters contrast remarkably with the letters that Harper sent to William Still and the *Christian Recorder* from the same places at the same time. While Harper extols wage labor, supports working women, and blames sexual discrepancies on white men rather than the myth of the sexually aggressive black female, Pillsbury speaks with great distaste for African Americans in the South. In one letter that is emblematic of his 1869 correspondence, he describes working black women who had "little on above the waist and nothing below the knees . . . doing day's works that not a white man in New England or New York could perform" (225). The descriptions of their attire disregard the reality of the oppressively hot working conditions in South Carolina fields as the implications of "scantily clad" point toward a lack of sexual virtue on the part of black women. By no means championing these scantily dressed laborers, he expresses disgust toward their ramshackle homes and personal hygiene. Forgetting AERA demands for equal pay for equal work and a fair wage, Pillsbury instead vilifies the freedwomen for their poverty despite their obvious hard work.

That the women perform work that would be impossible for white men in New England not only fails to inspire Pillsbury's respect, but he seems repulsed by their unladylike behavior. Pillsbury plays into the genre of folk comedy to depict black womanhood as crude, uncivilized, and unvirtuous (he reports that they not only refuse to marry, but also allegedly commit infanticide). In light of such perceived extreme difference between black and white women, particularly when moral purity served as a major argument for white woman suffrage, Pillsbury foresees no future in which votes for *black* women could be a reality. His hypocritical evaluation of South Carolina blacks concludes with a description of two black women waiting for a train: "One old woman laid her head in the lap of a younger one, and then a regular Ku Klux Klan search was instituted through it, with results, too, of which I need not speak" (225).

Particularly when Harper's letters, also from South Carolina, describe numerous scenes of mob violence incited by alleged sexual transgressions, it seems unthinkable for Pillsbury to joke about the Klan. Equating the ostensible vermin on an old woman's scalp with the more industrious and educated blacks subject to a Ku Klux Klan muster, Pillsbury dehumanizes black working women in South Carolina and connotes cleanliness and purification with the actions of the Ku Klux Klan as they comb the countryside looking for victims. While, in other writings, Pillsbury attempted to construct an empathetic stance toward suffering freed people, his rhetoric of taste in this piece resembles the "party line" of AERA members who supposedly champion poor women, and, through their mistress narrative, claim to support black women. Pillsbury's reference to "a regular Ku Klux Klan search" to describe what was probably an intimate scene of a younger woman braiding an older woman's hair also makes light of white-supremacist violence in the South. For Harper, of course, this was no joking matter.

As I mentioned above, a notable feature of the work ethic in Harper's letters and in *Minnie's Sacrifice* is an implied demand that the nation pay its dues to former slaves. Her challenge to the AERA reflects her commitment to labor and the idea that one merits citizenship through work rather than education or class status, yet she is equally concerned with what the nation owes African American citizens. Like Sojourner Truth, who downplays the significance of literacy as a voter qualification, Harper locates virtuous citizenship in the context of piety and hard work rather than cultural sophistication and elite education.[18] Minnie's work in the South and loyalty to the freed people informs her voice and her articulations of citizenship rights. She represents the future of a political body that recognizes the contributions of women as well as African Americans, although her tragic demise illustrates that the United States cannot see such a future without paying its debt to the black South.

Minnie and Louis identify a debt that they, and perhaps all Americans who benefited from slave labor, owe the freed people. The chapter immediately preceding Minnie's assertion that "I will help you pay it" is missing, but in all likelihood Louis tells Minnie that he must repay his debt to the black men and women whose work built his father's fortune and whose loyalty to the Union helped him escape the Confederacy (65). Her willingness to join him demonstrates that she wants to work rather than live the decadent lifestyle that Louis's background and inheritance affords. Since both were schooled in the North, they have the education that helps them forgo a life of leisure in favor of repaying their debt to the black South.

Just as Minnie dedicates her life to these responsibilities, Harper's letters offer ample heartening evidence of African American men and women who work side by side to purchase their own land and build self-sufficient families. The forgotten mothers of the South, furthermore, are black women whose agrarian, domestic, and reproductive labor built this interracial nation; thus, to them the nation is indebted. She models what Elsa Barkley Brown calls an "ethos of mutuality," a focus on the well-being of the community (one equally invested in men's and women's rights) that characterized black women's activism ("What" 298). While many white women sought equality through individual rights like the vote and equal status in the marriage contract, Harper considered land ownership, fair labor practices, and public safety as central issues in black men and women's civil rights.

The idea that Americans in general and middle-class blacks in particular had a debt to pay the freed people negates the mistress narrative's claim that white women were due rewards for "freeing the slaves."[19] While the *Revolution* heralds white women's reform efforts as the most significant "work" performed on behalf of former slaves, Harper offered an alternate vision of work and of the female worker. She believed that the changes required within the black community exceeded political transformation, and she advocated a vast cultural transformation in the black South, even urging middle-class northern blacks to emigrate and participate in building up of this new culture. Although "uplift" projects such as this often have a connotation of "Christianizing and civilizing" that perpetuates bourgeois ideals, Harper's idea of uplift in the South includes economic advancement for the freed people as well as for the northern blacks whose families have been free, sometimes, for generations.

In this sense, I would say she is inspired, not only by the memory of the Haitian Revolution, but by the recently recognized free black nation of Haiti and its agrarian workforce. Creating a majority African American culture in the South, she suggests, will improve the economic opportunities for northern émigrés, who might also have considered emigrating to Haiti.[20] In a letter to Henry Tanner written from South Carolina in August 1869, she asks: "Why couldn't some of our young men who will always be overshadowed in Philadelphia by the enterprise, wealth, and commercial activity which has got the start of them resolve that they will try their fortunes in some of these communities where our people are beginning to rise in the scale of life?" ("Letter").

Referring to the freed people in the South as "our people" despite the cultural and class differences between middle-class northerners and newly emancipated southerners, Harper envisions the communities of the South as places where racial and gender boundaries can be realigned. Not only can black businessmen improve their stakes and escape the shadow of the white majority in Philadelphia, black women can join in this work as equal partners. In "Truth Is Stranger than Fiction," a letter written from Mobile, Alabama, in 1871, Harper describes a particularly successful man whose "wife took on her hands about 130 acres of land, and with her force she raised about 107 bales of cotton" (Foster, *Brighter* 132). Adding 130 acres of land to the domestic sphere empowers this woman and betters her community, although the idea of a woman laboring to produce cotton received far less approbation in the *Revolution*. Celebrating her ability to work and create profit also reminds the reader of the tremendous financial contribution that unpaid African American labor made to the national economy before the war.

The novel states that the goals of self-sufficiency and freedom were within reach, for "the Reconstruction Act, by placing votes in the hand of the colored man, had given him a new position," not as tyrants, as was the case with enfranchised white men, but as companionate partners with wage-earning wives (74). As the novel attests, Harper viewed black male suffrage as a way to quell violence, ensure just pay for labor, and work toward universal equality; racial advancement likewise offered the conditions for African American women to rise to a position of power in the South. In reality, one cannot "go for sex" without recognizing its inseparability from race.

Harper's letters indicate that she spent most of her time during Reconstruction in the South and that, although she was in New York in May, she was back in South Carolina by August 1869.[21] She most likely attended the annual meeting of the AERA before returning to her work in the South and despite her busy writing schedule so she could participate in the debate over whether or not the AERA should endorse the Fifteenth Amendment to the U.S. Constitution. This debate reflected a pivotal moment not only in women's history, but in American history in general because the definition of citizenship was going through radical revision. A careful reading of *Minnie's Sacrifice*, which deals with issues almost identical to the ones Harper faced as an activist in the Reconstruction South, adds texture and nuance to Harper's loaded statement that "the white women all go for sex." The novel reverses the logic of Reconstruction sexual politics, rejecting the *possibility* that black men might become tyrants and recalling the fact that white men had, *in reality*, acted as sexual tyrants toward black women for hundreds of years. Roslyn Terborg-Penn, Louise Newman, and many other literary scholars and historians have gone to great lengths to locate and decipher the muffled black women's voices within the women's rights campaign; to this end, Harper's novel (combined with her letters and speeches) offers a rich field from which to mine insight into her political views and position as a black feminist during Reconstruction.

As *Minnie's Sacrifice* and Harper's personal correspondence suggest, gains for newly emancipated black women were stifled by sexual stereotypes and the discourse of dependency; in fact, the confluence of the two effectively denied black women's rights in the interest of placing the vote on a pedestal, accessible only to white women. The rhetoric of the *Revolution* in the period leading up to and immediately following the 1869 AERA meeting deployed the language of black hypersexuality as well as a discourse of black dependency to depict African Americans as incapable of self-government, thus less worthy of the vote than educated, bourgeois white women. Hence the radical break that Harper's main characters make from their white families in *Minnie's Sacrifice* very much symbolizes Harper's break from affiliations with the women of the AERA. Restored to her black mother, Minnie pivots away from reform efforts that require her proximity to her white "former friends." In its place, Harper imagines a new black community that is a nation within the nation. Rather than looking past the flesh to find an equal soul or imagining the commingling of black and white "blood" to create a radically egalitarian society, Harper pauses to consider the significance of African American embodiment. Blackness, in this historical context, signifies virtue, an honest labor ideology, free and flexible gender identities, and independence from the hypocrisy and contradictions of a nation built on slavery and the subordination of women. The project of historicizing Harper's fiction as well as her extant nonfiction enables us, nonetheless, to catch a glimpse of her political vision at the intersection of race, class, gender, and sexuality—an indispensable precursor to contemporary black feminist thought.

Conclusion

Un petit blanc, que j'aime,
En ces lieux est venu.
Oui oui c'est lui meme!
C'est lui! je l'ai vue!
Petit blanc! mon bon frère!
Ha! ha! petit blanc si doux!
—Lydia Maria Child, *Romance of the Republic*

AFTER THE CIVIL WAR, Lydia Maria Child attempted to convert the genre of tragedy—the tragic mulatta story that she helped shape in her short story "The Quadroons"—into a historical romance that resolved the problems of slavery. But as Frances Harper's *Minnie's Sacrifice* clearly articulates, the romantic ideals of racial and gender equality that inspired Julia Collins's Reconstruction optimism or Elizabeth Livermore's millennial Christian republicanism had little currency in a decade when the Ku Klux Klan formed, former abolitionists and suffragists went at one another's throats, and the nation reeled from the violence and destruction of a catastrophic war. There was little to romanticize about rebels, and, for more and more white writers and historians, the memory of the Haitian Revolution would become an object lesson in the consequences of civil war and the dangers of racial equality.

Perhaps what ushered the United States into the modern era—and marked the demise of American romanticism's quest for freedom—was the relative abandonment of antiracist work by white reformers. Elizabeth Cady Stanton invoked the myth of the black rapist; her cousin Gerrit Smith (who bankrolled a colony for John Brown and a community of free blacks in Upstate New York in the 1840s) recapitulated; and journalistic realism took the place of romantic idealism as a literary form. For this reason, the insidious racist images that romance and rebellion had challenged during the era of reform continued to evolve and thrive in a newly redefined white space.

The similarities between the 1860s and the second decade of the twenty-first century, furthermore, are eerie. Not unlike the infamous

New Yorker cover entitled *America's Worst Nightmare*, representations of Abraham Lincoln from the 1860s cast the president as an insurgent, an Islamic sympathizer, and a secret conspirator against the most "sacred" tenets of democracy. For example, a Confederate etching that was first printed in 1861 (and republished as late as 1890 in *Cosmopolitan*) features Lincoln in his office in stocking feet, one of which rests on the Constitution. The artwork surrounding him includes a portrait of "Ossawatomie" Brown and a landscape of "St. Domingo" that depicts naked Haitians sacrificing infants. Entitled *Writing the Emancipation Proclamation,* this visual image places the perceived race radicalism of the Civil War in an insurgent and international context. Several images in the same series depict black Union soldiers kidnapping and assaulting southern white women. These reactionary caricatures provide a dramatic counterpoint to the way that radical abolitionists imagined the Haitian Revolution, cross-racial coalitions, and Christian republicanism as symbols that could shape a postslavery United States culture of universal emancipation.[1]

By the 1860s, the romantic hero in Anglo-American fiction could no longer be a race rebel or, by any means, a woman. As J. Michael Dash has pointed out, Lydia Maria Child's *The Freedman's Book* (1865) presented an extremely pacifist version of Toussaint Louverture (*Haiti and the United States* 9). Child claims his "harshest action" was to execute his own nephew, General Moyse, for slaughtering whites (*Freedmen's* 55). More importantly, Toussaint "knew that the freedom of his race depended on their good behavior after they were emancipated" (56). This post-Emancipation pedagogy of passivity reemerges in 1867. Child's *Romance of the Republic* subtly invokes the gothic and dark memories of the Haitian Revolution, but quells those dark images of the past with the intervention of benevolent and reliable white heroes. The story begins in the 1840s in New Orleans and seems to whisper a didactic message. The epigraph of this conclusion, "Un petit blanc, que j'aime," is a song that the almost-tragic mulatta Flora sings to a suitor. It subtly and perhaps even inadvertently reminds the reader of the dangers of integrating the Caribbean past into the historical romance of North and South. Described by the novel's hero, Alfred King, as a song from the "French West Indies" about a "young negress" who falls in love with a white man, the fact that this white man is a "petit blanc" makes the song far more ominous (31). Flora, an "octoroon" and technically a "negress" herself, sings the song in a manner described as "roguish" and "mercurial" if not devilish or bewitching (17, 19, 72).

As Child and her abolitionist contemporaries well knew, there was not much love lost between mulattos and petit blancs. The passage of "republican" laws in prerevolutionary Haiti that deprived free blacks of many forms of public employment privileged petit blancs and ushered them into the labor market at the expense of free black men. The term "petit blanc," even when conjured by the "bewitching" Flora, has a dangerous history; the idea of a romance between a negress and a petit blanc is essentially a premonition of doom. The mischief of a "negress" who loves a "petit blanc" is a reminder of inequality and the dangers of cross-racial union, even if no one overtly reminds the singer that she is a "black sheep" (910). Benevolent white Americans rescue Flora. While not as obviously connected to her insurgent Haitian ancestry as her maid, who answers the door and serves tea in a "bright turban" (a headdress that became fashionable in prerevolutionary Haiti when proud mulatta women were forbidden to wear hats), Flora clearly embodies the enticing, exotic, yet irrepressible sexuality of the beautiful white-looking black woman.

But this is not to say that images of cross-racial romance and rebellion against injustice, or even the racially amalgamated hero or heroine, disappear from the literatures of the Americas. In a more heroic aspect, the danger and power of Flora's amalgamated sexuality resurfaces at the turn of the century, when Alice Dunbar Nelson's dark-eyed (racially ambiguous) Creole Manuela seeks aid from the "Wizened One" (8), an elderly woman whose charms and spells enable her to lure her beloved away from the blue-eyed Claralie. In Pauline Hopkins's *Contending Forces*, the idea of romance contends, once again, with racial and sexual inequality. The only feminine force more powerful than the enchantments of racially ambiguous heroines like Sappho Clark is the "turbaned" New Orleans priestess, Madame Frances. As the root of Sappho's hidden origins, Madam Frances, or Aunt Sally, retains the knowledge and traditions of New Orleans and of Sappho's amalgamated past.

In Hopkins's and Dunbar's work, furthermore, we find a transnational, often mystical aspect. They literally conjure what José David Saldívar calls "oppositional codes" (7). Hopkins's codes convert the romantic idealism of the nineteenth century (the hallmark, according to Saldívar, of José Martí's work as well) into the secret history of resistance—converging the worlds of voodoo, spiritualism, and anti-imperialism. The superstitions of Charles Chesnutt's *Tales of Conjure and the Color Line* provide a source of hidden power not unlike that which appears in Alejo Carpentier's work fifty years or so later, or even in

Ntozake Shange's work one hundred years later (a connection Saldívar originally drew as well).

Even in ostensibly realistic African American fiction, the discourse of resistance emerges from its rebellious roots. While Minnie, Harper's octoroon heroine, meets her death in an encounter with the Ku Klux Klan, the focus on the freed people who mourn her passing suggests that her spirit, like John Brown's, goes marching on. Among Harper's literary progeny—Thomas Fortune, Chesnutt, Hopkins, and W. E. B. Du Bois, an insurrectionary tradition continued in United States literature just as it prevailed in the work of Martí, José Rizal, and other opponents of American exceptionalism.[2]

Indeed, African American print culture and an ongoing familiarity with the de facto struggles for freedom and equality in the Caribbean provided the real enlightenment in the era of reform and continued to do so thereafter. As Scott Bradfield argues: "Europeans never found a 'free space' in the New World because they took too many Old World stories along with them to light the way. By presuming to 'transgress' European laws and traditions, Americans acted out a story originally generated by class conflict in Europe" which amounts to a "transatlantic recoding" of the "conceptual meaning of transgression" (xiii). The quest, essentially, gets recoded as a clash with the landscape or wilderness or with Native Americans. Bradfield, like Michael Davitt Bell, studies the usual subjects—Charles Brockden Brown, Cooper, and Poe primarily, omitting Hawthorne, Irving, and Melville. Perhaps the canonization of these figures has to do with their implicit or explicit support of the regime of whiteness, which is why my critical attention is focused, for the most part, on the noncanonical.

Yet if American literature has become the literatures of the Americas—and if our greatest living writers include Nobel Prize winners Toni Morrison, Derek Walcott, and Gabriel Garcia Márquez—then the noncanonical has certainly struck back at the empire. Each carries on the work of romance and rebellion in a variety of ways, always positioning the complexity of love in dialogue with the reality of oppression and violence, always rebelling against the national or cultural borders of knowledge. If the story of the Haitian Revolution, or of Harriet Jacobs's attempt to negotiate equality through cross-racial love, or the geographic mobility and equally expansive imagination of Livermore's Zoë do not still inform and influence a hemispheric, egalitarian longing for freedom in this New World, then it is difficult to understand what makes literature great.

As I was finishing this book, I read Isabel Allende's 2010 novel, *Island beneath the Sea*. This historical romance both depicts the realities of unfreedom that still exist in the world and magically realizes the radical freedom that spirit and imagination avail. Allende's twenty-first-century novel transports her biracial eighteenth-century heroine, Zarité, from slavery in revolutionary Haiti to the relative liberty of a free person of color in New Orleans. Zarité prevails because she knows how to conjure a glimpse of the freedom that resides in her spirit and enact it in the world. Like Harriet Jacobs, she rebels against and eventually escapes the abusive sexual power of her white master. At the same time, however, she understands that the process of freedom in the New World is an ongoing one; she abandons white space to forge an imaginary domain, one where Erzulie's powers reign and her a priori knowledge of freedom and natural right fortify her soul and move her body. Allende's representation of this Haitian woman in this historical moment—after the catastrophic 2010 earthquake—refutes the images of helplessness and despair that so many in the United States and beyond have wrongly accepted as the natural state of hopeless Haiti.

If Allende's story represents a pervasive connection between the Caribbean and the United States and depicts Haitians with dignity and spirit, her depictions of colonizers might also force the privileged to consider their complicity in the situation. Like Allende, Martí, Du Bois, and Hopkins, the main authors in this book should change the way we think about American literatures, perhaps even inspiring our protest against American exceptionalism today. What Gustavo Pérez Firmat has described as a generic approach to hemispheric literary studies—one that uses "as a point of departure a broad, abstract notion of wide applicability" (3)—seems to link nineteenth-century African American writers like Harriet Jacobs to Allende, thus placing them on points in a literary web that also includes Alejo Carpentier, Cirilo Villaverde, and Lydia Child as well as Harper, Hopkins, and Alice Dunbar-Nelson. In such a web, the materialism that construes realistic readings of miscegenated texts, those marked by what Eduardo González calls "American theriomorphia," opens up a "spectral rapport with romantic ideology" (Pérez Firmat 180). But this is not the romanticism of Coleridge—it is one whose mysticism inspires direct action; it is the radical potential of Dutty Boukman's soul reincarnated in the imagination and relived in the actions of those who sanctify the ongoing process of freedom.

Whether the link between Allende and Jacobs is generic or genetic, there is certainly an appositional confluence (Pérez Firmat 4) of concerns about threats to bodily integrity, its geographic parallel with the invasive creation of white space, and the longing for freedom that is both a desire for geographic mobility and the right to choose whom one will love. Like the other nineteenth-century women authors discussed but also like Allende's Zarité, Jacobs's quest for freedom from racial and gender restrictions leads her to precarious romantic relationships and dangerous journeys through white space. Yet she also seeks a home outside of white space by any means necessary. Her narrative begins with a family history wherein her emancipated grandmother seeks refuge from Anglo-America in Spanish Florida and ends with her incomplete quest for freedom in the supposedly emancipated North. Similarly, Avellaneda's hero and heroine venture from the plantation to indigenous villages in the Cuban countryside, where they participate in the mythology of the conquered population, and also visit cities where they engage with the capitalist culture of Anglo-American émigrés. Livermore's quadroon heroine makes a circum-Atlantic voyage from St. Croix to Denmark, then to England, and back across the Atlantic to Mobile, Havana, Kingston, Barbados, and home to St. Croix before she ascends to heaven with her Jewish lover. Collins's characters move, generation by generation, up and down the Mississippi from New Orleans to New England, amalgamating the Creole South with the Anglo North. Although Harper and Child ultimately mourn the passing of these romantic and revolutionary ideals and shift into the realism that would prevail until the century's end, their requiem for a moment of radical potential, with Haiti at its epicenter and cross-racial union as its goal, preserves the romantic, rebellious, amalgamated, and ever-expanding beauty of the ideal.

Notes

Preface

1. Of course, other scholars have emphasized the impact of the Haitian Revolution on American culture. As Eric Sundquist says of the era of reform, "especially in the wake of Nat Turner's uprising in 1831 and the emancipation of slaves in British Jamaica in the same year, Haiti came to seem the fearful precursor of black rebellion throughout the New World" (32). Alan Gilbert's work, *Black Patriots and Loyalists*, also establishes the presence of large numbers of African American soldiers in the War of Independence.

2. I want to emphasize that I take the term "amalgamation" to have primarily cultural meanings as I use it in this study, much as Monica Kaup and Debra Rosenthal stipulate in *Mixing Race, Mixing Culture*.

3. While other books, such as Suzanne Bost's *Mulattas and Mestizas* (2003), Jennifer Brody's *Impossible Purities* (1998), and Elise Lemire's *"Miscegenation"* (2002) have considered the way representations of interracial relationships reflect the political milieu in which they are produced, the connection between these relationships, or "romances," and stories of rebellion has not been explored or explained, nor has the role of geographic expansion.

4. Amalgamation, because it invokes the presence of white women and African Americans in the production of national subjects, contributes to pluralistic political philosophy and critique of liberal democracy as the exclusive purchase of white men. In *The Spirit of the Laws*, Andrew Fraser summarizes Hannah Arendt, explaining: "By acting and speaking together, we disclose our identity and establish a web of relationships with other persons. It is through action and speech that . . . the identity of the human agent is revealed. . . . Each person needs to act and speak in order to distinguish himself from others. That distinction would be impossible without a fundamental equality between persons" (177).

5. Neither Hawthorne nor any of the authors chosen for this book follow Choate's prescription for historical romance. As Emily Budick points out, "American historical romance . . . recognizes that words and events cannot

possess determinate meanings" (200). Similarly, Michael Davitt Bell uses the term "radical romance" to address "the question of meaning—of its status in relation to verbal artifice [which]—is of course crucial to any discussion of literary art . . . with its dissociation of rational "reality" and imaginative language" (107).

6. According to Leslie Rabine, "the traditional romantic quest narrative, which puts at its center the development of a single, individual hero, and which rests on strongly end-oriented, rationally ordered, monolinear chains of cause and effect, provides the conceptual form in which history is thought to happen" (3). In this vein, the editors of *Doubled Plots: Romance and History* look for feminist romances that challenge the master narrative of history—they "explore the ways in which all discourses of romance—the seemingly subjective, sentimental, and private—and history—the seemingly objective compendium of public fact—are implicated in and vitally necessary to each other." The book "represents the necessary next step in theorizing the functions, constructions, and interpenetrations of romance and historical plotting" (Carden and Strehle xxv).

7. Michael Davitt Bell argues that romantic heroes are often in a quest to find a home, which is particularly significant when we consider the dispossessed status of heroic figures like Frederick Douglass or Harriet Jacobs.

8. Although I don't discuss Hawthorne, Melville, or Poe in this book, recent scholarship has noted their innovations in the romance genre. Far from embodying typical romantic heroes, as Douglas Anderson points out, some of the male protagonists in Hawthorne's stories convey a "complex emotional response" to the unique moral and historical dilemma" of Hawthorne's generation (33).

Introduction

1. As president, nonetheless, Adams would sign the 1799 Toussaint Clause into law, an act that the diplomatic historian Gordon Brown explains "opened up a period of unparalleled cooperation between the U.S. government and a rebel regime, amounting to de facto recognition" (151). Perhaps motivated more by the lucrative trade with Saint-Domingue from which the merchants of Boston, Philadelphia, or Charleston profited than by a recognition of black sovereignty, Adams's foreign policy, according to Brown, eventually cost him the presidency. Thomas Jefferson, alternately, wrote to Alexander Hamilton: "We may expect therefore black crews, & supercargoes & missionaries thence into the southern states. . . . If this combustion can be introduced among us under any veil whatever, we have to fear it" (qtd. in Brown 148).

2. I am thinking about Silvio Torres-Saillant's extensive work on Caliban in this reference as well. Torres-Saillant makes the point that, by imagining Caliban only as a romantic hero, "we cannot remain unmindful about the deleterious effect of allowing the trope of 'romance' to guide the logic of our remembering" (206). I use the term "Caliban" as synecdoche, in this case, to anticipate the

potential for rebellion in the Caribbean, the response to the colonial discourses of white space.

3. Michael Bennett's study of "the various democratic discourses unleashed by black and white radical abolitionists" that "were woven into antebellum U.S. culture" draws, as I do, from Carroll Smith-Rosenberg's use of the term. Her Bakhtinian analysis supposes that "divergent, at times conflicting, narratives and imagery will proliferate as marginal social groups, speaking the 'language' of their experiences, challenge their culture's 'traditional' discourse" ("Writing" 35).

4. Notably, in "Romance and Real Estate," Walter Benn Michaels addresses the relationship between a fantasy of inalienable property and Hawthorne's musings on the romance genre. See also Jan Cohn.

5. The reason for including both kinds of representations is one that John Ernest describes in *Liberation Historiography*. The project of "African American historical writing, even more than national histories written by white historians in the age of national self-definition, would need to identify the terms of its own existence—asking what it might mean to write a history of African Americans, defining the African American community both with and against the terms used by white Americans by which African Americans found themselves with common experiences set off from but fundamental to the white national story" (40). I think historical romances work in a similar way, as does some women's history.

6. John Stauffer, quoting John Thomas's seminal essay "Romantic Reform in America," writes: "'Accepting for the most part Emerson's dictum that one man was a counterpoise to a city, the transcendentalists turned inward to examine the divine self and find there the material with which to rebuild society' (Thomas 671). The turn inward and the emergence of a modern self represented a precondition for reform. A modern self certainly did not have to lead to reform, but all romantic radicals exhibited traits of a modern self. . . . The degree to which romantic radicals were able to dismantle the various dualisms that had traditionally provided a source of order, structure, and hierarchy to society paralleled the degree to which they were able to escape the dualism of the social control paradigm" ("Beyond Social Control" 239).

1. "What Mischief Would Follow?"

1. See "Wendell Phillips to Ralph Waldo Emerson," Beinecke Library. The unnamed volumes were delivered to Phillips by Benjamin Hunt, a Harvard schoolmate of Emerson who would publish *A Plea for Hayti* in 1853. This text advocated both the geographical amalgamation of the New World through annexation of Haiti and the biological amalgamation of black and white citizens to expand the mulatto population and diminish the various differences between black and white. Hunt was engaged in profitable commercial enterprises in Port au Prince. I have not identified a specific set of volumes about

Haiti that fit Phillips's description, but Hunt donated a collection of volumes about the West Indies to the Boston Public Library in 1877 (see George Willis Cooke, *An Historical and Biographical Introduction to Accompany the Dial* 179). Considering Phillips's eventual use of Haiti as a model of equality, particularly his 1861 speech "Toussaint L'Ouverture," the fact that Waldo introduced him to material about the island is remarkable.

2. *Freedom's Journal*, known as the first African American newspaper and published in New York in 1827, featured many articles about Haiti's history and present condition. James McCune Smith, a New York doctor and journalist, published his own lecture on Haiti in pamphlet form in 1841. In the late 1850s, authors including Theodore Holly published material about Haiti in the *Anglo-African Magazine*. James Redpath, Franklin Sanborn, Elizur Wright, and Hunt would also publish volumes about Haiti in the 1850s and early 1860s.

3. In addition to Leon Higginbotham, Teresa Zackodnik's recent work goes into great detail about the expansion of antimiscegenation laws in the United States from the seventeenth to the nineteenth century.

4. Sexton's focus is primarily on the contemporary world—on how the idea of "multiracialism" provides an easy erasure of the history of the one-drop rule and the construction of blackness through violence and coercion. As Saidiya Hartman notes, the violent and sexually exploitative history of slavery provides an allegory of the present. The myth of blackness as absence of self-sovereignty prevails in caricature-like representations of blackness; Sexton lists, for example, "coddled criminals," "welfare queens," and the like (7). Patricia Hill Collins's work also illustrates the contemporary currency of biological constructions of racialized sexuality.

5. Edgar Allen Poe's story "The Ragged Mountains," which features a fantastic flashback to the insurrection and massacre in Bengal, and Senator William Seward's reference to Edmund Burke's 1794 speech on the Impeachment of Warren Hastings in his famous 1851 "Higher Law" speech, which condemned the governor of Bengal's alleged tyranny toward colonial subjects, evidence a critical stance toward Britain's colonial policies throughout the empire.

6. Critics such as Russ Castronovo and Dana Nelson have elaborated on the ideological construction of a masculinist, Anglo-American nation and on certain authors' resistance to it. While amalgamation plays a role in these constructions, particularly because it (to use Lauren Berlant's language) "expose[s] the unsettled and unsettling relations of sexuality and American citizenship— two complexly related sites of subjectivity, sensation, affect, law, and agency" ("Queen of America" 560), a solely national model of citizenship belies the transnational interests of these texts. Whether the very idea of sexuality was wedded to a sense of belonging within the nation obscures the question of how some writers may have envisioned the nation, not as we know it now, but as a synergistic circum-Atlantic entity encompassing far more of the Caribbean and perhaps even Latin America, but not necessarily in an imperialist context.

Although John Carlos Rowe identifies "internal colonialism" as a distinctive feature of Anglo-masculine nationalism and incipient imperialism, is it not possible that the people who perceived themselves as constituents of those "internal colonies" envisioned a different future? As Levine argues, furthermore, "writers of the past can be just as knowing about their culture" and able to critique its "Anglo-Saxon whiteness"; there was not necessarily a "white" literary nationalism (or, I would add, nationality) that "was uncritically accepted by all whites" (*Dislocating* 2, 6).

7. See also Matthew Clavin, who notes that abolitionists "marginaliz[ed] the role of Dessalines and other rebel leaders, as well as the nameless and faceless black masses" in favor of creating an image of Toussaint as a "Great Man, a slave who compared favorably to other Great Men of the Age of Revolution" ("Race, Rebellion" 2; "A Second" 118). This is not to say that Toussaint really was saintlike; recently, Philippe Girard has depicted him as an ambitious emancipated slaveholder bent on his own self-preservation, willing to use force to put former slaves back to work, and as ready to strike deals with the slaveholding British as he was to foil plans for insurrection on other islands. According to Laurent Dubois, "committed to defending liberty at all costs, Louverture had turned himself into a dictator, and the colony he ruled over into a society based on social hierarchy, forced labor, and violent repression" (250).

8. I think the images of Charles's lecture remained in Ralph Waldo's mind, though dormant, throughout the latter's career. In 1844, Ralph Waldo revived his deceased brother's arguments on immediate emancipation, which Len Gougeon summarizes as knowledgeable quotes "from various works dealing on emancipation in the West Indies" followed by an approving reference "to Toussaint, the liberating hero of St. Domingo, as a symbol of the worthy spirit of the black race" (see Gougeon 27). Ralph Waldo and Charles were particularly close during the time period when Charles was working on the antislavery lecture. According to Ronald Bosco and Joel Myerson, they roomed together as they embarked on their lecturing careers and planned to create a family compound, their "Arcadia," where they could raise their children when each married (see *The Emerson Brothers* 172–73).

9. As Susan Belasco points out: "Martineau's Toussaint slowly began to serve as a model for the members of the Transcendentalist circle as well as many other Americans involved in the antislavery movement during the 1840's (180). This model, however, had rather complicated dimensions, and one aspect of it revealed the fear of violent confrontation. As George F. Tyson has argued, white abolitionists were much more inclined to view the middle of Toussaint's career with enthusiasm and ignore the beginning (when Toussaint was actively involved in the bloody rebellion)" (183). Focusing on Toussaint as the embodiment of abstract ideals of freedom glorifies the Haitian event, participating in what Elizabeth Rauh Bethel calls the "Haytian myth" (832)—a romanticized representation of its liberatory ideals.

10. Emerson was familiar with both aspects of the story of the ongoing civil war in Haiti that began as a massive slave insurrection in 1791. The favorable aspect focused on how Toussaint joined insurgents and the Spanish side against France in 1793, switched sides in 1794 when the French Assembly declared emancipation, was appointed governor-general in 1797, and was deported to France in 1802. The less favorable aspect focused on how Dessalines declared independence from France in 1804, followed by the massacre of the remaining white colonists. From 1807 to 1820, the island nation was split in at least two hostile factions (North and South) and sometimes four. It occupied neighboring Santo Domingo from 1822 to 1844 and was not officially recognized by the United States until 1862.

11. Some reformers showed an interest in biological amalgamation as a political strategy. Ralph Waldo Emerson and Child first applied the idea of moral sentiment to political decisions by pleading on the behalf of Native Americans. Child's historical novel *Hobomok* (1824) suggests what Carolyn Karcher calls "the possibility of reconciling Indian and white through a marriage of cultures," a theme that recurs in Child's abolitionist work (xv). Ralph Waldo surmised, in his 1838 "Letter to Martin Van Buren," that the African, like the Cherokee, could assimilate, endeavoring to "redeem their own race . . . to borrow and domesticate in the tribe the inventions and the customs of the Caucasian race" (*Antislavery* 2).

12. A belief in inherited and immutable racial characteristics drove the concept of race science, which invoked the supposed authority of reason and knowledge to categorize human beings in a hierarchy of progress and potential; one of its tenets touted a system of moral development that further justified the subordination and exploitation of African and Native Americans, in particular, whose alleged propensity for violence or lasciviousness required constant vigilance on the part of whites. What A. Leon Higginbotham calls a legal "discourse of inferiority" converted this obsession with flesh into the word of law. Race science supported the economic interests of chattel slavery for a variety of reasons: it correlated supposed physical attributes with human suitability for different kinds of agricultural, mechanical, and reproductive labor; it tied those physical attributes to mental or intellectual propensities for learning, self-government, and cultural production; and it created a specter of the black body that required surveillance and control, as Charles Emerson describes, in light of the black propensity for violence and hypersexual behavior (see Higginbotham, *Shades of Freedom*).

13. Sibylle Fischer recounts Boisrond Tonnerre's notorious statement about penning the Haitian declaration of independence when the Haitian generals, including Dessalines, proclaimed their official break from France (202).

14. "From Hayti," *Vermont Gazette*, 23 March 1830, 1.

15. See "Important from Hayti," *Pittsfield Sun*, 25 July 1844, 3. Other reports in New England newspapers indicate that Haiti was a test case of sorts

in emancipation and free labor. While Charles and Waldo were adamant about the moral benefits of emancipation, their contemporaries debated whether free labor ideology applied to people of African descent and offered a viable economic system for the U.S. South. The potential for blacks to participate in building U.S. "civilization" is implicitly denied in an 1831 report that "Port-au-Prince, which was once the most flourishing city in the Western hemisphere, is now almost desolate, and the poverty and misery, which exist in its present ruinous condition, are a strong proof of the effect of free labor in the Colonies" (see "Rebellion in Hayti," *Farmer's Cabinet,* 23 April 1831, 2). Discussions of the suitability of blacks to citizenship often lapse into images of cross-racial marriage. In Richmond, Virginia, a harangue of British abolitionists notes that they condemn "American repugnance" toward "what they call 'amalgamation' —but we take the liberty of doubting whether [they] would willingly bestow [their] own sister in marriage upon the most polished specimen of the negro race . . . Comte Marmalade, or Marquis de Molasseville at the Court of Hayti" (see "National Gazette," *Richmond Enquirer* 13 November 1835, 4).

2. Colored Carpenters and White Gentlemen

1. All information about Kingsley is drawn from Daniel Stowell's extensive research on both Zephaniah and Anna Jai, which is published in *Balancing Evils Judiciously.*

2. This strategic narration reflects the religious worldview and political aspirations of the 1850s more than the desire of a young girl in the 1820s to escape slavery. Jacobs published *Incidents* pseudonymously, using the name Linda Brent. The fictionalization of names—Brent for Jacobs, Sands for Sawyer (the white man who fathered her children), and Flint for Norcom (her despicable master)—does more than protect the identity of the characters. Renaming her subjects signifies a sense of narrative control over them and the opportunity to retell the story truly but strategically, attenuating both the potential and the failure of radical romance to usher in racial and gender equality.

3. According to Cornell, narrative acts empower people to reclaim their bodies from the public sphere of social proscription. Her assertion that "the chance to become a person is dependent on the imagined projection of one's self as whole" in terms of reproductive and sexual rights in this century corresponds with Jacobs's right to love whomever she chooses (*Imaginary Domain* 35).

4. Carla Kaplan questions the actual subversive value of Brent's "desperate plunge" into a relationship with Sands and her self-willed incarceration in the tiny garret. While Kaplan characterizes Jacobs as a skeptic who has little faith in an "ideal reader," a white northern woman who will be transformed by reading her narrative, her argument that "Jacobs' presumption seems to be that narration lacks power" (94) omits one of the most stunning aspects of the text: the veritable moral manipulation of the white male in the form of Jacobs's strategic juxtaposition of the carpenter, Sawyer, and Norcom. She takes it upon herself to

name her persecutors in the public realm of literature and thereby exerts control over them.

5. Jennifer Rae Greeson also considers *Incidents* from the perspective of the 1850s. Greeson, however, notes Jacobs's use of the term "degradation" and the way it resonates in urban gothic fiction, particularly reform stories that emphasize the sexual exploitation of women in American cities (276).

6. As Frances Smith Foster points out, "It was only after the Compromise of 1850 created the Fugitive Slave Law, which made it possible for slave owners to claim individuals as their private property even in states where slavery was illegal, that Jacobs agreed to publicize some of her most personal experiences" ("Resisting *Incidents*" 61). Jacobs "used her own experience to create a book that would correct and enlist support against prevailing social myths and political ideologies" (62) about black promiscuity and Anglo-American moral superiority.

7. Gerrit Smith, who was also Elizabeth Cady Stanton's cousin, refused to join Stanton's movement because he felt that women, although entitled to equal rights through religious and constitutional ideals, were unsuited to independence: "not high-souled enough to consent to those changes and sacrifices in themselves . . . essential to the attainment of this vital object" (Gerrit Smith to Elizabeth C. Stanton, n.p.). Jacobs proves otherwise. Unlike Collins, however, she does not make extensive gestures toward including white women in her articulation of women's rights.

8. Karen Sánchez-Eppler credits "feminist-abolitionist discourse" with "a conception of the corporeality of the self" (48). This corporeal feminist and abolitionist Christianity takes on great significance in Jacobs's work. She makes it clear that she, and her children, have hybrid bodies, but rather than be devastated by her black "blood," Jacobs incorporates the fraught scene of the relationship between her white male grandfathers and black female grandmothers; unlike in Stowe or Child's work, where discovering black ancestry devastates the "tragic mulatta" heroine, Jacobs accepts the unfortunate circumstance of her white ancestry but never represents herself or the other women in her family as victims of rape. Franny Nudelman argues that "Abolitionist depictions of the tragic mulatta provide the paradigmatic instance of how the abused body reveals collective sin . . . the only action that the female slave is capable of . . . is the revelation of her victimization" (946–47). Jacobs's body, however, is not marked by "collective" sin, nor does her master have the right to accuse her of sin; she casts the sin and shame upon white men. In radical contrast to Stowe's understanding of respectability—which, according to Gillian Brown, characterized female sexual virtue in terms of a "spiritual, bodiless existence"—Jacobs describes a corporeal Christianity, one that accounts for women as sexual beings as it recognized the specifically interracial sexual activity that characterized American society (64).

9. Robert Stepto has challenged *Incidents'* "subversive" qualities on the grounds that it was written, supposedly, for a white abolitionist audience and

a potential cadre of northern sympathizers. Considering that "northern sympathizers" such as Livermore and Ralph Waldo Emerson also engaged in the active construction of an ideal social and political world, however, suggests that whiteness, or association with it, does not negate subversiveness. Hazel Carby argues: "Novels of black women should be read not as passive representations of history but as active influence within history . . . not only determined by the social conditions within which they were produced but also as cultural artifacts which shape the social conditions they enter" (95). The practice of altering conventional narratives of race, gender, and civic virtue was indispensable to black feminist writers. For example, Sandra Gunning points out that Ida B. Wells's "goal was to call into question white supremacist narratives of nation, history, and community by providing an alternative reading of events for the purpose of influencing public opinion" (*Red Record* 8). The imagined infiltration into the psyche of the white gentleman, men who were very often community leaders and demagogues of civic virtue, provided for black women a vehicle to reshape and render more inclusive the definition of responsible citizenship. The theorist Nancy Harstock suggests that the critical project that bridges personal experience with political power continues into the twentieth century. "When the various minority experiences have been described and when the significance of these experiences as a ground for critique of the dominant institutions and ideologies of society is better recognized," writes Harstock, "we will have at least the tools to begin to construct an account of the world sensitive to the realities of race and gender as well as class." (172).

10. A. Leon Higginbotham cites an 1855 case regarding an enslaved woman named Celia who was hung for murdering her master in an attempt to stop him from raping her. The court found that she, as property, had no right to self-defense. Indeed, the court could not imagine Celia's concept of "self" as legal subject; her legally invisible concept of "self" explains the legal denial of her bodily integrity (100). For Jacobs, in the aftermath of this case, to imagine her "self" as proud, defiant, and righteous is in itself a radical act of narration.

11. As Dana Nelson notes, white males (particularly the president) symbolically embody democracy right up until the Civil War ("Representative/Democracy" 225). Barkley Brown's scholarship on concepts of freedom within black women's political history also points out that demands for equality and citizenship significantly rewrite the republican male image, exceeding the parameters of "conceptualizations of republican representative government and liberal democracy" ("To Catch" 127).

3. Desire, Conquest, and Insurrection in Gertudis Gómez de Avellaneda's *Sab*

1. Like Margaret Fuller, Avellaneda used literature and everyday life to assert and pursue her personal desires, both intellectual and sexual. Avellaneda's autobiography, for example, is written in epistolary form and narrates

her rather unconventional behavior. The autobiography was originally a series of letters to a young man with whom she was in love; it describes her refusal to marry the man her family chose for her, her frustration with the male-centered literary world, and her goal of wooing and winning the young man to whom the letters are addressed. Although this particular love affair did not work out, Avellaneda (like Fuller) later had an illegitimate child with another lover. One of the unique characteristics of *Sab* and *The Autobiography* is the way Avellaneda exceeds the socially proscribed limits of the female intellect and imagination to argue for a sexually desiring and embodied subjectivity for herself and her heroine.

2. As Fischer illustrates, the act of conceptualizing the Haitian Revolution as a political moment of revolutionary antislavery makes a radical difference in how we understand the history of the Americas. Sundquist writes: "San Domingo thus offered both a distilled symbolic impression of the legacy of the American and French Revolutions, a realization of the Rights of Man, and a fearful prophecy of black rebellion throughout the New World" (141).

3. Debra Rosenthal's work is one of the first to approach the topics of mestizaje, indianismo, race mixing, and the mulatta in a hemispheric context (5–6, 14, 19–26). She explores white American and Latin American literature to argue that "racial hybridity can be situated at the heart of the literature of the Americas" (1). She also reads *Sab* as antiracist rather than antislavery, but she sees Sab's insurgent desires as dangerous rather than exciting to the narrator (78, 88). Rosenthal cites Fivel-Démoret, who points out that Avellaneda "established the causal relation between white oppression and black aggression" as a cautionary tale rather than an expression of desire for radical change (qtd. in Rosenthal 78).

4. Doris Sommer's foundational readings of *Sab* illustrate that Sab stands in for Avellaneda, in many ways, and that both represent the national identity of Cuba. Characterized, in part, as a "spiritual mimesis," Sommer's reading of the merger between author and protagonist results in the conception of a new Cuba "through their shared productive function, their literary labor" (114–15).

5. Susan Kirkpatrick elucidates Avellaneda's use of romantic paradigms of subjectivity to construct a female self who is representable, a lyrical "I" who could "portray socially oppressed subjectivity" (147).

6. According to Carolina Alzate Cadavid, critics often talked about Avellaneda as if she were a male. Her identification with a male protagonist whose maleness reflects her literary desire coincides with the socially acceptable canvas on which Avellaneda might project her sexual desire due to his race.

7. By the 1850s, as W. Caleb McDaniel illustrates, polite society, including Harriet Beecher Stowe, saw radical abolitionists as "crazy, promiscuous, and wild" because they believed in racial integration (129). The significance of a culture of manners and respectability among reformers made representations of radical romance, depicted as consensual cross-racial love, scandalous.

8. *Lugarto* seems to have some plot and character elements in common with French novelist Joseph Marie Eugène Sue's *Mathilde, Memoirs d'une jeune femme* (1845), a revenge novel, although the character of Lugarto does not appear.

4. Republicanism and Soul Philosophy in Elizabeth Livermore's *Zoë*

1. The last issue of the *Independent Highway* lists Livermore's address as the home of a rabbi who led a large Jewish congregation in Cincinnati. It is possible that she, like Zoë, found love with a Jewish man. This would explain "Mrs. Livermore's" disappearance from the public world.

2. Similarly, Stauffer's narrative of the emergence of the Radical Abolition Party in 1855 outlines a "Bible Politics," a term that Smith and McCune Smith often used to "characterize their belief that the government of God and earthly states should be one in the same" (*Black Hearts* 11).

3. According to the U.S. Senate website, Seward's pathetic oratory technique emptied the galleries within twenty minutes, but the arguments of the document itself gained immediate public popularity and notoriety: "Within three weeks, more than 100,000 pamphlet copies were distributed, with roughly an equal number reprinted in newspapers throughout the country" (Seward, *Classic*).

4. Extracted from its colonizationist context, this looks very much like Livermore's definition of the "Feminines," discussed below. Keeping in mind Mrs. Pumpkin's stipulation that this civilization comprises the very best of men and women, black and white, however, the chaos of racial meaning in the 1850s comes forth. Can we call something romantic racialism or reject its feminizing associations when we have been told by the author that the category is not specific to race or sex?

5. Their story, however, is as reminiscent of Moses as it is of Jesus. As Eddie Glaude illustrates, the Exodus story took on a secular function in African American political writing: "The ritualization of the story in African American political culture represented a set of common interests arrayed against particular interests: their natural right of liberty and equality against the racial order of American society" (81). Livermore seems well aware of this significance.

6. Unlike Livermore, Swisshelm had no interest in comparing white women's condition to slavery because she did not savor the idea of likening herself to a "negro."

7. Both Pricilla Wald, in *Constituting Americans,* and, more recently, Robert Levine, in *Dislocating Race and Nation,* critique the literati known as "Young America" in the decade prior to Livermore's appearance on the literary scene. Wald and Levine also consider how better-known authors including Melville resisted the literary nationalism promoted by O'Sullivan and the Ducyckinks.

8. For a convincing ethnography of the Anglo-American as this particular ethnic identity developed prior to 1850, see Kaufman.

9. For more on the politics of respectability, particularly as they apply to black women's lives, see Elsa Barkley Brown, Evelyn Higginbotham, and Claudia Tate. Higginbotham considers women's religious activity in the latter half of the nineteenth century; her analysis thus provides interesting connections to the issue of religion and respectability in the 1850s.

5. Reconstruction Optimism in Julia Collins's *The Curse of Caste*

1. Army major and Freedman's Bureau agent Martin Delany was, according to Robert Levine, "convinced that the possibilities for black elevation in the United States were never better than right after the Civil War" (*Martin Delany* 227).

2. Claire's grandfather Frank, referred to only as "Colonel" Tracy after chapter 5, inherits his wealth from his father, John, who emigrated from Connecticut to Louisiana. The name "Colonel" represents Frank's deep investment and privileged status within the social structure of the antebellum South. His connection to the South is something he seems to feel in his bones, for, after visiting relatives in Connecticut as a young man, he decides: "The North was too bleak and cold for him, that he should soon seek his sunny, Southern home, where roses bloomed the year round" (*Curse of Caste* 17). With (presumably blue and Anglo-Saxon) New England blood and a great fortune made up of vast property "well-stocked with slaves, that indispensable appendage of southern life" (15), Colonel Tracy brings a young Connecticut-born wife to Louisiana where their son, Richard, is born.

3. The term "miscegenation" was coined in 1864. Jon-Christian Suggs also cites an 1888 essay by black activist Aaron Mossell declaring the unconstitutionality of miscegenation laws. While black leaders like Mossell would criticize laws forbidding interracial marriage on principle, because the spirit of the law degraded blacks, dominant white society participated in the hysteria over black men's alleged social goal to marry white women. Even suffragists used the panic rhetoric of miscegenation to oppose the Fifteenth Amendment. Many black activists punctuated demands to abolish antimiscegenation laws with assurances that the issue was one of equal protection and the basis of social equality rather than interracial sexual desire. The topic continued in African American rights discourse well into the twentieth century, when Alain Locke demanded the abolition of miscegenation laws in "Enter the New Negro."

4. No such black newspaper of this title appears in *African American Newspapers and Periodicals: A National Bibliography* (Danky and Hady). The *Inquirer* probably refers to the *Philadelphia Inquirer* (founded 1829).

5. The library plot measures up with the conventions of several British novels, as Lynch illustrates, and the trope of a portrait and a family curse bears similarity to Hawthorne's *House of the Seven Gables* (see Susan Williams for more on Hawthorne).

6. Collins seems skeptical that the law could provide the ultimate means toward social and political equality. Her immediate sphere of interest—family

ties and sexual virtue as well as the sanctity of legitimate Christian marriage—has legal implications, but Collins creates a narrator whose concerns and sphere of influence circulate in the private realm. What Kimberlé Williams Crenshaw calls "racial marketplace ideology"—the concept that "if social equality were to be achieved, blacks would essentially have to earn the respect of whites in the private social sphere" seems to operate in the Collins text especially (Lubiano 284). While Crenshaw refers to this ideology in a negative context regarding the Supreme Court's legal laissez-faire opinion in *Plessy v. Ferguson* (1896), Collins, a middle-class black woman living in central Pennsylvania in 1864, may have seen this racial uplift strategy as a viable contribution that black women in particular could make toward attaining citizenship.

6. The End of Romance in Frances Watkins Harper's *Minnie's Sacrifice*

1. Southworth's novel also has a subplot involving a quadroon woman from Cuba who, like the other women in these novels, is the daughter of a slave owner. She, like Harper's protagonist, is named Minny. Harper's revision of Minny's story and her renaming (as Minnie) deserve further consideration but are not within the purview of this project.

2. Melissa Williams also observes that black political rhetoric during Reconstruction reflected an "initial belief that their equal citizenship would be protected" but eventually "yielded to a profound distrust of whites in general, a distrust that increasingly extended to their only political allies, the Republicans" (155).

3. This particular meeting marks what is known as "the great schism" in woman suffrage—the historical moment when suffragists who supported the Fifteenth Amendment (including Harper, Lucy Stone, and Mary Livermore) and those who opposed it without the simultaneous adoption of a Sixteenth that would enfranchise women (including Stanton, Anthony, Parker Pillsbury, and Paulina Davis) declared irreconcilable differences and parted ways. The "schism" between suffragists and abolitionists is well documented (see Angela Davis, Du Bois, Isenberg, and Kraditor).

4. Thomas Organ, a medical doctor writing for the *Revolution,* best sums up the connection between political rights and sexual self-sovereignty: "Every woman possesses the right to the full and perfect control of her own person, in or out of the marriage relation. This is Revolution" (214).

5. For a thorough analysis of the contemporary discourse of black sexuality, see Patricia Hill Collins.

6. Sexual tension pervaded the debates throughout the day. In fact, only minutes before the issue of the Fifteenth Amendment came up, Lucy Stone had denied the charge that woman suffrage was synonymous with Free Love. Just as the issue of miscegenation—interracial sex—had become a favorite vehicle through which to slander radical abolitionists, it functioned to deny social and

political equality in the form of black male suffrage. Of course, after Stone broke from Stanton and Anthony, Stanton would go on to embrace Victoria Woodhull and support, to a certain extent, the tenets of Free Love. Rumors of Stanton's fondness for Woodhull may have encouraged the antisuffrage propaganda that equated suffrage with Free Love (see Horowitz 342–57).

7. Stokes goes on to explain that the proximity of Eve (assumed in these stories to be a white woman) to a black man implied that women wandering beyond domestic space posed a danger to racial purity and national integrity because they were tempted by black male sexual prowess when they shared the public sphere. Douglass's postlapsarian rhetoric demeans women's role as political leaders because it calls into question the validity of the feminine tactic of moral suasion as it invokes an antireformist language of women as insurrectionary, disorderly, and threatening to political stability. Douglass usually refuted these antireformist versions of the story.

8. See Kern. Stanton made it a personal project to combat misogynist exegesis. She may have borrowed some of her ideas about Eve from Margaret Fuller.

9. Ellen DuBois describes Stone's "middle principle," that endorsing the Fifteenth Amendment with the intent to work toward a Sixteenth Amendment later on negotiated between Douglass's assertion that black male suffrage was absolutely more urgent than woman suffrage and the Stanton/Anthony position that votes for women should precede the franchise for black men. The New England Woman Suffrage Association, including Stone and Blackwell, believed that manhood suffrage was an important step in the road toward universal suffrage (see chapter 6).

10. Harper contributed to and read dozens of periodicals; while there is no irrefutable evidence that she was reading the *Revolution*, the fact that she was one of the AERA's most visible public lecturers suggests that it would be very unlikely for her *not* to read its major publication (see "Equal Rights Convention for New York State").

11. Harper addressed the problem of white men's sexual abuse of black women during slavery and had been traveling in the South; she witnessed the brutally violent consequences of the KKK discourse of sexual politics in the South and knew that black men and women lived in terror. As Bettye Collier-Thomas suggests, "Harper felt that the efforts of some suffragist leaders to create such images of black men and to imply that white women without the ballot were more susceptible to rape by ignorant black males left black women open to continual sexual exploitation and black men more vulnerable to lynching" (50–51).

12. At the 1869 meeting, Harper proceeded with her second concern, questioning the AERA's allegiance to working and colored women, at which point "Anthony and several others" tried to assure, and perhaps silence, her by interjecting, "Yes, yes" ("Annual Meeting"). Without missing a beat, Harper offered evidence to the contrary, stating "that when she was at Boston, there were sixty

women who rose up and left work because one colored women went to gain a livelihood in their midst (Applause)" ("Annual Meeting"). For the second time in only a few sentences, Harper challenges *white* women's stated goals and objectives in reform, subtly illustrating that white women repeatedly fail to advocate black women's rights.

13. In August 1869, writing from Georgetown, South Carolina, she says, "I am not content for colored men only to be represented in legislative halls" ("Letter"). While suffrage was certainly important to Harper, it was most of all a means toward an end, and that end was freedom from economic reliance on whites as well as freedom from racial violence. bell hooks rehearses a similar argument in her classic essay "Black Women: Shaping Feminist Theory." Deemphasizing the liberal ideology of competitive acquisition of rights propounded by Stanton, Harper instead focused on what hooks would call the "social collective" consisting of the freed people.

14. Interestingly, Harper often marks people as "white" but rarely specifies when someone is black. In this case, the man was black.

15. The *Revolution* also reflected Anthony and Stanton's disdain for the Republican Party. In 1867, Stanton and Anthony sought support from the Democratic Party as they toured Kansas urging woman suffrage in that state. According to Stacey Robertson, they were "driven to take drastic measures as a result of the indifference of abolitionists [toward woman suffrage] and the opposition of Republicans . . . even if [this] meant abandoning their commitment to racial equality" (144).

16. Like Broca and Walker, cited in earlier chapters, Croly's book was published in the United States and Europe.

17. See "White Woman Suffrage," "Republican Pusillanimity," and "Let Blacks Rise—Lift Them" for examples of white women's elitist claims to citizenship.

18. For more on Truth's distinct rhetorical construction of self in contrast to her mostly middle-class, educated cohort, see Painter, "Voices of Suffrage." For more about white feminist misrepresentations of her voice, see Deborah Gray White and Painter. In reference to Truth's concern that the AERA and women's rights groups in the 1850s subordinated black rights to women's rights, and a discourse analysis of the ways Truth used spoken language as a multifaceted, heteroglossic form of expression, see Peterson, *Doers of the Word*; and Zackodnik, "Sojourner Truth."

19. Numerous *Revolution* essays, mostly written anonymously, deride the way former abolitionists handle white northern women's rights after these women's work "freed the slaves."

20. Another one of Harper's objectives in writing *Minnie's Sacrifice* is to enlist middle-class black support in the effort to "uplift" the freed people as well as to locate a space in which those middle-class émigrés can find equality for themselves. Kevin Gaines is very critical of the politics and ideology of uplift. Its

bourgeois and quasi-evolutionary goals and assumptions, according to Gaines, "implicitly faulted African Americans" if "lowly" blacks did not succeed. To understand uplift as "a self-appointed personal duty to reform the character and manage the behavior of blacks" complicates one's understanding of the motivations behind Harper's uplift ideology. He finds in Harper's "egalitarian Radical Republicanism" the roots of "conservative civilizationist self-help ideologies that, by the 1890's, endorsed educational and property qualifications for citizenship" (see Gaines 8, 20, 21). Harper's complicity in such ideologies, however, is up for debate. *Minnie's Sacrifice* upholds the exemplary moral character of the freed people, for Minnie must learn from them about evangelism, and explicitly disavows the notion that literacy or property ownership are prerequisites for the vote or for virtuous citizenship. Harper was more interested in black self-help as a means toward eschewing dependency or white cultural influence.

21. Although Harper had a deep investment in the South, she tried to maintain a connection to northern reformers as well. In a letter written to Wendell Phillips from Augusta, Georgia, dated August 1866, she expresses regret that she did not receive an invitation from him to lecture in time, assuring him that she would have taken a stagecoach after her speaking engagement in Rockland (probably a plantation near Charleston, South Carolina) and traveled all night to appear. She had been in New York in May, which suggests that it was not uncommon for her to travel between the North and South in her work.

Conclusion

1. Some of the prints in this series were featured at the National Portrait Gallery in Washington, D.C., in an exhibit commemorating the 150th anniversary of the Civil War. The exhibit, *The Confederate Sketches of Adalbert Volck,* ran from 30 March 2012, to 21 January 2013.

2. Susan Gillman draws a similar parallel in "The Squatter, the Don, and the Grandissimes"; she locates Martí "somewhere between the high sentimentality of white feminists from Stowe to Matto de Turner and the critical adaptations of sentimentality practiced by African American writers from Harriet Jacobs to Pauline Hopkins" (Kaup and Rosenthal 148). The reciprocity between Hopkins and Martí is fascinating, since Hopkins's involvement with the *Colored American Magazine* has a similarly transnational reformist spirit. The magazine also published at least one essay about Martí.

Bibliography

Abbot, Abiel. *Letters Written in the Interior of Cuba*. Boston: Bowles and Dearborn, 1829.

Adams, Abigail, to John Adams, and John Adams to Abigail Adams. In Brooks, Moore, and Wigginton *Transatlantic Feminisms*, 165–66.

Agamben, Giorgio. *States of Exception*. Chicago: University of Chicago Press, 2005.

Alzate Cadavid, Carolina. *Desviación y Verdad: La re-escritura en Arenas y la Avellaneda*. Colorado: Society of Spanish and Spanish-American Studies, 1999.

Anderson, Douglas. "*The Blithedale Romance* and Post-Heroic Life." *Nineteenth Century Literature* 60.1 (2005): 32–56.

Andolsen, Barbara Hilkert. "*Daughters of Jefferson, Daughters of Bootblacks*": *Racism and American Feminism*. Macon: Mercer University Press, 1986.

"Annual Meeting of the American Equal Rights Association." *Revolution* 27 (May 1869): 247.

Another American. "Negro Suffrage." *Christian Recorder*, February 25, 1865, 49.

Anthony, Susan, and Elizabeth Cady Stanton. *History of Woman Suffrage II*. New York: Fowler and Wells, 1881.

"Apology." *Anglo-African Magazine* 1 [1869]. New York: Arno Press, 1968.

Appleby, Joyce Oldham. *Liberalism and Republicanism in the Liberal Imagination*. Cambridge: Harvard University Press, 1992.

Austin, James Trecothick. *Remarks on Dr. Channing's Slavery. By a Citizen of Massachusetts*. Boston: Russell, Shattuck and Co., and John H. Eastburn, 1835.

Avellaneda, Gertrude Gómez. *Sab and Autobiography*. Translated and edited by Nina Scott. Austin: University of Texas Press, 1993.

Bakhtin, Mikhael M. *The Dialogic Imagination*. Austin: University of Texas Press, 1981.

———. *Problems of Dostoevsky's Poetics*. Minneapolis: University of Minnesota Press, 1997.

Ballou, Maturin Murray. "The Sea Witch; or The African Quadroon: A Story of the Slave Coast." *Ballou's Monthly Magazine.* New York: S. French, 1855.

Barreto, Reina. "Subversion in Gertrudis Gomez de Avellaneda's *Sab*" *Decimonónica* 3.6 (2006): 1–10. www.decimononica.org/VOL_3.1/Barreto_V3.1.pdf.

Bauer, Ralph. *The Cultural Geography of Colonial American Literatures: Empire, Travel, Modernity.* New York: Cambridge University Press, 2003.

Bay, Mia. *The White Image in the Black Mind: African-American Ideas about White People, 1830–1925.* New York: Oxford University Press, 2000.

Belasco, Susan. "Harriet Martineau's Black Hero and the American Antislavery Movement." *Nineteenth Century Literature* 55.2 (September 2000): 157–94.

Bell, Michael Davitt. *The Development of American Romance.* Chicago: University of Chicago Press, 1980.

Benjamin, Walter. *The Arcades Project.* Translated by Howard Eiland and Kevin McLaughlin. Cambridge: Belknap Press of Harvard University Press, 1999.

———. "Theses on the Philosophy of History." *Illuminations.* Translated by Harry Zohn. New York: Schocken, 1965.

Bennett, Michael. *Democratic Discourses: The Radical Abolition Movement and Antebellum American Literature.* New Brunswick: Rutgers University Press, 2005.

Berlant, Lauren. *The Anatomy of National Fantasy.* Chicago: University of Chicago Press, 1991.

———. "The Queen of America Goes to Washington City: Harriet Jacobs, Frances Harper, Anita Hill." *American Literature* 65.3 (1993): 549–74.

Berzon, Judith. *Neither White nor Black: The Mulatto Character in American Fiction.* New York: New York University Press, 1978.

Bethel, Elizabeth Rauh. "Images of Hayti: The Construction of an Afro-American Lieu De Mémoire." *Callaloo* 15.3 (1992): 827–41.

Bloch, Ruth. "The Gendered Meanings of Virtue in Revolutionary America." *Signs* 13 (1987): 37–58.

Bosco, Ronald, and Joel Myerson, eds. *Emerson: Bicentennial Essays.* Boston: Massachusetts Historical Society, 2006.

———. *The Emerson Brothers: A Fraternal Biography in Letters.* New York: Oxford University Press, 2005.

Bost, Suzanne. *Mulattos and Mestizos: Representing Mixed Identities in the Americas, 1850–2000.* Athens: University of Georgia Press, 2005.

Boyd, Melba Joyce. *Discarded Legacy: Politics and Poetics in the Life of Frances E. W. Harper.* Detroit: Wayne State University Press, 1994.

Bradfield, Scott. *Dreaming Revolution.* Iowa City: University of Iowa Press, 1993.

Brickhouse, Anna. *Transamerican Literary Relations and the Nineteenth-Century Public Sphere.* New York: Cambridge University Press, 2004.

Broca, Paul. *On the Phenomena of Hybridity in the Genus Homo.* London: Longman, Green, Longman, and Roberts, 1864.

Brody, Jennifer DeVere. *Impossible Purities: Blackness, Femininity, and Victorian Culture.* Durham: Duke University Press, 1998.

Brooks, Joanna, Lisa L. Moore, and Caroline Wigginton, eds. *Transatlantic Feminisms in the Age of Revolutions.* New York: Oxford University Press, 2012.

Brown, Elsa Barkley. "Negotiating and Transforming the Public Sphere: African American Political Life in the Transition from Slavery to Freedom." *Public Culture* 7 (1994): 107–46.

———. "To Catch the Vision of Freedom: Reconstructing Southern Black Women's Political History, 1865–1880." In *Unequal Sisters: A Multicultural Reader in U.S. Women's History*, edited by Ellen Carol DuBois and Vicki Ruiz, 124–46. New York: Routledge, 2000.

———. "'What Has Happened Here?' The Politics of Difference in Women's History and Feminist Politics." *Feminist Studies* 18.2 (1992): 296–312.

Brown, Gillian. *Domestic Individualism: Imagining Self in Nineteenth-Century America.* Berkeley: University of California Press, 1990.

Brown, Gordon. *Toussaint's Clause.* Jackson: University of Mississippi Press, 2005.

Brown, William Wells. *Clotel; or The Colored Heroine.* Miami: Mnemosyne, 1969.

Bruce, Dickson D., Jr. *The Origins of African American Literature 1680–1865.* Charlottesville: University Press of Virginia, 2001.

———. "Print Culture and the Antislavery Community: The Poetry of Abolitionism, 1831–1860." In *Prophets of Protest: Reconsidering the History of American Abolitionism*, edited by Timothy Patrick McCarthy and John Stauffer, 220–34. New York: New Press, 2006.

Budick, Emily Miller. "Hester's Skepticism, Hawthorne's Faith; or; What Does a Woman Doubt? Instituting the American Romance Tradition." *New Literary History* 22 (1991): 199–211.

Burns-Watson, Roger. "The Unitarian Clergy and Anti-Slavery in Antebellum Cincinnati." First Unitarian Church of Cincinnati. lists.firstuu.com/LetFreedomRing/essay1.pdf

Carby, Hazel. *Reconstructing Womanhood.* New York: Oxford University Press, 1987.

Carden, Mary Paniccia, and Susan Strehle, eds. *Doubled Plots: Romance and History.* Jackson: University of Mississippi Press, 2003.

Cassara, Ernest. "Hosea Ballou." Unitarian Universalist Historical Society. 2007. www25.uua.org/uuhs/duub/articles/hoseaballou.html.

Castronovo, Russ. *Fathering the Nation: American Genealogies of Slavery and Freedom.* Berkeley: University of California Press, 1995.

Chambers, Ross. *Room for Maneuver.* Chicago: University of Chicago Press, 1991.

Child, Lydia Maria. *An Appeal in Favor of That Class of Americans Called Africans.* Boston: Allen and Ticknor, 1883.

———. *The Freedmen's Book*. Boston: Ticknor and Fields, 1866. Project Gutenberg.

———. *Hobomok and Other Writings on Indians*. Edited and introduction by Carolyn Karcher. New Brunswick: Rutgers University Press, 1986.

———. "The Quadroons." The Online Archive of Nineteenth-Century U.S. Women's Writings, edited by Glynis Carr. Summer 1997. www.facstaff. bucknell.edu/gcarr/19cUSWW/LB/Q.html.

———. *Romance of the Republic*. Boston: Ticknor and Fields, 1867. Project Gutenberg.

"Classic Senate Speeches: William H. Seward, 'Freedom in the New Territory.'" United States Senate. www.senate.gov/artandhistory/history/common/ generic/Speeches_Seward_NewTerritories.htm.

Clavin, Matthew. "Race, Rebellion, and the Gothic: Inventing the Haitian Revolution." *Early American Studies* (Spring 2007): 2–30.

———. "A Second Haitian Revolution: John Brown, Toussaint Louverture, and the Making of the American Civil War." *Civil War History* 54.2 (2008): 117–45.

———. *Toussaint Louverture and the American Civil War*. Philadelphia: University of Pennsylvania Press, 2010.

Clifford, Deborah. *Crusader for Freedom: A Life of Lydia Maria Child*. Boston: Beacon Press, 1992.

Cohn, Jan. *Romance and the Erotics of Property: Mass-Market Fiction for Women*. Durham: Duke University Press, 1988.

Cole, Jean Lee. "Information Wanted: *The Curse of Caste, Minnie's Sacrifice*, and *The Christian Recorder*." *African American Review* 40.4 (2006): 731–42.

Collier-Thomas, Bettye. "Frances Ellen Watkins Harper: Abolitionist and Feminist Reformer." In *African American Women and the Vote*, edited by Ann D. Gordon et al., 50–51. Amherst: University of Massachusetts Press, 1997.

Collins, Julia. *The Curse of Caste; or, The Slave Bride: A Rediscovered African-American Novel by Julia C. Collins*. Edited by William Andrews and Mitch Kachun. New York: Oxford University Press, 2006.

Collins, Patricia Hill. *Black Sexual Politics: African Americans, Gender, and the New Racism*. New York: Routledge, 2005.

Cooke, George Willis. *An Historical and Biographical Introduction to Accompany the Dial, Volume 2*. Cleveland: Rowfant Club, 1902.

———. *Ralph Waldo Emerson: His Life, Writings, and Philosophy*. Boston: James R. Osgood, 1881.

Cornell, Drucilla. *At the Heart of Freedom: Feminism, Sex, and Equality*. Princeton: Princeton University Press, 1998.

———. *The Imaginary Domain*. New York: Routledge, 1995.

Coviello, Peter. *Intimacy in America: Dreams of Affiliation in Antebellum Literature*. Minneapolis: University of Minnesota Press, 2005.

Coyle, William. *Ohio Authors and Their Books.* Cleveland: World, 1963.

Crane, Gregg. *Cambridge Companion to the Nineteenth-Century American Novel.* New York: Cambridge University Press, 2007.

———. *Race, Citizenship, and Law in American Literature.* New York: Cambridge University Press, 2002.

Croly, David Benjamin. *Miscegenation: The Theory of the Blending of the Races.* New York: H. Dexter, Hamilton, 1864.

Dalleo, Ralph. *Caribbean Literature and the Public Sphere: From the Plantation to the Postcolonial.* Charlottesville: University of Virginia Press, 2011.

Danky, James, and Maureen Hady, eds. *African American Newspapers and Periodicals: A National Bibliography.* Cambridge: Harvard University Press, 1998.

Dash, J. Michael. *Haiti and the United States: National Stereotypes and the Literary Imagination.* New York: Palgrave Macmillan, 1997.

———. *The Other America: Caribbean Literature in a New World Context.* Charlottesville: University of Virginia Press, 1998.

Davies, Catherine. "On Englishmen, Women, Indians and Slaves: Modernity in the Nineteenth-Century Spanish-American Novel." *Bulletin of Spanish Studies: Hispanic Studies and Researches on Spain, Portugal, and Latin America* 82.3–4 (2005): 313–33.

Davis, Angela. *Women, Race, and Class.* New York: Vintage, 1983.

Davis, Cynthia. "Nation's Nature: 'Billy Budd, Sailor,' Anglo-Saxonism, and the Canon." In *Race and the Production of Modern American Nationalism*, edited by Reynolds Scott-Childress, 43–66. New York: Garland, 1999.

Davis, David Brion. *The Problem of Slavery in Western Culture.* Ithaca: Cornell University Press, 1966.

Dayan, Joan. *Haiti, History, and the Gods.* Berkeley: University of California Press, 1995.

de Man, Paul. "Autobiography as De-Facement." In *The Rhetoric of Romanticism.* New York: Columbia University Press, 1984.

"The Degradation of Woman." *Revolution* 15 (January 1868): 25–26.

Douglass, Frederick. "Zoe; or, the Quadroon's Triumph." *Frederick Douglass Paper*, October 5, 1855.

DuBois, Ellen Carol. *Woman Suffrage and Women's Rights.* New York: New York University Press, 1998.

Dubois, Laurent. *Avengers of the New World: The Story of the Haitian Revolution.* Cambridge: Harvard University Press, 2004.

Du Bois, W. E. B. *John Brown.* New York: Modern Library, 2001.

DuPlessis, Rachel Blau. *Writing beyond the Ending: Narrative Strategies of Twentieth-Century Women Writers.* Bloomington: Indiana University Press: 1985.

Emerson, Charles Chauncy. "Lecture on Slavery." April 29, 1835. Houghton Library MS Am 82.6.

Emerson, Ralph Waldo. *Emerson's Antislavery Writings*. Edited by Len Gougeon and Joel Myerson. New Haven: Yale University Press, 1995.

———. *Emerson's Prose and Poetry*. Edited by Joel Porte and Saundra Morris. New York: Norton, 2001.

"Equal Rights." *New York Tribune*, 23 May 1869, 5.

Equal Rights Convention for New York State. 1865 (?). Pamphlet. Gerrit Smith Broadside and Pamphlet Collection. Syracuse University Special Collections Research Center.

Ernest, John. *Liberation Historiography: African American Writers and the Challenge of History, 1794–1861*. Chapel Hill: University of North Carolina Press, 2011.

Faulkner, Carol. *Women's Radical Reconstruction*. Philadelphia: University of Pennsylvania Press, 2004.

Ferguson, Ann. "Feminist Communities and Moral Revolution." In *Feminism and Community*, edited by Penny Weiss and Marilyn Friedman, 367–98. Philadelphia: Temple University Press, 1995.

Field, Susan L. *The Romance of Desire: Emerson's Commitment to Incompletion*. Teaneck: Fairleigh Dickinson University Press, 1997.

"The Fifty Fourth Massachusetts." *Christian Recorder* 5 (23 September 1865): 149.

Finseth, Ian. "Evolution, Cosmopolitanism, and Emerson's Antislavery Politics." *American Literature* 77 (2005): 729–60.

Firmat, Gustavo Pérez, ed. *Do the Americas Have a Common Literature?* Durham: Duke University Press, 1990.

Fischer, Sibylle. *Modernity Disavowed: Haiti and the Cultures of Slavery in the Age of Revolution*. Durham: Duke University Press, 2004.

Fletcher, John. *Studies on Slavery, In Easy Lessons*. Natchez: Jackson and Warner; Charleston: McCarter and Allen; New Orleans: John Ball; Philadelphia: Thomas Cowperthwait and Company, 1852.

Foner, Eric. *Tom Paine and Revolutionary America*. London: Oxford University Press, 1977.

Foreman, P. Gabrielle. "Who's Your Mama? 'White' Mulatta Genealogies, Early Photography, and Anti-Passing Narratives of Slavery and Freedom." *American Literary History* 14.3 (2002): 505–39.

Foster, Frances Smith, ed. *A Brighter Coming Day: A Frances Ellen Watkins Harper Reader*. New York: Feminist Press, 1990.

———. "Resisting *Incidents*." In *Harriet Jacobs and Incidents in the Life of a Slave Girl*, edited by Deborah Garfield and Rafia Zafar. Cambridge: Cambridge University Press, 1996.

Fowler, O. S. *Hereditary Descent: Its Laws and Facts Applied to Human Improvement*. New York: Fowlers and Wells, 1847.

———. *Love and Parentage, Applied to the Improvement of Offspring*. 40th ed. New York: Fowler and Wells, 1857.

Fraser, Andrew W. *The Spirit of the Laws: Republicanism and the Unfinished Project of Modernity.* Toronto: University of Toronto Press, 1990.

Fraser, Nancy, and Axel Honneth. *Redistribution or Recognition? A Political-Philosophical Exchange.* London: Verso, 2003.

———. "Rethinking the Public Sphere: A Contribution to the Critique of Actually Existing Democracy." In *Habermas and the Public Sphere*, ed. Craig Calhoun, 109–142. Cambridge: MIT Press, 1992.

Fredrickson, George. *The Black Image in the White Mind.* New York: Harper-Collins, 1971.

"From Hayti." *Vermont Gazette*, March 23, 1830, 1.

Frye, Northrop. *The Anatomy of Criticism: Four Essays.* Princeton: Princeton University Press, 1957.

Fuller, Margaret. *Woman in the Nineteenth Century.* Edited by Larry Reynolds. New York: Norton, 1998.

Gaines, Kevin Kelly. *Uplifting the Race: Black Leadership, Politics, and Culture in the Twentieth Century.* Chapel Hill: University of North Carolina Press, 1996.

Garfield, Deborah M., and Rafia Zafar, eds. *Harriet Jacobs and "Incidents in the Life of a Slave Girl."* New York: Cambridge University Press, 1996.

Garland, Libby. "'Irrespective of Race, Color, or Sex': Susan B. Anthony and the New York State Constitutional Convention of 1867." *Magazine of History* 19.2 (2005). www.oah.org/pubs/magazine/gender/index.html.

Garrity, Doris. *The Libertine Colony: Creolization in the Early French Caribbean.* Durham: Duke University Press, 2005.

Gilbert, Alan. *Black Patriots and Loyalists.* Chicago: University of Chicago Press, 2012.

Gilbert, Sandra, and Susan Gubar. *The Madwoman in the Attic: Women in the Nineteenth Century Novel.* New Haven: Yale University Press, 2000.

Gilyard, Keith, and Anissa Wardi, eds. *African American Literature.* New York: Penguin, 2004.

Girard, Philippe. "Black Talleyrand: Toussaint Louverture's Diplomacy, 1798–1802." *William and Mary Quarterly* 661 (January 2009): 87–124.

Glaude, Eddie. *Exodus: Religion, Race, and Nation in Early Nineteenth-Century Black America.* Chicago: University of Chicago Press, 2000.

Goddu, Teresa A. *Gothic America.* New York: Columbia University Press, 2002.

Goldman, Anita. "Jacobs, Douglas, and the Slavery Debate." In Garfield and Zafar, 251–74.

Goudie, Sean. *Creole America: The West Indies and the Formation of Literature and Culture in the New Republic.* Philadelphia: University of Pennsylvania Press, 2005.

Gougeon, Len. *Virtue's Hero: Emerson, Antislavery, and Reform.* Athens: University of Georgia Press, 1990.

Greeson, Jennifer Rae. "The 'Mysteries and Miseries' of North Carolina: New York City, Urban Gothic Fiction, and *Incidents in the Life of a Slave Girl.*" *American Literature* 73.2 (2001): 277–309.

Gunning, Sandra. *Race, Rape, and Lynching: The Red Record of American Literature 1890–1912.* New York: Oxford University Press, 1996.

———. "Reading and Redemption." In Garfield and Zafar, 131–55.

Hale, Dorothy. "Bakhtin in African American Literary Theory." *ELH* 61.2 (1994): 445–71.

Hale, Sarah Josepha, ed. *Liberia, or, Mr. Peyton's Experiments.* New York: Harper and Brothers, 1853.

Hanlon, Christopher. "'The Old Race Are All Gone': Transatlantic Bloodlines and *English Traits.*" *American Literary History* 19.4 (2007): 800–825.

Harper, Frances E. W. *Minnie's Sacrifice, Sowing and Reaping, Trial and Triumph: Three Rediscovered Novels by Frances E. W. Harper.* Edited by Frances Smith Foster. Boston: Beacon Press, 1994.

———. "Letter from Mrs. F. E. W. Harper." Frances Harper to Henry Tanner. *Christian Recorder,* 25 September 1869, 3.

———. "F. E. W. Harper to Wendell Phillips." The Wendell Phillips Papers. Series 2, Item 659. Courtesy of the Houghton Library, Harvard University.

Harris, Cheryl I. "Whiteness as Property." *Harvard Law Review* 106 (June 1993): 1707–91.

Harstock, Nancy. "Foucault on Power: A Theory for Women?" In *Feminism/Postmodernism,* edited by Linda J. Nicholson, 157–75. London: Routledge, 1990.

Hartman, Saidiya. *Scenes of Subjection: Terror, Slavery, and Self-Making in Nineteenth-Century America.* New York: Oxford University Press, 1997.

Henderson, Mae Gwendolyn. "Speaking in Tongues: Dialogics, Dialectics, and the Black Woman Writer's Literary Tradition." In *Changing Our Own Words: Essays on Criticism, Theory, and Writing by Black Women,* edited by Cheryl Wall, 16–37. New Brunswick: Rutgers University Press, 1989.

Higginbotham, A. Leon. *Shades of Freedom.* New York: Oxford, 1994.

Higginbotham, Evelyn Brooks. *Righteous Discontent.* Cambridge: Harvard University Press, 1993.

Hildreth, Richard. *The Slave; or, Memoirs of Archie Moore.* Boston: Whipple and Damrell, 1840.

Hobsbawn, E. J. *Nations and Nationalism since 1780.* Cambridge: Cambridge University Press, 1990.

Hode, Martha. "The Sexualization of Reconstruction Politics: White Women and Black Men in the South after the Civil War." *Journal of the History of Sexuality* 3 (1993): 402–17.

Hoeller, Hildegard. "Self-Reliant Women in Frances Harper's Writings." *ATQ* 19.3 (2005): 205–20.

Holquist, Michael. "Bakhtin and Rabelais: Theory as Praxis." *Boundary 2* 11.1–2 (1982–83): 5–19.

hooks, bell. "Black Women: Shaping Feminist Theory." *Feminist Theory: From Margin to Center*, edited by Manning Marable, 1–15. Cambridge, Mass.: South End Press, 1984.

Horowitz, Helen Lefkowitz. *Rereading Sex: Battles over Sexual Knowledge and Religion in 19th Century America*. New York: Knopf, 2002.

Horton, Lois. "Avoiding History: Thomas Jefferson, Sally Hemings, and the Uncomfortable Public Conversation on Slavery." In *Slavery and Public History*, edited by James Horton and Lois Horton, 135–49. New York: New Press, 2006.

Hunt, Benjamin. *Plea for Hayti, with a Glance at Her Relations with France, England and the United States, for the Last Sixty Years*. Boston: Eastburn Press, 1853.

———. "Remarks on Hayti as a Place of Settlement for Afric-Americans: And on the Mulatto as a Race for the Tropics." Philadelphia: T. B. Pugh, 1860.

Ignatiev, Noel. *How the Irish Became White*. New York: Routledge, 1995.

"Important from Hayti." *Pittsfield Sun*, 25 July 1844, 3. Volume XLIV, issue 2288, America's Historical Newspapers.

Isenberg, Nancy. *Sex and Citizenship in Antebellum America*. Chapel Hill: University of North Carolina Press, 1998.

Jackson, Cassandra. *Barriers Between Us: Interracial Sex in Nineteenth-Century American Literature*. Bloomington: Indiana University Press, 2004.

Jacobs, Harriet. *The Harriet Jacobs Family Papers*. 2 vols. Edited by Jean Fagan Yellin. Chapel Hill: University of North Carolina Press, 2008.

———. *Incidents in the Life of a Slave Girl*. Edited by Jean Fagan Yellin. Cambridge: Harvard University Press, 1987.

Jacobson, Matthew Frye. *Whiteness of a Different Color*. Cambridge: Harvard University Press, 1998.

Jameson, Frederic. *The Political Unconscious: Narrative as a Socially Symbolic Act*. Ithaca: Cornell University Press, 1982.

Jefferson, Thomas. *Notes on the State of Virginia*. New York: Penguin, 1998.

Kaplan, Carla. "Narrative Contracts and Emancipatory Readers: *Incidents in the Life of a Slave Girl*." *Yale Journal of Criticism* 6.1 (Spring 1993): 93–120.

Karcher, Carolyn. Introduction to *Hobomok*. New Brunswick: Rutgers University Press, 1986.

Kaufman, Eric. "American Exceptionalism Reconsidered: Anglo-Saxon Ethnogenesis in the 'Universal' Nation, 1776–1850." *Journal of American Studies* 33.3 (1999): 437–57.

Kaup, Monica, and Debra J. Rosenthal, ed. *Mixing Race, Mixing Culture: Inter-American Literary Dialogues*. Austin: University of Texas Press, 2002.

Kern, Kathi. *Mrs. Stanton's Bible*. Ithaca: Cornell University Press, 2001.

Kirkpatrick, Susan. *Las Romanticas: Women Writers and Subjectivity in Spain 1830–1850*. Berkeley: University of California Press, 1989.

Kraditor, Aileen S. *The Ideas of the Woman Suffrage Movement, 1890–1920*. New York: Columbia University Press, 1965.

Lazo, Rodrigo. *Writing to Cuba: Filibustering and Cuban Exiles in the United States*. Chapel Hill: University of North Carolina Press, 2005.

Lebsock, Suzanne. "Woman Suffrage and White Supremacy: A Virginia Case Study." In *Visible Women: New Essays on American Activism,* edited by Nancy Hewitt and Lebsock, 62–100. Urbana: University of Illinois Press, 1993.

Lemire, Elise. *"Miscegenation": Making Race in America*. Philadelphia: University of Pennsylvania Press, 2002.

Levine, Robert. *Dislocating Race and Nation*. Chapel Hill: University of North Carolina Press, 2009.

———. *Martin Delany, Frederick Douglass, and the Politics of Representative Identity*. Chapel Hill: University of North Carolina Press, 1997.

Levine, Robert, and Ivy Wilson. *Works of James M. Whitfield*. Chapel Hill: University of North Carolina Press, 2011.

Lewis, Leslie. "Biracial Promise and the New South in *Minnie's Sacrifice*: A Protocol for Reading Julia Collins's *Curse of Caste*." *African American Review* 40.4 (2006): 755–68.

Livermore, Elizabeth. *The Independent Highway: Truths for the People, Liberty, Law, Love*. Cincinnati, 1856.

———. *Zoë; or, The Quadroon's Triumph*. 2 vols. Cleveland: Truman and Spofford, 1855.

Locke, Alain. "Enter The New Negro." *Survey Graphic*, March 1925, 631–34.

Looby, Christopher. *Language, Literary Form, and the Origins of the United States*. Chicago: University of Chicago Press, 1998.

Lubiano, Wahneema, ed. *The House That Race Built*. New York: Vintage, 1998.

Lynch, Deidre. "Gothic Libraries and National Subjects." *Studies in Romanticism* 40.1 (2001): 29–48.

Malone, Dumas. *Jefferson the President: First Term, 1801-1805*. Boston, Little Brown, 1970.

Mann, Susan A. "Slavery, Sharecropping, and Sexual Inequality." *Signs* 14 (1989): 774–98.

Marsh, James. Introduction to *Aids to Reflection*, by S. T. Coleridge. Burlington: Chauncy Goodrich, 1829.

McCarthy, Timothy Patrick, and John Stauffer, eds. *Prophets of Protest: Reconsidering the History of American Abolitionism*. New York: New Press, 2006.

McClaurin, Irma ed. *Black Feminist Anthropology*. New Brunswick: Rutgers University Press, 2001.

McDaniel, W. Caleb. "The Fourth and the First: Abolitionist Holidays, Respectability, and Radical Interracial Reform." *American Quarterly* 57.1 (2005): 129–51.

McHenry, Elizabeth. *Forgotten Readers: Recovering the Lost History of African American Literary Societies*. Durham: Duke University Press, 2002.

Michaels, Walter Benn. Romance and Real Estate." In *The American Renaissance Reconsidered*, edited by Walter Benn Michaels and Donald Pease. Lewisburg, Pa.: Bucknell University Press, 1983.

Mossell, Aaron A. "The Unconstitutionality of the Law against Miscegenation." *A.M.E. Church Review* 5.2 (1888): 72–79.

Mullen, Harryette. "Optic White: Blackness and the Production of Whiteness." *Diacritics: A Review of Contemporary Criticism* 24.3 (1994): 71–89.

———. "Runaway Tongue." In *The Culture of Sentiment: Race, Gender and Nineteenth-Century Literature*, edited by Shirley Samuels, 244–64. New York: Oxford University Press, 1992.

Murray, Meg McGavran. *Margaret Fuller: Wandering Pilgrim*. Athens: University of Georgia Press, 2008.

Nelson, Dana. *National Manhood: Capitalist Citizenship and the Imagined Fraternity of White Men*. Durham: Duke University Press, 2002.

———. "Representative/Democracy: The Political Work of Countersymbolic Representation." In *Materializing Democracy*, edited by Russ Castronovo and Nelson, 218–47. Durham: Duke University Press, 2002.

"National Gazette." *Richmond Enquirer*, 13 November 1835, 4.

Nesbitt, Nick. *Universal Emancipation*. Charlottesville: University of Virginia Press, 2008.

Newman, Louise Michelle. *White Women's Rights: The Racial Origins of Feminism in the United States*. New York: Oxford, 1999.

Noll, Mark. *America's God: From Jonathan Edwards to Abraham Lincoln*. New York: Oxford University Press, 2002.

Nott, Josiah. *Two Lectures on the Natural History of the Caucasian and Negro Races*. Mobile: Dade and Thompson, 1844.

Nudelman, Franny. "Harriet Jacobs and the Sentimental Politics of Female Suffering." *ELH* 9 (1992): 939–64.

Nyong'o, Tavia. *The Amalgamation Waltz: Race, Performance, and the Ruses of Memory*. Minneapolis: University of Minnesota Press, 2009.

O'Bryan, Charles. *Lugarto the Mulatto*. London: Charles Haile Lacy, 1850.

Organ, Thomas. "Woman Wronged." *Revolution*, 9 April 1868, 214.

Packer, Barbara. *The Transcendentalists*. Athens: University of Georgia Press, 2007.

Painter, Nell Irvin. "Difference, Slavery, and Memory: Sojourner Truth in Feminist Abolitionism." In *The Abolitionist Sisterhood: Women's Political Culture in Antebellum America*, edited by Jean Fagan Yellin, 139–158. Ithaca: Cornell University Press, 1994.

———. *Sojourner Truth: A Life, A Symbol*. New York: Norton, 1996.

———. "Voices of Suffrage: Sojourner Truth, Frances Watkins Harper, and the Struggle for Woman Suffrage." In *Votes for Women: The Struggle for Suffrage Revisited*, edited by Jean Baker, 42–55. New York: Oxford University Press, 2002.

Paton, Diana, and Pamela Scully. *Gender and Slave Emancipation in the Atlantic World*. Durham: Duke University Press, 2005.

Patterson, Orlando. *Slavery and Social Death*. Cambridge: Harvard University Press, 2005.

Paxson, James. "(Re)Facing Prosopopeia and Allegory in Contemporary Theory and Iconography." *Studies in Iconography* 22 (2001): 1–20.

Peterson, Carla. *Doers of the Word*. New Brunswick: Rutgers University Press, 1995.

———. *Reconstructing the Nation: Frances Harper, Charlotte Forten, and the Racial Politics of Periodical Publication*. Worcester, Mass.: American Antiquarian Society, 1999.

Pillsbury, Parker. "South Carolina: A Letter from Parker Pillsbury." *Revolution*, 14 October 1869: 225–26.

Popkin, Jeremy. *Facing Racial Revolution: Eyewitness Accounts of the Haitian Insurrection*. Chicago: University of Chicago Press, 2007.

Pratt, Frances Hammond. *La Belle Zoa, or, The Insurrection of Hayti*. Albany: Weed, Parsons, and Co., 1854.

Rabine, Leslie. *Reading the Romantic Heroine: Text, History, Ideology*. Ann Arbor: University of Michigan Press, 1985.

Read, Malcolm K. "Racism and Commodity Character Structure: The Case of *Sab*." *Tesserae: Journal of Iberian and Latin American Studies* 10.1 (2004): 61–84.

"Rebellion in Hayti." *Farmer's Cabinet*, 23 April 1831, 2.

Redpath, James. *Guide to Hayti*. Boston: Haytian Bureau of Emigration, 1861.

———. *The Pine and the Palm* 1.1 (1861)–2.36 (1862).

Reynolds, David S. *Beneath the American Renaissance: The Subversive Imagination in the Age of Emerson and Melville*. Cambridge: Harvard University Press, 1988.

Rifkin, Mark. "'A Home Made Sacred by Protecting Laws': Black Activist Homemaking and Geographies of Citizenship in *Incidents in the Life of a Slave Girl*." *differences* 18.2 (2007): 72–102.

Robertson, Stacey M. *Parker Pillsbury: Radical Abolitionist, Male Feminist*. Ithaca: Cornell University Press, 2002.

Robinson, David M. "Margaret Fuller and the Transcendental Ethos: *Woman in the Nineteenth Century*." *PMLA* 97.1 (1982): 83–98.

Roe, Elizabeth A. *Aunt Leanna, or, Early Scenes in Kentucky*. Chicago: self-published, 1855.

Roediger, David R. *The Wages of Whiteness: Race and the Making of the American Working Class*. New York: Verso, 1991.

Rosenthal, Debra J. *Race Mixture in Nineteenth-Century U.S. and Spanish American Fictions: Gender, Culture and Nation Building*. Chapel Hill: University of North Carolina Press, 2004.

Rowe, John Carlos. *Literary Culture and U.S. Imperialism: From the Revolution to World War II*. New York: Oxford University Press, 2000.

————. "Nineteenth-Century United States Literary Culture and Transnationality." *PMLA* 118 (2003): 78–89.

Saldívar, José David. *The Dialectics of Our America: Genealogy, Cultural Critique, and Literary History*. Durham: Duke University Press, 1991.

Sale, Maggie. *The Slumbering Volcano: African Slave Ship Revolts and the Production of Rebellious Masculinity*. Durham: Duke University Press, 1997.

Samuels, Shirley. *Romances of the Republic*. New York: Oxford University Press, 1996.

————. "Women, Blood, and Contract." *American Literary History* (2007): 57–75.

Sanborn, Franklin. *The Life and Letters of John Brown; Liberator of Kansas and Martyr of Virginia*. New York: Negro Universities Press, 1969.

Sanchez, Maria. *Reforming the World*. Cedar Rapids: University of Iowa Press, 2009.

Sánchez-Eppler, Karen. *Touching Liberty: Abolition, Feminism, and the Politics of the Body*. Berkeley and Los Angeles: University of California Press, 1993.

Sansay, Leonora. *Secret History; or, the Horrors of St. Domingo and Laura*. Edited by Michael Drexler. Peterborough, Ontario: Broadview Press, 2007.

Saunders, Prince, ed. *Haytian Papers: A Collection of the Very Interesting Proclamations and Other Official Documents; together with some Account of the Rise, Progress and Present State of the Kingdom of Hayti*. 1816; Westport: Negro Universities Press, 1969.

Sawyer, Michael. "The Noble Savage as Hegelian Hero: Dialectic Process and Postcolonial Theory." *Hispanic Journal* 24.1–2 (2003): 65–74.

Saxton, Alexander. *The Rise and Fall of the White Republic: Class Politics and Mass Culture in Nineteenth-Century America*. London: Verso, 2003.

Scott, David. *Conscripts of Modernity*. Durham: Duke University Press, 2004.

Scott, Nina. Introduction to *Sab and Autobiography*. Austin: University of Texas Press, 1993.

Sedgwick, Eve Kosofsky. "The Character in the Veil: Imagery of the Surface in the Gothic Novel." *PMLA* 96.2 (1981): 255–70.

Seward, William H. "Freedom in the New Territories." In *The Senate, 1789–1989: Classic Speeches, 1830–1993*, edited by Robert C. Byrd. Washington, D.C.: Government Printing Office, 1994. www.senate.gov/artandhistory/history/resources/pdf/SewardNewTerritories.pdf.

Sexton, Jared. *Amalgamation Schemes*. Minneapolis: University of Minnesota Press, 2008.

Shakespeare, William. *The Tempest*. New York: Signet, 1998.

Sizer, Lyde Cullen. *The Political Work of Northern Women and the Civil War, 1850–1872*. Chapel Hill: University of North Carolina Press, 2000.

Sklar, Kathryn Kish. *Women's Rights Emerges within the Antislavery Movement 1830–1870*. New York: Bedford/St. Martins, 2000.

Smith, Gerrit. "Gerrit Smith to Elizabeth C. Stanton, Peterboro, December 1

1855." Gerrit Smith Broadside and Pamphlet Collection. Syracuse University Special Collections Research Center. Digital Edition.

Smith, James McCune. *A Lecture on the Haytien Revolutions; with a Sketch of the Character of Toussaint L'Ouverture.* New York: Daniel Fanshaw, 1841.

Smith, Valerie. *Self-Discovery and Authority in Afro-American Narrative.* Cambridge: Harvard University Press, 1987.

Smith-Rosenberg, Carroll. "Writing History: Language, Class, and Gender." In *Feminist Studies/Critical Studies*, edited by Teresa de Lauretis. Bloomington: Indiana University Press, 1986.

Sommer, Doris. *Foundational Fiction: The National Romances of Latin America.* Berkeley: University of California Press, 1993.

Sorisio, Carolyn. *Fleshing Out America.* Athens: University of Georgia Press, 2002.

Southworth, E.D.E.N. *Retribution: A Tale of Passion.* New York: Lupton, 1889.

Spelman, Elizabeth V. *Fruits of Sorrow: Framing Our Attention to Suffering.* Boston: Beacon Press, 1998.

Spillers, Hortense. "Changing the Letter: The Yokes, the Jokes of Discourse, or, Mrs. Stowe, Mr. Reed." In *Slavery and the Literary Imagination*, edited by Deborah McDowell and Arnold Rampersad. Baltimore: John Hopkins University Press, 1989.

Spurlock, John. *Free Love: Marriage and Middle-Class Radicalism in America, 1825–1860.* New York: New York University Press, 1988.

Stanley, Amy Dru. *From Bondage to Contract.* New York: Cambridge University Press, 1998.

Stanton, Elizabeth Cady. "To Our Radical Friends" *Revolution*, 14 May 1868, 296.

Stanton, Elizabeth Cady, and Susan B. Anthony. *The History of Woman Suffrage.* Vol. 2. New York: Fowler and Wells, 1882.

Stauffer, John. "American Responses to British Emancipation: The Problem of Progress." Address. The Gilder Lehrman Center, Yale University. 2001. www.yale.edu/glc/conference/stauffer.pdf.

———. "Beyond Social Control: The Example of Gerrit Smith, Romantic Radical." *American Transcendental Quarterly (ATQ)* 11.3 (1997): 234–60.

———. *The Black Hearts of Men.* Cambridge: Harvard University Press, 2002.

Stepto, Robert. "Distrust of the Reader in Afro-American Narratives." In *Reconstructing American Literary History*, edited by Sacvan Bercovitch, 300–322. Cambridge: Harvard University Press, 1986.

Stokes, Mason. "Someone's in the Garden with Eve: Race, Religion, and the American Fall." *American Quarterly* 50 (1998): 718–44.

Stowe, Harriet Beecher. *Uncle Tom's Cabin.* New York: Norton, 1994.

Stowell, Daniel W., Eugene D. Genovese, and Gary R. Mormino, eds. *Balancing Evils Judiciously: The Proslavery Writings of Zephaniah Kingsley.* Gainesville: University Press of Florida, 2000.

Suggs, Jon-Christian. *Whispered Consolations: Law and Narrative in African American Life*. Ann Arbor: University of Michigan Press, 2000.

Sumner, Charles. "On the Crime against Kansas." University of Virginia. www.iath.virginia.edu/seminar/unit4/sumner.html.

Sundquist, Eric. *To Wake the Nations: Race in the Making of American Literature*. Cambridge: Harvard University Press, 1993.

Tate, Claudia. *Domestic Allegories of Political Desire*. New York: Oxford, 1993.

Tate, Gayle. *Unknown Tongues: Black Women's Political Activism in the Antebellum Era, 1830–1860*. East Lansing: Michigan State University Press, 2003.

Terborg-Penn, Roslyn, and Ann D. Gordon, et al., ed. *African American Women and the Vote*. Amherst: University of Massachusetts Press, 1997.

Thomas, John L. "Romantic Reform in America, 1815–1865." *American Quarterly* 17.4 (1965): 656–81.

Tompkins, Jane. "The Other American Renaissance." In *The American Renaissance Reconsidered*, edited by Walter Benn Michaels and Donald Pease. Baltimore: Johns Hopkins University Press, 1985.

Torres-Saillant, Silvio. *An Intellectual History of the Caribbean*. New York: Palgrave, 2006.

Trouillot, Michel-Rolph. *Silencing the Past: Power and the Production of History*. Boston: Beacon Press, 1995.

Tucker, Veta Smith. "A Tale of Disunion: The Racial Politics of Unclaimed Kindred in Julia C. Collins's *The Curse of Caste: or, The Slave Bride*." *African American Review* 40.4 (2006): 743–54.

Tyson, George F. *Toussaint L'Ouverture*. New York: Prentice Hall, 1973.

Wald, Priscilla. *Constituting Americans*. Durham: Duke University Press, 1995.

Walker, Alexander. *Intermarriage: or, The mode in which and the causes why beauty, health, and intellect result from certain unions and deformaty, disease, and insanity from others . . .* New York: J. H. Langley, 1839.

Waters, Hazel. *Race and the Victorian Stage*. Cambridge: Cambridge University Press, 2007.

Weigman, Robin. "Intimate Publics: Race, Property, and Personhood." *American Literature* 74.4 (2002): 859–85.

Welter, Barbara. *Dimity Convictions: The American Woman in the Nineteenth Century*. Athens: Ohio University Press, 1976.

"Wendell Phillips to Ralph Waldo Emerson." Beinecke Library. Yale Collection of American Literature Manuscript Miscellany. YCAL MSS MISC Group 453 F-1.

White, Deborah Gray. *Ar'n't I a Woman? Female Slaves in the Plantation South*. New York: Norton, 1999.

White, Hayden. *Metahistory: The Historical Imagination in Nineteenth Century Europe*. Baltimore: Johns Hopkins University Press, 1975.

"White Woman's Suffrage Association." *Revolution*, 4 June 1868, 337.

Williams, Melissa. *Voice, Trust, and Memory: Marginalized Groups and the Failures of Liberal Representation*. Princeton: Princeton University Press, 1998.

Williams, Patricia J. *The Alchemy of Race and Rights*. Cambridge: Harvard University Press, 1992.

Williams, Susan. "The Aspiring Purpose of the Ambitious Demagogue: Portraiture and *The House of the Seven Gables*." *Nineteenth Century Literature* 49.2 (1989): 221–44.

Wright, Elizur. "The Lesson of St. Domingo: How to Make the War Short and the Peace Righteous." Boston: A. Williams & Co., 1861.

Yellin, Jean Fagan. *Harriet Jacobs: A Life*. New York: Basic, 2004.

———. "Written by Herself: Harriet Jacobs's Slave Narrative." *American Literature* 53 (November 1981): 479–86.

Zackodnik, Teresa. *The Mulatta and the Politics of Race*. Jackson: University Press of Mississippi, 2004.

———. "'I Don't Know How You Will Feel When I Get Through': Racial Difference, Woman's Rights, and Sojourner Truth." *Feminist Studies* 30.2 (2004): 49–73.

Index

abolitionism, radical, 44–46, 48, 51, 158, 167n8; criticism of, 103, 172n7, 175n6. *See also* Radical Abolition Party

Adams, Abigail, 1

Adams, John, 1–2, 97, 164n1

AERA. *See* American Equal Rights Association

Agamben, Giorgio, 2

Allende, Isabel, 161–62

Alzate Cadavid, Carolina, 172n6

amalgamation, x, 6–7, 112, 119–22, 163n4; Collins's views on, 127–29, 132; cultural, 23, 84, 163n2; denounced by antireformers, 18–19, 77; geographic, x, 30, 57–58, 61, 102, 162, 165n1; Livermore's views on, 93–95, 98–99, 101–3; racial, 15–16, 159; reformers' views on, 20, 26, 168n11; and slavery. *See also* cross-racial romance; interracial marriage; miscegenation; mulattos and mulattas; octoroons; quadroons; and sexuality: racialized

American Colonization Society, 25

American Equal Rights Association, 137–43, 145, 150, 152–53, 155–56, 176n10, 176n12

American exceptionalism, xi, 84, 160, 161

Anderson, Douglas, xi, 164

Anglo-American: aggression, 17–18, 26; capitalism, 43, 69–70; ethnic identity, xiii, 173n8; imperialism, xii, 61; nationalism, xiv, 2, 6–9, 40, 166n6, 167n6; property rights, 28; racialized representations, 84, 90–95; sovereignty challenged, 4–5, 12, 29–36, 39–42, 47, 72, 76; supremacy, xi, 19. *See also* whiteness; white space

Anthony, Susan B., 137, 139–43, 150, 175n3, 175n12, 177n15

antireform writing, 7, 8, 14–19

Arendt, Hannah, 163n4

Attucks, Crispus, 2

Austin, James Trecothick, 7, 18, 61, 77, 122

Avellaneda, Gertrudis Gómez de, xii, 108–9, 171n1, 172n6; autobiography, 9, 172n1; *Sab*, x, 7, 9, 56–81, 162, 172nn3–4

Bakhtin, Mikhael, 17

Ballou, Maturin Murray, 7, 104–8

Bauer, Ralph, 58

Bay, Mia, 87

Belasco, Susan, 167n9

Bell, Michael Davitt, 160, 164n5, 164n7

Bennett, Michael, 165n3

Berlant, Lauren, xi

Berzon, Judith, 77

Bethel, Elizabeth Rauh, 167n9

Blackwell, Henry, 137, 141, 176n9

Bloch, Ruth, 107

Bonaparte, Josephine, 5

Bosco, Ronald, 167n8

Bost, Suzanne, 88, 163n3

Boukman, Dutty, 161

Boyer, Jean-Pierre, 5

Bradfield, Scott, 160

Brickhouse, Anna, 61, 68

Broca, Paul, 7, 14

Brody, Jennifer, 163n3

Brown, Elsa Barkley, 44, 154, 171n11, 174n9

Brown, Gillian, 103, 170n8

Brown, Gordon, 164n1